MOZAMBIQUE

Mozambique

A War against the People

Hilary Andersson

MACMILLAN

First published 1992 by
MACMILLAN PRESS LTD
Houndmills, Basingstoke, Hampshire RG21 2XS
and London
Companies and representatives
throughout the world

Copy-edited and typeset by Cairns Craig Editorial, Edinburgh

ISBN 0–333–56811–7 (hardcover)

A catalogue record for this book is available
from the British Library

Printed in Hong Kong

This book is dedicated to my Father who made it possible, and to both my parents, for everything

Contents

List of Maps and Figures

Maps

Figure

Acknowledgements

Thanks are due to Muhendra Sheth, Johan Viljoen, Tony and Phillipa of Care, Alex Vines and the many others who were so generous with time, material and hospitality. I am grateful too to all those who gave their time to be interviewed, particularly the refugees; and to the United Nations for the use of its maps. I would like also to thank Katharine Simpson and Thomas Case for their editorial help in the preparation of this book.

List of Abbreviations

AIM	Agencia Informação de Mozambique
ANC	African National Congress
BOSS	Bureau of State Security
CCB	Civil Co-Operation Bureau
CCM	Christian Council of Malawi
CIO	Central Intelligence Organisation
DGS	Direção de Segurança (PIDE renamed DGS in 1969)
GD	Grupa Dinamizador
ERP	Economic Rehabilitation Programme
FRELIMO	Frente de Libertação de Moçambique
MNR	Mozambique National Resistance; Originally Movimento Nacional de Resistência de Moçambique, later Resistência Nacional Moçambicana (RNM or RENAMO)
NGO	Non-Governmental Organisation
PALMO	Partido Liberal e Democratico de Moçambique
PIDE	Polícia Internacional e de Defesa do Estado (Portuguese secret Police renamed DGS)
OMM	Organisação da Mulher Moçambicana
REMO	Resistência Moçambique
RENAMO	Resistência Nacional Moçambicana
SACC	South African Council of Churches
SADCC	Southern African Development Co-Ordination Conference
SADF	South African Defence Force
UNAMO	Mozambique National Union
UNDP	United Nations Development Programme
UNHCR	United Nations High Commission for Refugees
WFP	World Food Programme
WHO	World Health Organisation
ZANU	Zimbabwe African National Union

Chronology

1960	Massacre at Mueda by Portuguese
1962	25 June, Frelimo Founded; September, First Congress held
1964	September, armed struggle for independence begins
1968	July, Frelimo Second Congress
1968	Frelimo war spreads into Tete
1969/70	First Rhodesian raids into Mozambique
1970–73	Frelimo war spreads south of the Zambezi, into Manica and Sofala
1974	September, Frelimo dominates transitional government.
1975	June 25, Independence for Mozambique
1975	September, *Magaia* first appears
1976	March, Mozambique imposes sanctions on Rhodesia
1976	July 5, Radio station set up in Rhodesia
1977	February, Frelimo Third Congress held
1979	Renamo 'Statutes' printed
1979	December, Lancaster House Agreement
1980	April 18, Independence for Zimbabwe
1979/80	André Matsangaissa killed, Afonso Dhlakama becomes President of Renamo
1980	March, Renamo 'handed' fully to South Africa
1982	Renamo conference held
1983	April, Frelimo Fourth Congress held
1983/4	Renamo war spreads north
1983/4	Droughts reach their peak
1984	March 16, nKomati Accord signed
1984	October 3, Pretoria Declaration Talks
1986	October 19, Samora Machel is killed, November 6, Joaquim Chissano takes over as President
1986/7	Massive influx of Refugees to Malawi starts
1987	July, Renamo massacre at Homoine, 424 slaughtered
1987	August, Renamo massacre at Manjacaze, 92 slaughtered
1987	October, Renamo massacre at Taninga, 278 slaughtered
1987	Economic Rehabilitation Programe embarked on
1989	June, Renamo 'First' Congress held
1989	July, Frelimo Fifth Congress held
1990	December, Rome partial ceasefire agreement

1 Background – a Land of War, a Land of Hope

I never saw a man who looked
With such a wistful eye
Upon that little tent of blue
That prisoners call the sky

Oscar Wilde

Looking East over the Chimanimani mountains of Zimbabwe into neighbouring Mozambique, the spectacular beauty of this forbidden land is striking. Down by the South African border at Komatipoort the lush quality of the banana-growing farm land on the South African side makes it hard to believe that the same potential is not also found on the Mozambican side. One wonders what the problem is.

Yet, further up north, where Mozambique borders Malawi, impressions are less positive. The well used road running between Malawi's two main cities, Lilongwe and Blantyre, actually forms the border with Mozambique. On this road the most unusual contrast is on view. On the Malawian side thriving markets nestle in amongst the hundreds of round thatched huts, and there is a sense of activity unique to this small and populated country. The Mozambican side of the road is deserted. Only one or two people are ever to be seen at once; usually they are hurrying across the road back to safety for the night after spending the day farming their land in Mozambique. The Mozambican side is littered with abandoned and ruined colonial buildings, some of them double storied, all of them distinctively Portuguese in style. According to the locals, these used to be shops. It is difficult to imagine that before Mozambique gained its independence from Portugal, in June 1975, this was the more active side of the road.

The negative images become even sharper inside Mozambique. In Maputo, the capital, skyscrapers decay and threaten collapse while no one can afford to revamp them. Deep holes, where once a European had started to lay the foundations of a dream, litter the ground. The only way of telling how old and abandoned the dreams are is by measuring the height of the trees which have grown out of the partially laid foundations. Presently the trees are seventeen years high. For it was in 1975 that what had been Mozambique's life stream, fled.

The slums of Maputo harbour a million unwilling inhabitants who have fled to their capital in search of refuge from their war-ravaged villages. The dislocated live in shanties not made, even, of solid mud bricks, but of discarded plastic sheeting or cardboard. When the heavy tropical rains come, the cardboard comes down, the ground that the shacks stand on slips away in the muddy slime, and through all this mothers with babies on their backs have to start again to build some shelter.

Not all refugees can even make it to the dubious sanctuary of the Maputo slums, so many flee to neighbouring countries. Sometimes they end up better off, sometimes worse, than those who headed for the capital. Whatever the case the rainy season is still a trial for temporary residents in temporary huts. The dry season is little better, as so many who abandoned farmland of their own, live now, frustrated, in arid and overcrowded patches. Humanity is piled on top of humanity, and need on top of need.

Mozambique today, the origin of so much misery and suffering and the sixth poorest country in Africa with a per capita income of $170, could not be a more perfect contrast to the Mozambique of thirty or even eighty years ago for the prosperous Portuguese and British colonists. Little wonder then that so many who look at Mozambique today express horror at how people could make such a mess of their country. Yet, very much like South Africa today, Mozambique's real economy in those days was not nearly as glittering as it appears in the tales of the colonists. Though it often escapes people's notice, the vast majority of people in Mozambique are native Africans. For them life then, as now, was about survival, not luxury.

Mozambique, situated in the east of southern Africa, has a coastline stretching along 1500 miles of the Indian ocean. With an area of some 300 000 square miles it is comparable in size to Britain and France combined. Its population, however, stands at a mere 15.3 million. Along its borders are the six southern African countries of South Africa, Swaziland, Zimbabwe, Zambia, Malawi and Tanzania. All but two of them are landlocked, providing Mozambique with a ready market for its ports.

To know anything about any of these countries is to know a little about Mozambique. The weather, topography, geology and tribal divisions of each country overlap with the relevant part of Mozambique. Borders in southern Africa are largely a reflection of the colonists' concern with economic advantage, and have little to do with the patterns of indigenous people. Thus Mozambique has come to harbour nine main different ethnic groups, and many more different languages.

Mozambique is a country of contradictions. The beautiful and the ugly live side by side. It is a land still where the witch doctor's legends hold

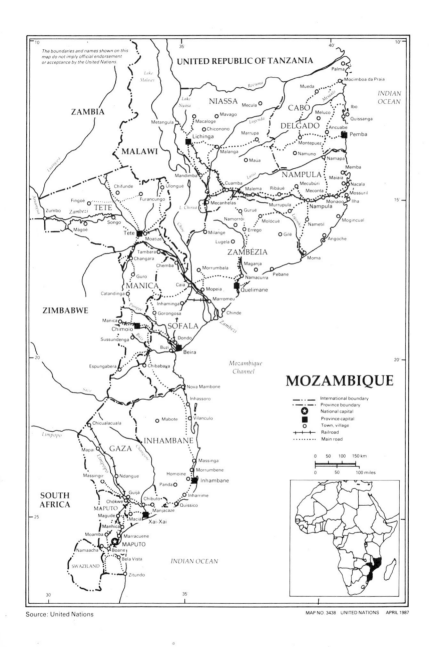

The boundaries and names shown on this map do not imply official endorsement or acceptance by the United Nations.

UNITED REPUBLIC OF TANZANIA

ZAMBIA

MALAWI

NIASSA

CABO DELGADO

ZIMBABWE

TETE

NAMPULA

ZAMBÉZIA

MANICA

SOFALA

INHAMBANE

GAZA

SOUTH AFRICA

MAPUTO

SWAZILAND

INDIAN OCEAN

Mozambique Channel

MOZAMBIQUE

International boundary
Province boundary
National capital
Province capital
Town, village
Railroad
Main road

0   50   100   150 km
0   50   100 miles

Source: United Nations

MAP NO. 3438   UNITED NATIONS   APRIL 1987

MAP 1.1   Mozambique

the most sway, and black magic has a large following. It is the country
that Livingstone wrote of: where once wild animals roamed over wild land,
full of savages and cannibals, and a place where wars of mutilation raged
between tribes. Even so, it has probably the safest capital in Africa, in
terms of criminality, which is frequently attributed to the gentle nature
of the Mozambican people. Its past is ravaged by slavery, and its present
by war and poverty, yet it has natural resources which, if only they were
exploited, would be the envy of many more developed countries.

To many, perhaps, it is a typical Third World country: a neo-Marxist
turned socialist government, warring against a group of guerrillas; a bankrupt economy, a suffering people, and little hope of recovery. All of this
is true, but there is much more to it; for one thing, there is its potential.

Under the sometimes arid ground of Mozambique, particularly in the
north-western province of Tete, lies an abundance of unexploited wealth.
This is wealth which, if the speed with which foreign investors acted when
Mozambique paved the road for them by liberalising its economy in 1987
is anything to go by, foreign investors seem to have been waiting to get
their hands on for some time.

Significant reserves of coal, copper, graphite, asbestos, marble, iron ore,
titanium, tantalite, nephaline-syenite, semi-precious stones and even gold,
lie under Mozambique's soil. It is also blessed with only partially exploited
natural gas reserves. There is hope too that Mozambique has oil, and explo-
rations are presently being conducted by foreign interests.

The strategically important minerals such as titanium could provide significant export earnings, while resources such as iron ore and coal offer
the opportunity for Mozambique to produce its own steel. Portugal, as
one of the poorest colonial powers, could not afford to exploit resources
in Mozambique which required great industrial development. Many of the
larger industrial projects operating in colonial Mozambique were British
owned. Since independence, Mozambique has not been able to afford to
exploit its resources either, and so they lie there, waiting.

Mozambique has southern Africa's largest rivers running through it, providing natural transportation opportunities. The great Zambezi River is at its
widest in eastern Mozambique and is navigable for some 450 kilometers all
the way from the Indian Ocean to the city of Tete. Tete lies half way along
the main road between the capital of Zimbabwe, Harare, and the capital of
Malawi, Lilongwe. The potential that this provides for the transportation
of imports and exports is obvious. Potential for internal distribution is also
great, for the Zambezi River cuts Mozambique neatly into two, dividing the
north from the south. Moreover, from Zimbabwe, the Zambezi runs into the
Mozambican dam of Cahora Bassa, host to one of the largest hydro-electric

power plants in Africa. This dam is potentially Mozambique's single most significant industrial asset.

The Limpopo, the Save and the Pungoe rivers in the north, the Lurio and the Rovuma rivers, combine to provide Mozambique with a natural water supply network. There is even a section of the Limpopo that is theoretically navigable and used to be used quite regularly by small craft, though the mouth has been silted up for some time now, making access impossible. Yet, in spite of all these rivers, Mozambique suffers more than its fair share of droughts. The provinces of Gaza and Inhambane, dry always and better suited to animal husbandry than crop growing, contrast with some of the more northerly parts of the country which are covered in cool and moist forests; yet both are susceptible to fearsome droughts.

Malawi, a large part of whose population of eight million survives from the bounty of enormous Lake Niassa (or Lake Malawi) which runs from north to south through most of the country, should look over the water at its Mozambican neighbours with envy. For while only about one seventeenth of Mozambique's inland border runs along the side of Lake Niassa, the entire population of Mozambique is only twice as large as that of small and overcrowded Malawi. Thus, a relatively small number of Mozambicans enjoy a whole third of Lake Niassa. Today, a far cry from this scenario, it is the Mozambicans who look across to their Malawian neighbours' side of the lake with envy. Such is their envy that they brave the crocodile-infested lake to swim across to the safe side. There is a tiny island in Lake Niassa, Likomo Island, which is host to over a thousand such refugees from Mozambique.

Forbidden though much of Mozambique is today, only a few years ago it had a thriving tourist industry. Rhodesians and South Africans used Mozambique as their holiday playground. For Rhodesians the nearest beaches were in Mozambique (they dubbed it Rhodesia-by-the-sea), and for both Rhodesians and South Africans the famous Mozambican Tiger prawns were an irresistible attraction. Mozambique has a natural tourist industry. It has miles of beautiful and unspoilt beaches, wonderful fishing, sea food and islands. On top of all this it has huge game reserves, which used to be famous for their attraction as hunting spots. Nowadays, in eastern and southern Africa, hunting is a luxury sport, and earns host countries significant sums of foreign currency.

Unfortunately for Mozambique, its history has not been kind to its game. Hunting, to the colonists' minds, was supposed to provide the settler with sufficient meat to adequately feed himself and his labourers. This belief inspired a policy which instructed that hunting licences should be given to almost anyone who applied. Many took advantage of the system and started hunting commercially and selling the meat for profit, thus killing a huge proportion of Mozambique's game. Recent years of war too have helped deplete Mozambique's resources, as the chaos has turned the country into a poacher's paradise. The old herds that used to roam the inlands of Mozambique have been butchered for their meat and tusks[1].

Most of the game and the Portuguese, as well as the tourist industry, have gone. Old hotels, like Maputo's famous Polana Hotel, retain little more than a hint of their previous grandeur. The faded gilt lettering on the plates which no one has been able to afford to replace since the Portuguese left, tells the tale. Breakfast, in another such hotel, in which the breakfast room had been built on the top floor so as to command the best view of the Maputo harbour, is now a nightmarish experience. Without the air-conditioning that it was designed to have, the heat that the enormous glass windows reflect makes it like a greenhouse, turning the luxuries meant to be enjoyed in it, sour.

Even so, the beaches have not faded away, and neither has Mozambique's share of natural scenic beauty. The tourist industry waits to be rebuilt. People all over southern Africa still ask about the beaches and the prawns – they have not forgotten. Nor has the present government or foreign investors. The tourist industry is of great interest to all.

The fishing industry is another of Mozambique's natural assets, although it is evident that the fish too have suffered from the country's politics. Soviet fishermen, allowed fishing rights in exchange for Soviet aid to Mozambique, overexploited Mozambique's fish reserves. Nonetheless, as 84 per cent of Mozambicans are rural people[2] agriculture is the most important sector of Mozambique's economy. Although during colonial times it was considered more important for the foreign currency it provided from exports than for feeding the population, agriculture has long been considered crucial to Mozambique's economy. Because the economy was so heavily structured towards the export market in the years before independence, the export of agricultural products has remained crucial to the economy. This is despite the fact that the Frelimo government has been trying to restructure the economy to reduce dependence on exports since independence.

Mozambique exports cashew nuts, raw cotton, and wood in significant quantities. It used to export sugar but now, despite the huge sugar factories left by the settlers, has to import it. Sisal, tea and copra are also major agricultural products. There is a host of other products which Mozambican soil can grow such as bananas, sunflower seeds, beans, pineapple, sesame, rice, sweet tobacco, potatoes, sorghum, wheat, groundnuts, millet, citrus fruits and many others. Some of these, such as rice, pineapples, cashews[3] and cotton, were not grown by the indigenous population until the Portuguese introduced the idea, and sometimes the seed.

It is interesting to note how distant the factors have sometimes been that have determined what Mozambique has grown. Rice, for, example was first grown on a large scale in Mozambique in the 1940s as a reaction to the fall of Singapore and the associated problems in South East Asia which caused rice to become scarce, and thus expensive.

Because the economy has been geared to the export of primary produce, Mozambique, like many similarly structured African countries, is very vulnerable to the rise and fall of world commodity prices. Thus during the world recession of the 1980s, Mozambique's foreign currency earnings plummeted, and the sting of the recession was felt very sharply. The most visible manifestation of Mozambique's export geared economy is that all the main railways, and most of the main roads, run from east to west: from the coast to the neighboring countries. These railways used to service the export and import needs of the greater part of southern Africa: indeed the transport industry was at one time Mozambique's biggest foreign currency earner.

However, the fact that the railways and roads run mostly from east to west in a country that is far longer than it is wide, was a sad reflection of the neglect of the needs of the bulk of the Mozambican people. Because most Mozambicans were rural and did not live in capitals or near major ports, they were bypassed by the country's transport infrastructure. The infrastructure was not geared at all to distribute Mozambique's bounty among its people. The lack of an infrastructural base for an internal trading system made Mozambique's goal of developing into a self-sufficient nation, rather distant.

Other legacies, such as the level of education of Mozambicans left by the Portuguese, also frustrated the achievement of this goal. At independence illiteracy stood at 95 per cent. The Portuguese, with their access to good education, are, astonishingly, included in this figure. There was one black doctor and one black agronomist at independence.[4] Furthermore, out of 4000 university students, only 40 were native Mozambicans. When the majority of the Portuguese fled after independence, they left very little in the way of skilled manpower.

The lack of education on the part of the blacks was as serious as it could be. The Portuguese settlers tended to be of a lower socio-economic class than, for example, British colonists. They therefore took not only the top jobs in their colonies, but also the vast majority of the semi-skilled and unskilled jobs, which left the native Mozambicans with only the lowest of jobs. The long term effects, in terms of the size of the educational task ahead, and inefficiency caused by lack of expertise, have proved devastating.

If shoes are being made by untrained staff, leather is wasted, if beds are being made, wood is wasted. Lack of expertise in maintaining technical equipment necessitates frequent replacement. At the managerial level the same lack of professionalism prevails. A trip into hotel reception quickly reveals this. Even if there is only one person wanting to check in, it will take half an hour, because the receptionist has no concept of the need to get things done quickly, nor of how to skip the unnecessary parts of the paper work.

The prevalence of time-consuming procedures and inefficiency is less to do with a lack of an innate incentive to be fast and efficient than it is with the bureaucratic legacy of the Portuguese, and the lack of managerial education. Evidence enough of the latent set of production incentives is the existence of the thriving black market. Mozambique's black market truly represents a second economy. On the *cadonga*, as it is called, a huge spectrum of goods that cannot be obtained elsewhere, are available. If there is no maize available in official shops at official prices, there surely is at a different price on the black market. Many Maputo slum dwellers have a stash of Rands hidden away for a future trip to South Africa to visit their relatives or to buy goods unavailable in Mozambique. Well known corners in the shanty towns have always got three or four people waiting to do deals.

The lack of foreign currency is a very real problem for Mozambique, and the government has taken strict measures in the past to try to curb the cadonga. Even basic food supplies like grain, milk and fertilizer must now be imported, yet there is not even enough foreign currency to pay for these. The foreign currency now required for such essentials, limits the amount left for fueling the continued and efficient operation of the industries that generate foreign currency.

Foreign currency earnings were slashed when South Africa cut the number of Mozambican immigrant labourers allowed from 115 000 to less than 40 000 in 1976. Two years later, Mozambique suffered another devastating blow to its foreign currency earnings when the South Africans decided to stop linking the payment for immigrant mining labour from Mozambique to current gold prices. In spite of this, foreign currency earnings from immigrant labour to South Africa still represent a large proportion of Mozambique's total foreign currency earnings. The Mozambican Foreign Trade Representative in Johannesburg describes 90 per cent of his job as being concerned with the immigrant miners.

The economies of the southern Mozambican provinces of Inhambane and Gaza have long been dominated by the massive movements of immigrant labour to the South African mines. It seems to be almost a ritual requirement for a young man to go off to the mines for several years before he can consider starting up a family. The fact that so much young and energetic labour has always left these two provinces has had an adverse effect on their local economies.

This channelling of labour into an area not directly productive for Mozambique, together with the suppression of initiative throughout the colonial, and much of the recent, period, explains a good deal. It explains in part why, when you walk down the streets of Maputo, you do not see the thriving bustle of hawkers and street sellers that are so common in many African and Asian countries. Indeed, aid workers believe that even the rural Mozambicans' natural understanding of how to grow and eat a balanced and healthy diet, has been undermined by, amongst other things, long years of being forced to grow certain crops for export. If there is truth in this, it goes to show how profoundly the people of Mozambique have been affected by their history.

During the travels of the Portuguese explorer, Vasco da Gama, at the beginning of the sixteenth century, sophisticated cultures were found along the coast of Mozambique. More recently, coins and other relics have been found to prove the existence of ancient and prosperous cities and ports. There were extensive trade links at least 400 years ago between the Arab world and East Africa. The Chinese and Indians too traded with Mozambique, in the much sought after ivory and gold. Quelimane, one of Mozambique's operating ports today, was chosen to be the first East African-Indian port. Remains of a four-hundred-year-old Portuguese settlement, are visible on the Island of Mozambique to this day.

But this age of prosperity ended in ignominy for Mozambique, as the Chinese, and eventually the Portuguese, realised that there was another commodity in East Africa that could be traded in: humans. It is hard to quantify the damage that the slave trade wrought on the nation. Suffice to say that the export of its people was in the devastatingly large numbers of up to 25 000 a year. Mozambique was lucky, perhaps, that it was situated on the east coast of Africa, and not the west coast, where far larger numbers of slaves were taken due to the west coast's proximity to Europe and the Americas. However, historians[5] believe that in addition to the recruiting done directly from the east coast ports, slaves were taken from the eastern countries and walked to the west for shipping overseas. Thus Mozambique, with such a long coastline making it particularly vulnerable, suffered on both fronts.

The Portuguese, like the Afrikaners in South Africa, had settled in Mozambique long before the eighteenth century 'scramble for Africa', when Europe carved up the continent into nations and divided it amongst themselves. Unlike the Afrikaners, however, the Portuguese, to keep their territory, joined in the rush, carving off a bit of Africa for themselves and calling it a nation. Before the Portuguese made Mozambique into a unified territory, the native people did not know each other as people of one nation. The people of the north and the south were very little concerned with each other. In order to rule effectively over their newly conceived nation inhabited by so many tribes, the Portuguese adopted a classic and very effective method of government: divide and rule. Tribal chiefs were co-opted by the system and given power that they already had. However, now they were colonial administrators too, and maintaining their power was subject to their obedience to their Portuguese masters.

This method of government has proven itself in many countries to be an extremely effective method of minority government, but its exercise makes the road to democracy a very rocky one. Its effects are still visible today in Mozambique, in the ploys of the Renamo rebels who use the very same tactics that the Portuguese had used, to attempt to gain power for themselves, and to further their immediate goal of disrupting the country.

The Portuguese interest in Mozambique, initiated four hundred years ago, remained fairly stable until 1926 when a military coup led to António Salazar taking power in Portugal in 1932. Development until then had been a slow process, with much of the interior inaccessible due to the dangers presented by the tsetse fly and rampant malaria. With the type of sweeping approach to problems peculiar to fascist dictators, Salazar saw the solution to Portugal's overpopulation problem and the possibility for a more prosperous colony at once. By enticing large sections of the population to relocate in the Portuguese colonies, not only would the overpopulation problem be solved but the colonies would become more productive, and thus would better serve the needs of Lisbon. Between 1940 and 1960 Mozambique saw settlers, most of whom were fairly poor, some without even shoes, arriving en masse, more than tripling Mozambique's white population.

Actually, Portugal preferred not to think of Mozambique and its other acquired territories, as 'colonies', but rather as 'provinces of Portugal': integral parts of the mother country. A striking monument to this particular brand of colonialism used to be plainly on view to any visitors to Lourenço Marques. In the city's central square the massive Portuguese letters 'Here Is Portugal' were emblazoned on the ground. This washed a little sour in the mouths of those who saw that Mozambique was not being developed as a territory important in itself, but only in so far and in such a way as it suited Portugal's needs.

Huge sums of money were poured into Mozambican projects even to satisfy the most trivial of Portuguese needs, while little was spent on the needs of the territory itself. It was thus that the economy became so heavily orientated to exports, while infrastructure for domestic needs was not developed, and it was thus that native Mozambicans were forced to grow crops of no use to themselves, from which they earned little money, and which they could not eat. Mozambique became further and further estranged from itself and its own needs as a territory. The need to produce exports so that the settlers could afford to buy materials necessary to live in the style to which they were accustomed, dominated.

When it was decided that cotton would make a profitable export if only it could be produced in sufficient quantities, the worst side of the Portuguese colonists came out. Measures were taken to force the Africans to grow cotton. As one settler himself put it[6] 'The African simply did not understand . . . only by obliging him, therefore, was it possible to get any results at all, but unfortunately this had the boomerang effect of reducing the planting of his other normal crops'. Perhaps the African understood better than some people thought. In what was considered his 'primitive' way, he understood at least the basics extremely well: that he wanted to grow things that he could sustain himself with.

To enforce their will, the colonists instituted a system of forced labour, called *chibalo*. In this system it became obligatory for each African to work six months of the year for a settler farmer. The alternative was to pay a high tax in foreign currency. Natives did not have access to foreign currency. Of course, it was phrased the other way around: pay the tax or do the penance. Either way it amounted to the same thing. Given the institutionalized impossibility of a native being able to raise the foreign currency to pay the tax, it is not unfair to call this a system of slavery.

Remarkably, even with all this estrangement between whites and blacks in Mozambique, the Portuguese language became thoroughly embedded in Mozambican culture. It has become the national language, not just officially, but as one which is voluntarily and spontaneously spoken by the masses, most of whom are uneducated.[7] This spontaneous adoption of the settlers' language is unusual in the southern African context. In South Africa there is nothing like this. When a black speaks to a white it is in English or Afrikaans. But when he speaks to a fellow black it is in an African language, be it Zulu, Xhosa, Sotho or any of the other languages. If the Portuguese were better at mental colonisation than at economic colonisation, the opposite is true of South Africa. Part of the reason for such a deep penetration of the language into the native culture may have been the lack of an 'apartheid' (or separate development) philosophy on the part of the Portuguese colonists.

The Portuguese were very proud of the fact that the laws which governed their colonies were not explicitly colour-coded, and considered themselves extremely liberal because their laws were not overtly racist. It is true that, before it became fashionable to consider all races theoretically equal, the Portuguese were scorned by the world for their liberalism.[8] In all Lusitanian territories there was a legal provision by which the natives could become assimilated into Portuguese society. The few that succeeded in doing so were called *assimilados*. This, the Portuguese have been proud to announce, meant that an intelligent and well-mannered black could socially and economically surpass a lazy and stupid Portuguese settler. However, although these laws may have seemed liberal one hundred and fifty years ago, they do not now. The modern meaning of liberal is more exhaustive. For although the Portuguese did not directly discriminate against the natives, in the sense that they allowed a native to become assimilated if he showed the 'right' qualities, the Mozambicans did not have the necessary access to the education which would teach them what was, supposedly, expected of them. This is evidenced by the fact that less than one per cent of Mozambicans had reached *assimilado* status by the time of independence.

The claim that the system did not discriminate against race was no more than a sham. The discrimination was overt. There was one type of school for the vast majority of the native population, and another for the Portuguese. To an extent this is understandable in itself, for it would have been highly impractical to put a semi-educated Portuguese child in a class with a Mozambican who had never seen a word in his life. However, if the system was non-discriminatory, the difference would surely have levelled out after one generation.

There were two distinct levels of basic education, 'rudimentary' and 'primary'; the former was, in theory, supposed to lead on to the latter. The rudimentary level was specifically for teaching the Africans the three 'R's'. In 1941 African rudimentary education was handed over to the church. Primary schools, which were predominantly Portuguese, were mostly run by the state. After the rudimentary schools were handed over to the church, it often took twice as long for the children to complete the education necessary to reach primary level than it had before. This was because the great emphasis on religious education was very time consuming. This, coupled with the fees charged by these schools, meant that very few Africans even reached primary level, and thus even fewer, secondary level. The number of educated Africans existing at the time of independence speaks for itself.

Given the barriers to receiving the kind of education which was so easily accessible to the Portuguese, it is hardly surprising that few Africans reached the much valued *assimilado* status. *Assimilados* were effectively honorary Portuguese, much as the Japanese in South Africa today are categorised as 'Honorary Whites'. The Portuguese, influenced perhaps by their Catholicism, believed that they were in Mozambique on a 'civilising mission': the poor barbaric heathens had to be civilized, they believed, because they could not possibly be happy in their savage state, and certainly held no hope of eternal salvation in this state. These ideas may sound old fashioned, but, modified slightly, they are essentially the same ideas that were held out as justifications of Portuguese colonialism all the way until 1974 when the Portuguese exodus began. Only in more recent years, concerns for religious salvation have been replaced by concerns for economic salvation. It was believed by the Portuguese, as it is by many South Africans and Westerners today, that only a Westernized black could become economically successful. Thus all the privileges were saved for the *assimilados*. This is the crux of the whole matter. The laws did not discriminate between an *assimilado* and a real Portuguese. However there was one law for the 'civilised' and another for the 'uncivilised' and it was no easy matter to become 'civilised' if you were not born that way.

It is true that, at least in the eyes of the Western world, Mozambique became more economically successful after the Portuguese came. In the terms of the innovations that the Portuguese brought to Mozambique, wide promenades in town and such things as cotton-ginning factories, Mozambique was richer. However, as many Mozambicans will tell you, 'economic success' is not so easily defined that it can be taken for granted that it is always good in every way and for all concerned. As 'economic success' for Mozambique meant forced labour for all native Mozambicans, which in turn meant that they could not grow the crops that they needed to keep themselves alive and healthy, it was not, in their eyes, such a wonderful thing. Likewise because the 'development' the colonists brought meant that Mozambique had to become culturally and in every other sense like Portugal, it was not much appreciated. In reality, the imposition of development on Mozambique from above, while the people of the country had no political say at all, made 'development' extremely unpopular.

When Mozambique finally became independent, the scale and suddenness of the Portuguese exodus was something to behold. The panic to get out in 1974/5 was fused by propaganda that had been spread around by the Portuguese security forces about Frelimo, the liberation force and government to be. The propaganda held, and many believed, that Frelimo was anti-white, and that the whites would suffer at their hands. Rumours were spread that, amongst other things, whites were all to be massacred and that babies were to be nationalised. Between September 1974 and July 1975 the number of whites in Mozambique declined from 230 000 to a mere 80 000, and soon after it fell to less than 25 000.

Frelimo, as a party eventually persuaded by Marxism, did not hold out racism as one of its beliefs; rather, it promised a safe future for the whites in its Mozambique. But, the Portuguese knew that even if they were not killed, staying on in Mozambique would mean suffering unbearable losses of the privileges that they had come to take for granted. They were right, of course. Life for the tiny minority of Portuguese that stayed, and remain today, is nothing like as good as it was before independence.

When the Portuguese fled they destroyed everything that they could on their way out. They slaughtered their cattle, burnt machinery, and dropped cement down lift shafts of buildings under construction, rather than leave Mozambique with anything they had given it. Their spite, according to them, was inspired by their belief that they had given Mozambique all that it had and so they had a right to destroy it. Certainly they were correct that the technical skills and know-how came from the Portuguese, but the sweat and blood came from the natives. The Portuguese had not built Mozambique, but masterminded its development. They had forced the Mozambicans to build up Mozambique in the way that they themselves saw fit.

In many ways, Mozambique was left worse off than it had been before the Portuguese ever came. It was left with an export oriented economy which could not support the country because the skilled workers who had run it had fled. Moreover, the people had been taught Western expectations without being educated into the means of achieving them. Worst of all, Mozambique was left with a rebel force which had sprung out of the tremendous conflicts going in the region at the time when white rule began to disintegrate. It is a poor epitaph to a unhappy story that the rebel movement is still supported by some of these very same ex-colonists.

Mozambique has been at war now for twenty-seven years. The warring for independence which started in 1964 came to a conclusion in 1974 with Frelimo dominating the transitional government, and finally taking power in 1975 in a newly independent Mozambique. There followed two relatively peaceful years, which have proved to be the only years of any respite in the last two and a half decades. But even they were not without problems. It was during these years that Renamo was born and, slowly, for the first time, reared its menacing head. The whole of southern Africa was severely disrupted by Rhodesia's war of independence, and Mozambique more than most. Renamo was formed by the white Rhodesians for the purpose of monitoring and disrupting the activities of one of the Zimbabwean rebel forces, ZANU, in Mozambique.

On 3 March 1976, Mozambique, in an act of solidarity with those fighting for independence in Rhodesia, closed its borders with its neighbour. Although this move cost Mozambique an estimated $139–$165 million in the first year,[9] (losses which, contrary to expectations, it was never fully compensated for), it was a move that had to be made since Mozambique could no longer survive economically whilst surrounded by hostile neighbours. Mozambique suffered with Zimbabwe during its war of independence through many air and land attacks, and continues to suffer today from those fatally intense days of the mid 1970s when the Rhodesians formed their back-up guerilla group, Renamo, and set it to work on Mozambique.

It is ironic that Mozambique was host to some 150 000 Zimbabwean refugees during these years, as Zimbabwe is now host to 84 500 of Mozambique's refugees. When Rhodesia finally became independent Zimbabwe, Renamo was in danger of losing both its *raison d'être* and its source of funding, and fizzling away. So its control and financing was handed over to South Africa, between the 5–7 March, 1980. It was at this point that Renamo first began to call itself a liberation movement which was working on behalf of Mozambicans for the removal of Frelimo from power in Mozambique. This, if anything, heralded the true beginning of the war as it is today.

In an attempt to quell the devastation being caused by South Africa's Renamo, the Frelimo government signed a truce, the nKomati Accord, in 1984. The signing of this accord was not popular with Mozambique's neighbours, who considered it a sell-out to South Africa. It was signed between the South African and Mozambican governments ostensibly for the sake of mutual expedience, for the agreement was to 'respect each other's sovereignty and independence, and, in fulfillment of this fundamental obligation, to refrain from interfering in the internal affairs of the other'. For Mozambique the commitment was to stop harbouring ANC exiles, while for South Africa it was to stop backing Renamo. South Africa's dominant economic position in the region, however, as well as the destruction that it was wreaking through Renamo, left Mozambique with little choice but to sign the agreement. Thus South Africa did not feel as much practical obligation to keep its part of the pact as Mozambique did.

The security situation in Mozambique has played an enormous part in preventing any sort of domestic development. While it has frustrated the government's goal of achieving independence from the rest of the world by dislocating millions from their homes and land, thus preventing them from producing, it has also, exacerbating restrictive government policies, discouraged foreign investment in many ways. It is not just the locals who are prevented from transporting and trading their goods by the dangers of overland travel, but the foreigners too. The likelihood of being ambushed by rebels, is very real and high. Maputo has long had a thirty kilometer radius beyond which few venture. As it is usually the only way of guaranteeing safe arrival at the other end, most traveling between provinces, and sometimes between districts, is done by air. Some would-be investors, less resilient perhaps than Lonrho which employs its own private army to protect its interests in Mozambique, find the security situation very uneconomical.

But for foreign investors contradictory forces are at work in Mozambique. The gravity of the economic situation in 1984 was not only enough to make the Mozambican government compromise with its hated neighbours, but also to make it lay down the socialist principles which it had cherished, in order to qualify for loans for rehabilitation. The IMF-sponsored Economic Rehabilitation Programme (ERP), which it finally embarked on in 1987, meant a complete reversal of the socialist economics which it had pursued since independence. While the security situation continued to worsen and deter investment, the government relaxed the laws governing private enterprise and, in a major policy change, went out of its way to attract foreign investment.

Mozambique's position had been very weak. Having suffered a large share of the worst drought that southern Africa had ever recorded during the mid-1980s, and with a devastating war of destruction on its hands, the Mozambican economy was all but bankrupt. The effects of the drought were horribly exacerbated by the war. In the worst hit areas, the two southern provinces of Inhambane and Gaza, and the north-westerly province of Tete, it is estimated that over 100 000 people died as a result of the drought, and the war's exacerbating effects.

While foreign investment is increasing as a result of the policy changes, it still faces serious obstacles. The economic infrastructure is limited, and much of it has been ruined by Renamo. The Portuguese-built roads and railways leading inland from the ports are constantly harassed by rebel sabotage, and many are unusable. Mozambique's most basic requirements for development are being frustrated by the war. In April 1990, not an atypical month, there was not one day of uninterrupted power supply to Maputo. Apart from being expensive, this has severely interrupted the normal operation of business and industry. These are the constraints within which Mozambique's development has to take place.

Mozambique's position with regard to South Africa, or anyone else for that matter, is not much less vulnerable now than it ever has been. That there is a separate government department in Mozambique for the handling of 'National Calamities', says much in itself. In November 1989, the southern African Economist magazine said that six million people faced starvation in Mozambique unless dramatic action was taken. The country's basic susceptibility to natural disasters remains unchanged. The curse of a drought is followed by the slap in the face of floods. This happened in 1984 when the worst drought in living memory broke with a cyclone that ripped through southern Mozambique leaving devastation in its trail. The Pungoe river, leading out of the main port of Beira in Sofala province, is easily flooded. When it floods, the main road leading to Zimbabwe is cut off. Recently, torrential rain, which lasted for three days, destroyed 450 hectares of crops in the districts of Dondo and Nyamatanda, by flooding fields of rice and potatoes.

Meanwhile, all the classic and unpopular short term effects of the IMF's 'short, sharp, shock' economics were taking place, including the introduction of minimal charges for health care, and a rise in the price of basic food stuffs resulting from devaluations of the Metacal. In January 1990, the discontent of people who had been accustomed to subsidised prices and 'free' social services, became very visible. There was a wave of strikes in which more than 20 000 workers from hospitals, buses, schools, mines and a host of other occupations, demanded higher wages to match the higher prices.

Frelimo reacted confidently to these strikes, passing new and more liberal labour relations laws, giving workers the right to strike on the condition that they provide three days notice. It is interesting to note that when these changes were announced, a liberal South African newspaper carried an article expressing surprise that Mozambique, an independent and socialist African nation, actually allowed its workers more trade union rights than their counterparts in South Africa had. The newspaper's surprise is reflective of the more usual tendency of even socialist African countries to curtail union rights as soon as strikes pose a political threat.

Frelimo's record on securing the rights of Mozambique's citizens has long been a relatively good one in African terms. However, as far as citizens' rights go, African standards are not much to be compared to. Frelimo too is guilty of having allowed contraventions of human dignity to take place in Mozambique. Sometimes these contraventions of rights have been attributable to the prevailing war situation, at other times simply to the attempts of a one party state to enforce its political and economic beliefs on the unwilling. Along with Frelimo's change of stance on economic policy – which was prompted partially by self criticism – its treatment of human rights has improved markedly in recent years.

After independence, 're-education camps' were established in Mozambique, for people who had shown hostility to Frelimo. There are a number of prisoners who were sent to the re-education camps whose fate remains unknown. Conditions in normal Mozambican prisons today are extremely poor in terms of food and health, and reports that prisoners are maltreated in the prisons with beatings and torture, and that prison officials run prostitution rings with female prisoners, have been published. However, the International Committee of the Red Cross has, since 1988, been allowed to visit Mozambican prisons, a sign, at least, of some commitment to erase violations against human rights which do not conform to internationally expected standards.

In 1983 after the Fourth Party Congress, when the sense of Mozambique's devastation and the failure of policies pursued since independence was at its highest, various radical measures were taken as a last minute salvage operation. One of these was an act allowing the public flogging of black marketeers, armed robbers and child rapists. At the same time the Law Faculty at Maputo's Eduardo Mondlane University was abolished after the nation's President, Samora Machel, accused lawyers of defending the rich, saying, 'A revolution that does not know how to defend itself is not a revolution'.[10] This law, which prescribed such a severe punishment for an economic crime, was repealed in late 1989, after international human rights agencies complained. The public beatings had been extremely unpopular in Mozambique, particularly since even official reports evidenced the fact that policemen had been taking the law into their own hands and beating people before they had been tried.

It seems that Mozambique has been better at the fine tuning of the more sophisticated human rights, than at ensuring that more basic human rights are in order. For while laws have been amended to increase sexual equality, to allow more freedom of religion, and to increase trade union rights, academic freedom has been restricted, the people have not been allowed to choose their own government, and education has been thoroughly saturated with propaganda in favour of Frelimo and its policies.

The average person has not felt at ease to discuss politics freely in Mozambique in recent years, for fear that he may be labelled as 'the enemy'. However, people have felt free to discuss politics within defined limits. The national press openly criticizes certain policies pursued by the government. The parameters within which criticism is allowed encompassed, in the past, the criticism of methods used to achieve 'commonly accepted' goals, but not criticism of the goals themselves. This is more than can be said for even relatively respected African countries, Malawi for example, which, because it is not socialist or Marxist, is one of the West's favourite countries in

Africa. In Malawi, people are terrified to speak their minds or to even criticize the least important policy; this is even in the safety of a car with all the doors shut. Since 30 November, 1990, when the new democratic constitution was passed, Mozambicans have been protected by a bill of rights that covers basic issues from habeas corpus to true press freedom, and, effectively since 6 February 1991, by a law which recognises their right to form political parties.

A dramatic change has indeed taken place in Mozambique as a result of the changes which began in 1984, and were consolidated in 1987, leading to its closer alliance with the West, and also to the new constitution. The streets of Maputo still have old Aeroflot offices, and white faces on signs have distinctly Slavic or East European features, but these are all remnants of the old days. Now the offices are packed with French, British, American and Canadian advisors and aid administrators instead of East European ones. The road with all the Eastern bloc embassies on it has now been matched with one or two roads of Western embassies.[11]

Investment is rolling in from all directions. Ports are being upgraded, the Maputo tire factory, which has not operated at capacity since 1982, forecasts sales of over \$12 million this year. Timber growing projects, oil exploration, and a hundred other foreign funded projects are underway. In 1990, hawkers on the streets of Maputo became legal for the first time. Aid is flowing in in its millions, and Renamo and Frelimo have started peace talks. On the face of it, Mozambique is a changed world.

Yet war and its effects continue to ravage Mozambique. Nearly two million people are dislocated within the country, almost one and a half million people have fled the country and sought refuge somewhere else, and more than a further two million in Mozambique have been adversely affected by the war.

It is an old attitude that the vanquished are weak. Mozambicans have been vanquished for the last several hundred years, if not by outright slavery then by colonialism. Now, in spite of all the traumas going on in their country, they want to be strong. Every morning the refugee children, in one of the makeshift schools in a Malawian camp, stand up and spontaneously sing their national anthem. They all want to come back, only they do not dare. The words of the anthem belong to the deepest part of Africa's heart, asking for strength and unity. The words also allude to a dream of a self sufficient and prosperous Mozambique in which everyone participates. The children sing on, unaware that the revolutionary writings on the walls surrounding Samora Machel's memorial, which is in the middle of a roundabout on the outskirts of Maputo, have faded. What did it ever matter to them? The agony on their faces, a reflection of the war has ravaged their country, like the agonised pictures on that wall, has not faded. So much has happened in Mozambique, and we must ask ourselves, as they do, not just what, but why.

2 Frelimo – Idealism, Discipline, Pragmatism

A man may be very sincere in good principles without having good practice.

Dr Samuel Johnson, 1773

Frelimo (Frente de Libertação de Moçambique) is the internationally recognized government of Mozambique. It is also effectively the government of the capital and all the provincial capitals, and is the nervous master of most of the countryside. As can be seen from Map 2.1, which shows the accessibility of Frelimo-backed aid to Mozambique's interior, the Renamo rebels have confident control of a few rural areas, and thoroughly disrupt almost the entire remainder.

Frelimo is a political party, and not, as is commonly misconceived, the state itself. Until recently, however, the constitution dictated that it was the only party allowed, and that the leader of Frelimo was automatically also the Head of State. Since independence, up until the recent changes, there has been very little difference between the party and the state.

Exactly what Frelimo stands for is not as easily deciphered as some would have it. A recent visit to Mozambique would have revealed a government professing socialism, but overtly executing capitalist policies. A visit ten years ago would have found a Marxist-Leninist government in power, the very same party. A visit to Mozambique twenty years ago would have found a Portuguese government in power and a group of nationalist guerillas, run by revolutionary intellectuals, calling themselves Frelimo, fighting a bush war.

Remarkably, the very same figures who led the war against the Portuguese, and who were instrumental in forming Frelimo, are the people that run the party today. This is evidenced by the appointment of Joaquim Chissano as the President succeeding Samora Machel, as well as in the makeup of the Central Committee. Core members of the government such as Marcelino dos Santos, Jorge Rebelo, Mario Machungo, Chissano and, of course, Samora Machel, were all represented in early Frelimo governments and are all veterans of the war.[1] It is the same core of people who changed the party from a loosely defined nationalist movement to a

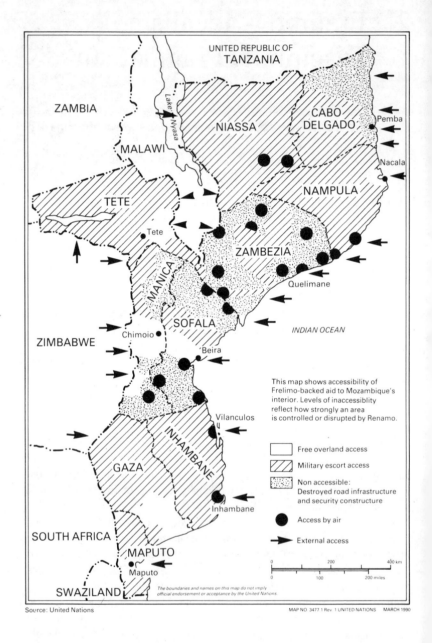

MAP 2.1 Mozambique: Conditions of accessibility, February 1990

Marxist-Leninist party, and now to a party which is struggling even to call itself socialist.

It is these same people who have presided over the miseries of their country for the last twenty seven years, and who have charged themselves with responsibility for the suffering of their people for the last seventeen years. They have seen the struggles of life under repressive Portuguese colonialism, they administered the bitter pill of the war of independence, and now they watch the suffering of the Mozambican people continue under their own rule.

Mozambique is ravaged by desperate poverty, and despite independence, Mozambicans continue to suffer, perhaps more than ever. Like the people, the economy is wasted; the trading structure has broken down almost entirely, and most real economic activity goes on in the thriving black market. Thousands of farmers have fled the land altogether, and millions face starvation. The country is in danger of turning into an aid-reliant economy where everyone tries to maximise their allocation of aid instead of working together to build up their country. For all of this Frelimo must take some blame.

One wonders what kind of philosophy could have guided a government to preside for years over the wholesale destruction of its own economy, while spending all its energy on trying to build up the country, to make basic foods, education and health accessible to everyone. What kind of principles, people might ask, guide a government to force peasant farmers to live in communal villages for the purpose of fostering large scale farming one year, and in the next decide that family farming should take priority; to rip mini-skirts off women in the streets whilst at the same time fighting for the rights of its women; to profess democracy, yet not allow people to chose their government, and to penalise church-goers and traditional ways of life; to flog people publicly for selling goods in the streets one day, and to condone it the next?

To understand Frelimo, and the principles under which Mozambicans' lives have been ordered in the years since independence, the origins of Frelimo and the party's leading figures must be briefly considered.

In 1962, Dr Eduardo Chivambo Mondlane, a Mozambican who had studied for several years in the West and returned to his own country in 1961, founded Frelimo in Dar es Salaam, in neighbouring Tanzania. The war of independence waged by Frelimo against the Portuguese was not started until two years later in September, 1964.

At the time of its formation, Frelimo was simply a nationalist movement whose sole objective was to release its people from the rule of the Portuguese colonists, and create a Mozambique in which all Mozambicans were independent from colonial shackles. As Marcelino dos Santos, a leading Frelimo figure, said in 1973: 'The minimum ideological framework when Frelimo was formed in 1962? Just to be against the colonial oppression and for national independence. Nothing else.' The latent Marxist-Leninist tendencies within Frelimo, which encompassed these goals and prescribed a logic and method of achieving them, did not become dominant until 1969.[2]

The offensive and repressive practices of Portugal's colonial regime in Mozambique stimulated an anger that was not to be stifled. The refusal of the Portuguese to recognise the existence of Mozambique as an entity in itself, insisting instead that it was an integral province of Portugal, helped define the core of Frelimo's goals as nationalist, as did the racist practices of the colonists. The Portuguese, unlike some other colonial powers in Africa, refused to accept the changing times and to back out of their colonies as smoothly as possible; instead, holding on. But, the pot of Mozambican resistance was boiling, and the tight lid that the Portuguese kept on it did not make it go away. Instead it boiled over.

By 1960 the Portuguese had already become extremely sensitive to rebellious political feeling amongst the native Mozambicans, and in that year butchered an alleged 600 Mozambicans at the infamous massacre at Mueda. In 1962 Frelimo encountered PIDE, the Portuguese security police, for the first time: the first taste of the long war between them that was to come.

For the first few years of the war, the only border friendly to Frelimo was the Tanzanian border. However, in 1964 with the achievement of Zambian independence, Frelimo, in theory at least,[3] gained a second friendly ally. Thus Frelimo was able to spread its war for independence into the province of Tete by 1968. Previously, guerilla activity had been mainly confined to the northernmost provinces of Cabo Delgado and Niassa. Once it reached Tete, the spread southwards was inevitable, and by 1973 the central provinces of Sofala and Manica were under fire.

Frelimo overcame the Portuguese forces against enormous odds. Eight thousand Frelimo guerillas were ranged against the much larger Portuguese force of sixty thousand. The war's turning point came in May 1970 when Frelimo survived the massive manoeuvre by the Portuguese: Operation Kualza de Arriaga (or Gordian Knot). For this operation, which was intended to be the final blow to the guerillas, forty to fifty thousand Portuguese troops were mobilised.[4] Perhaps it is a testimony to the tactical advantages of popular guerilla warfare over conventional warfare that Frelimo managed to withstand it, and to go on to win the war. By 1975 Frelimo was in government, most of the Portuguese had gone, and a new set of problems presented itself. Not the least of the new problems was the practical difficulty of changing a military force, many of whose leaders had spent the last eleven years living in the bush, into a government with an administrative capacity to carry out its emerging set of policies.

From the war's stimulants – colonialism and its practices – Frelimo had developed a clear idea of what it saw as the meaning of nationalism and independence. Nationalism to Frelimo meant one nation which was governed by itself and not by colonists. Independence to Frelimo meant a country which was free of the exploitative economic system by which the colonists justified their rule. The nature of this system which maintained and justified itself by achieving its goal of keeping the élite rich at the expense of the masses, defined Frelimo's opposition as socialist. Frelimo would not count Mozambique as independent until the majority of its people were engaged in developing themselves and their country.

But these were broad aims. How they were to be achieved was another matter. Already, out of the way that it had conducted its war, which resulted from blending practicality with the nationalistic principles which grew out of its negative experiences of colonialism, there had grown a degree of political cohesion and unity of ideas within Frelimo on this question, and on the question of many principles.

Because the guerillas had operated in small units, hiding out in the bush, they had relied heavily on local villagers to provide them with food and other basic requirements. Frelimo had formed 'dynamising groups' (known as GD's, *Grupo Dinamizador*) which activated people into supporting the guerrillas, and into building social structures, including schools and hospitals, in the liberated zones. It was necessary to have active popular support for the war both in practical terms and in terms of achieving the goal of building a Mozambique in which the people were truly independent. The need for popular support became, as the partial result of the practical lessons of the war, fundamental to Frelimo's political ideas.

Formative too of Frelimo's political principles, was the decision taken during the war to recruit women to fight as Frelimo soldiers. This step, like other early ones, was not easy. There were many rival factions in Frelimo vying for control of the party, most notably the faction controlled by Lazaro Nkavandame, which created a great rift in the party until 1969 when he was finally suspended from all his activities in Frelimo; on this issue of women soldiers, and many others, the party was split to the core.[5]

The arguments used in favour of the inclusion of women in the struggle, and the outcome of the women issue, were symbolic of what the future Frelimo held as its most basic values. It was Samora Machel himself, President-to-be, who argued the most vehemently and effectively for the inclusion of women. His argument was simply that they were needed if the struggle was to be won. Those opposing him argued that women in the army might cause a breakdown of discipline amongst the fighters, and a loss of concentration on the part of the men. Yet Machel held that discipline was so fundamental that it had to be made strong enough not to frustrate the political goals of the party. His view was, in essence, pragmatic: the women were needed and so they fought.

This curious mixture of high ideals and the realistic edge of hard-headed pragmatism showed itself again soon after independence. Machel, in spite of the fact that the Catholic church was an integral part of the Portuguese institutions that he had been fighting against for the last ten years, sent Marcelino dos Santos, Vice President of Frelimo, to meet the Pope, and court his support for Frelimo. He realised that, although it was extremely unlikely that the Vatican would befriend or indeed formally recognise what was seen as a group of neo-Marxist guerillas who had all but ejected the Portuguese Catholic establishment from Mozambique, it would be a remarkable *coup de grâce* if it did. To the great astonishment of the world, the Pope did choose to recognise his new Mozambique, announcing that the Catholic Church supported the struggle for justice, freedom and national independence.

In the light of Machel's reservations about the church some might call it hypocrisy, or weakness of principle on his part, but to him it was simply a practical move. To him the church was an institution always hiding its political motives behind hands folded in prayer, trying to appear harmless by shutting its eyes and bowing its head, while at heart it was tremendously political, powerful and pervasive. In one fiery May Day speech, Machel condemned the church as an imperialistic institution 'recruiting people against us, using its cassocks as disguise'.[6] Yet it was this, the highest establishment of the Catholic Church, that he approached for the recognition of his new country. This bold pragmatism is what has most characterised Frelimo's attitude to government over the last sixteen years, implying that even through its most Marxist years, its fundamental goals had always remained nationalist at heart, albeit with vivid disciplinarian and socialist strands.

It was Machel himself who moulded Frelimo to this form. Many Mozambicans referred to him as the 'father' of the nation; with his tremendous oratory, military and political skills he soon became a legendary figure. He was seen widely as a man of vision and hope, and as a strong and good man. His reputation for integrity spread so far that I have even heard hard-bred present day white Zimbabwean farmers, his most unlikely allies, single him out as praiseworthy. The slab of stone which sits amongst the deep grass of KaNgwane in South Africa where his plane tragically crashed in 1986, remembers him as 'A Hero of Africa'. He was an endearing disciplinarian, orator, politician, general and fighter.

His style was almost that of a demagogue,[7] and the personal touch which he gave to Frelimo characterised the party and its policies. He would often make up his own rules in his speeches without consulting his party, and would order instant and sweeping changes to solve local problems which he became aware of on his many journeys around the country. Even so, it was he who played the main role in building the party, demonstrating as he did so that his primary concern was with Frelimo, over and above himself. One of his paramount goals was that the Mozambican people should be organised, so that they could express themselves through the party or the adjoining mass movements. In this respect he was, thankfully, a benevolent dictator.

In other respects there was less to be thankful for. When Frelimo came to power, Machel was adamant that there was to be discipline within the party and without. This was an ambitious goal in a country which had just undergone an extremely violent and disruptive revolution. Mozambique's world had been turned upside down, and revolution to many was symbolised by chaos and the reign of indiscipline. At the time of independence, the world ran riot: people moved from slums into abandoned Portuguese flats and houses, they ransacked shops; whites and blacks shot each other on the streets of Maputo. A Portuguese woman who lived through the revolution told me that in the few days leading to independence, poles with severed heads and other body parts impaled on them, were planted and paraded in the streets of the capital.

Machel knew that he had been instrumental in bringing about this state of affairs, yet, given his own belief that a rigid and disciplined morality should guide one through life, he could not have wanted to be responsible for his people losing all sense of morality and values. Nor, one supposes, could he have wanted the country to miss the whole point of the revolution. For the idea behind the new one-party state was that it should rule on behalf of all the Mozambican people, who in theory were united as one nation behind its goals. Disunity in the country because of political or tribal differences, would certainly undermine the validity and purpose of the party, as the loss of moral values would undermine the purpose of the revolution. Proverbially, he wanted to have his cake and eat it: he wanted to stir people's emotions, excite their hopes, awaken their hatreds to incite them to revolution, but at the same time keep them in line.

The result was a massive clamp down on anything that symbolised loss of morality. Tight trousers or short skirts were considered to 'only cause temptation'.[8] What was called 'prostitution', but was often no more than a destitute woman who did not have the usual wraps of family to make her appear normal, was treated very severely. 'Prostitutes', along with any one else who dissented from the new Mozambique, were sent to the re-education camps. Many others, who were not politically motivated, were sent to the camps.

These policies, reflective largely of Machel's own personal morality, grated uncomfortably with the revolutionary zeal simultaneously being espoused by him and his party for a united Mozambique in which tribal differences and the yokes of traditional ways of life did not impede development. One of Frelimo's goals that grated particularly painfully with these strict moral codes was its commitment to 'liberate women'. Women in Mozambique have traditionally played a very secondary role to men. Frelimo pledged to work towards the prevention of such oppressive traditional practices as initiation rites [9] and the traditional paying of bride price.[10] Frelimo's idea of the liberation of women was unusual, in that it wished to take away all the 'bad' things from traditional tribal values and leave the bits that fitted with its, or rather Machel's, idea of morality. The result was that Frelimo espoused an odd mixture of liberalism and conservatism.

Machel's concern with discipline was, at least, symbolic of the fact that he, unlike some revolutionaries, had a strong idea of the chaos that was to come after the destruction of everything that had been. He had a strong sense of what his moral ideals were, and of the kind of Mozambique that he wanted to achieve, and he fought against the indiscipline of emotional or any other type of interference. His anti-racist stance is another example of his willingness to be both extremely pragmatic and disciplined in the pursuit of his broad goals. Like the women issue, it divided his party deeply in the days before independence; Machel faced battles trying to win consensus on his point of view. He knew personally that the whites were needed in Mozambique since only they had the education and skills required for development, so he fought the anti-white feelings in the townships at the peak of the revolution. His pro-white stance also fitted with his idea of a new, unified and non-discriminatory Mozambique.[11]

I met a Portuguese woman, Gracias, now living in Johannesburg, who, as a twelve year old shortly after the revolution was living in Mozambique. She was in a shop one day when two black Frelimo soldiers came up to her and started playing with her hair. They taunted her by telling her that whites did not belong in Mozambique. Gracias ran home crying, to tell her older brother, who was also a Frelimo soldier. He told her to report her molesters to the relevant officer. Gracias duly went to their commanding officer and told her story. He ordered all his soldiers to line up, and asked her to identify the culprits. She did so. He then told the culprits to lie down on the floor on their stomachs. He took out his long black rubber sjambok and beat the men till they wept.

At independence, many of Frelimo's representatives were guerrillas who had just returned from a military life in the bush and, in trying organise civilian life, they used crude measures. A telling rejoinder to this story is that, when the men were bleeding and screaming on the floor, the officer turned to Gracias and asked her if she was satisfied yet. The twelve year old replied that she wasn't yet satisfied and he should beat them more so that they would respect women in future. He did so.

Mozambique was different in many respects from other African countries which had recently, after bloody wars, become independent. One notable aspect, illustrated by the story, was the disciplined attitude that Frelimo had to government corruption. From the beginning, Frelimo made it clear to officials that they were not endowed with their office so that they could exploit the people, but on the contrary, so that they could be of assistance to them. The number of officials in Mozambique, both before and after Frelimo took over, was enormous, and the task of preventing corruption completely was nearly impossible; however, it is to Frelimo's credit it that it succeeded fairly well in its task. The main difference between the Mozambicans' attitude to the problem of corruption, and that of other African countries, is that Frelimo has not tried to sweep the whole issue under the carpet. On the contrary, every case is brought out into the open and made an issue of.

This tremendous and, in the African context, unusual, emphasis on discipline within Frelimo, was an attempt to make the party a body which the people of Mozambique could trust, and a body through which they could express their grievances. The argument runs that if discontent is expressed through the party rather than against it, then the one-party state is as democratic as a multi-party state, and also more effective. This kind of government is supposed to save the frustrating effects of negative forces working against each other, the very thing which propels competitive multi-party systems. Frelimo, in pursuit of the unity necessary to make this idea work, tried to organise the Mozambican people into a body which understood this principle and supported the party. Sometimes, as mentioned, this took the form of overt 're-education',[12] or propaganda in the schools. Its more congenial face was represented in the creation of the various 'mass movements' such as the OTM (organisation of workers), the OMM (women's movement) and the ONP (organisation of teachers).

The OTM was and still is supposed to represent the workers and to try to ensure decent wages and living standards for them. In a Western democracy the equivalent would be the umbrella organisation of the trade union movement, which would have to compete for higher wages and bargain for better working conditions. In Mozambique, however, the OTM is supposed to be an integral part of a cohesive society in which it does not have to bargain or fight for its members, but only to ask for fair treatment. Thus, in the wave of strikes in January 1990, the reaction of the government to the higher wage demands of the workers was to appeal to the workers' knowledge of the economic situation of the country. The strikes were considered an expression of democracy, but the demands were nevertheless seen as irresponsible because, as one government minister put it, 'although the demands are reasonable, the state cannot grant such claims, and I think the strike leaders know perfectly well the state of the country'.

Frelimo's unusually conciliatory attitude to its enemies, both the Portuguese army and Renamo, is also an expression of this attempt to mould the people of Mozambique together as one and, simultaneously, to quell dissent. Again, Frelimo's performance, when compared to the humanitarian records of ruling African counterparts, has been impressive. Often in African countries, enemies of the state are mutilated and killed in massive and brutal displays of power by the victors. The video of the barbaric murder of Samuel Doe in Liberia by his successors, matched by Doe's equally barbaric murdering of Tolbert[13] whom he succeeded, are amongst many such examples. Such displays are common after coups and uprisings as a crude method of re-establishing the superior power of the victors, and of making future dissent from the same people impossible.

Frelimo has not been tempted by such extravagances in its politics, instead behaving in the opposite manner. In 1982 a special reunion of ex-PIDE officers and other hard-liners was held in the presence of Frelimo; Frelimo encouraged them to talk over the atrocities that they had committed. Accounts of this reunion by fighters from both sides of the wars, recount it as an intensely personal experience for many. It was seen by Frelimo as a kind of secular version of forgiveness: of self-forgiveness through confession. Frelimo officially 'forgave' those who confessed and openly talked about their atrocious deed. The only drawback of confessing was that the picture of the confessor was hung in his work place for months afterwards, naming his crime. Humiliating though that no doubt was, it was certainly better than being killed.

That reunion, in its perverse way, was an attempt to forgive and forget, and to bring those people back into society. A similar attempt to bring back into the fold those whom Frelimo considered estranged, was the amnesty for Renamo supporters which was first announced in 1987.[14] The amnesty was, of course, a blatant attempt to win support from Renamo over to Frelimo, and, in this sense, was an overtly political move. But it was also an attempt to rehabilitate those who had fought for Renamo in the past, and who continued to do so out of fear of being punished by Frelimo. The promise was that if they came back out of the bush, all would be forgiven and no negative action would be taken against them. Although even Frelimo reports that only 3000 had responded to the amnesty by December 1988, it remained another demonstration of Frelimo's wish to unify Mozambique.

However, as Frelimo learned, intending to unify a country is not the same as actually doing it. Frelimo's belief in the democratic nature of its government of Mozambique for the last sixteen years of enforced one party rule, has always been severely undermined by the existence of significant anti-Frelimo feeling within the country.

Although there are very strong grounds for believing that Renamo, as we know it, is not a proper representation or expression of this discontent (see Chapter 3), serious discontent with Frelimo does exist. Unlike discontent with Renamo, however, which is expressed through the movement of populations away from it (and confirmed by an examination of its origins, tactics and targets), discontent with Frelimo has been left largely unexpressed. It is only discernible through a certain amount of passive and some positive action on the part of the peasants, and through the existence of the strong grounds for potential discontent.[15] The passive discontent has been the most destructive for Frelimo, as it has played a large part in bringing about Mozambique's economic collapse.

Frelimo made some crucial mistakes very early on, offending and thus alienating certain dangerous individuals who were not prepared to give up power that they had wielded prior to independence. The massive open dissent from Frelimo by people who felt they had not been given the power that they deserved after Frelimo took over, was adequately demonstrated by the open mutiny of 400 soldiers in December 1975.[16] Eventually, the most prominent of those who felt deprived of the political power that they had expected in post-independence Frelimo were Afonso Dhlakama, and André Matsangaissa, the present and former leaders of Renamo.[17] A less terminal but more profound mistake was Frelimo's failure to pay sufficient homage to the important power bases that the tribal leaders held. By failing to provide any place for them in the new Mozambique, Frelimo alienated them. This left a vital power base open to manipulation by Renamo.

Both creating and exacerbating genuine popular discontent with Frelimo were the harsh methods it used in trying to eradicate traditional tribal habits and affiliations. Christian Geffray,[18] who spent a year and a half living amongst the people of the Erati district of Nampula province, quotes a local man, called Yamaruza, in his damnation of Frelimo's anti-traditional practices:

> That is why we have stopped presenting *epepa* (ritual sorghum flour presented to ancestors to allay affliction): to let the masters do what they want . . . The *ekhavete* (ritual drums) were broken by the Frelimo soldiers. When the *epepa* was in a bottle, they broke the bottle and forced us to dilute the little amount of *epepa* left and drink it. Those were terrible events . . . [19]

In its earlier years, Frelimo showed a healthy respect and understanding for the pockets of tribal power. Once in government, it tried to change things too fast and, becoming overwhelmed by its own power, forgot how best to manage it. Frelimo lost its sensitivity, and quickly regressed into the heavy-handed approach. Machel's trips into the interior of the country, which used to be regular events in which he kept in touch with the feelings and complaints of local people, soon became Pope-like tours, with much pomp and hand waving. This was not Machel's style, and he did not appear happy with this situation.[20] But the demands on him were great at this time, and the party's inexperience at government showed through.

This new heavy-handedness, of which Machel's loss of touch with his countrymen provided the first glimpse, was directed against, amongst other things, the church. The church, like the tribal leaders, was another very important pocket of power. Christianity was wide spread in Mozambique, and it did not endear Frelimo to Christians that their religion was penalised. The churches were turned into storage rooms for the over-fertilized and inedible tomatoes which were the product of inept foreign advice intended to supplement the government's already disastrous agricultural policy. Church-goers would often only receive half their salary because of their religion, and were barred from membership of Frelimo.

Frelimo's abusive policies also helped isolate many of its urban supporters. Frelimo's original base was amongst the rural people who had supported it during the war of independence; support from city dwellers was something that had to be worked on. But Frelimo hardly made itself popular with city dwellers when it enacted its solution to the urban unemployment problem, and began forcibly removing hundreds of unemployed people at a time to the interior. Frelimo did not even take care to put people back in the villages that they had come from. Instead people were dumped, sometimes hundreds of miles from anywhere they had ever been, by government planes which took them to where Frelimo thought that they were needed most.

The introduction of public floggings for economic crimes, including black-market dealing, compounded urban discontent, instead of quelling it as intended. The black market thrived in the cities, and this public display of government hostility to the hundreds who lived by the black market – which thanks to government policy was the only place that many commodities were available at all – was not well received.

Meanwhile, even those whom Frelimo claimed as its most ardent supporters, the rural farmers, were having serious doubts about their government. In an attempt to modernise agriculture and operate farming projects on a large scale, Frelimo not only made one of the worst economic mistakes of the early years of its government, but also succeeded in eroding the support of the peasant farmers. Many of the farmers were forcibly moved from their family plots into communal villages. The communal villages had modern equipment which, because it could be shared, was supposed to herald the modernisation and increased productivity of Mozambican agriculture. A similar policy of forced 'villagisation' had been carried out in Tanzania just before it was tried in Mozambique. In both cases the policy of trying to force socialism onto people without appealing to them by offering incentives was disastrous.

Frelimo's goal however, was still essentially what it always had been: to forge a nation which was truly independent and free from colonialism, dependent economic relations, and in whose development all Mozambicans could play a part. The need to achieve this goal came to a climax in Frelimo's collective mind in 1977, when the party formally adopted Marxism as its ideology at the party's Third Congress. The belief that it was possible to achieve the goal became, temporarily, more important than the goal itself. For Machel's part, his disciplinarian streak got the better of his concern with the ultimate goals. Machel, it is said by his friends, although very shrewd, was a not a profound thinker; Marxism was to him less a set of ideals, than a way of achieving them. The problem, of course, was that it was precisely this dominating concern with achieving the goal, that lead to the failure to achieve it, not least in economic terms.

Because a crucial elements of Frelimo's idea of a truly independent Mozambique was that the people had to be economically productive and able in their own right, the elimination of poverty was seen as fundamental. Frelimo had hoped that development as a country independent of ties to richer countries could come about could come about by organising the economy so that everyone had access to the most basic requirements, like food, housing, health and education. The temptation to bypass years of painstaking development with huge injections of investment, in a place as desolate as Mozambique, was a gnawing one. However, effecting it was no mean task.

In order to enact the idea, the entire economy had to be highly centralised. Basic commodities had to be subsidised and social services had to be provided free of charge. To be able to do this, the economy had to be weaned off the 'wastefulness' of luxuries. Incentives therefore could no longer play a part in the system. Without incentives and market forces of demand and supply governing prices, the whole production system needed to be planned. This suited Frelimo, as it was convinced anyway that huge injections of investment and the most modern machinery into agriculture and industry were the answer to all its problems; these were things that market forces and private capital could not suddenly provide. So, Frelimo embarked on the massive restructuring of all sectors of the economy.

The lack of incentives in the system, to produce, or to live without luxuries, did not bother Frelimo. Again, the leaders were convinced that making their system work was only a matter of discipline. They were convinced, moreover, that the nation understood their cause and were prepared to be disciplined.

Since, in theory, Mozambicans unanimously understood and were united in the goal of creating the kind of Mozambique which Frelimo wanted, any 'stick' that had to be used by the government to motivate people to be disciplined would not be unpopular, but self-imposed. From the moment Machel's disciplinarian streak began to dominate, the revolution began to precede itself, imagining that it was happening when its was not; this false belief justified the use of force. In fact what happened was not a revolution, but just independence followed by disaster.

The belief was that so long as there were no cracks in the system, no leaks out of which unplanned economic activity could seep, all would be well. This meant that a black market could not be allowed to develop, as it would represent precisely such a leak. It also meant that when the government decided that farming should be concentrated in communal and state farms, and carried out with the use of modern methods, instead of in traditional ways on family plots, resistance and unwillingness to cooperate could not be afforded if the plan was to work.

Of course a black market did develop, and a huge one. There was also significant resistance to the communal farming idea as many people knew that their old methods of growing worked, and did not want to hear an urban bureaucrat telling them about a different way of doing it. The government's reaction to the resistance was predictably severe; there was much at stake by this point. If its plan did not work, the economy would be in even greater tatters and the government's credibility would wane. This is when it began to publicly flog black-marketeers, labelling them 'unarmed bandits', in an implicit comparison to the other enemies of the state the 'armed bandits' (Frelimo's term for Renamo). As mentioned, the problem of the unwilling farmers was solved by the use of force.

Indeed, it was in the agricultural policy that Frelimo's fundamental mistake – the use of force instead of incentives as a political tool – was the most crudely apparent and the most devastatingly destructive. As 84 per cent of Mozambicans were agricultural producers of one sort or another, Frelimo had decided that agriculture should be made the backbone of Mozambique's new economy. The failure of the agricultural policy represented the failure of the rock upon which the rest of the plan depended. The agricultural policy embarked on is a classic example of trying to change too fast, and with too much muscle. Frelimo attempted to increase agricultural output by organising production in much larger units. Three levels of farms were introduced. The biggest, and most important were the state farms. Next came the communal farms, and the smallest of all were the cooperatives.

The state farms were allocated huge quantities of investment. They were given up to date machinery and equipment, as were the smaller units on a smaller scale. In each case, and particularly with the middle level, the communal farms, the central problem was lack of technical ability to make use of their new equipment. The people who ran these new enterprises had often never set eyes on a tractor in their lives, and many could barely read or write. The lack of operating ability was exacerbated by an almost total lack of the ability to maintain the equipment. The machinery was mistreated, and the vast sums of foreign currency spent on buying it were wasted. In addition, the lack of managerial skills necessary to run the new organisations was severe. People did not know how to keep books and records, they had been used to simple crop growing on small family plots, and selling what they grew at the local market. With the earnings they would eat and buy next year's seed; their economies had always been very simple. Moreover, many people, especially in the north, were reluctant to move into communal villages as was required, because, as Otto Roesch put it, 'resettlement in the territory of another group had historically meant economic and political subordination'.[21]

The problems facing the new agricultural policy were fundamental. They were problems which could take many expensive years to overcome, by which time there would be no foreign currency left in the country to sustain the policy. Advisors were imported, but from Bulgaria and other East European countries whose own agricultural performances were unimpressive. It was these advisors who were supposed to help Mozambicans, who had learned to live off food produced from their own unique soil for hundreds of years, make the new policy work. Suffice to say that the advisors were not of top quality, and many mistakes were made.

Nor was it just the lack of skills, excessive investment in expensive machinery and the unpopularity of imposing the communal farming idea that lead to the failure of the policy. There was a deeper factor at work, even amongst Frelimo's 'supporters'. For many, their contribution to the failure of the agricultural policy stemmed less from a hatred of Frelimo than of a complete failure to understand what Frelimo had in mind. Years of Portuguese colonialism in which labour was forced, frequently with the butt of a stick, left much of Mozambique with the idea that work was purely something that one was forced to do. Thus when Frelimo freed Mozambicans from their colonial masters, giving workers higher wages and simultaneously abolishing colonial methods of work extraction, it was seen just as a holiday might be; Frelimo was associated with 'time off', and thus with the very opposite of work. This is eloquently described by a Zambezian peasant,

> The government used to cheat us. We used to work, but got paid very little. If you complained that the money was too little you would be put in prison. There you can work for six months and not get paid money or anything. Now Frelimo has taken the country. Now we are resting. The one who is giving us time to rest is Frelimo. [22]

The simplest equation between productivity and economic success, it seems, was entirely missed by all. This was no one's fault more than Frelimo's, for Frelimo had not yet explained itself fully to people; it had not had time perhaps to articulate even to itself quite what it was going to replace productivity and skills with. The need for success became increasingly urgent as decreased productivity, and high wages were pursued by a disintegrating economy. To an extent Frelimo became trapped within the need to nationalise [23] as lower productivity meant that the government had to borrow more and more from the Bank of Mozambique to keep plants and farms operating. Economic failure led to the regression into dogmatism, and the dogmatism quickly regressed into force.

Many of the same problems that caused the failure of the agricultural policy were evident in other sectors of the economy. The same large scale ideas that had been applied to agriculture were applied to industry, for example. Within projects, inefficiency caused by lack of skilled labour, and wages that did not reflect the amount of work done, was rife. Entire projects went to waste because of the lack of skilled labour needed to make them a success. Meanwhile, industrial projects suffered from the lack of foreign currency needed to maintain machinery and equipment.

Some sections of industry did actually grow during these years, for example the construction sector which grew by 32 per cent between 1981 and 1986. Most, however, went into drastic decline. Transport earnings, previously the most important foreign currency earner, declined by 50 per cent in the same period. This decline was largely due to the effect of Mozambique responding to the UN call for sanctions against Rhodesia, a move which cost Mozambique so much.[24]

Foreign currency earnings were further reduced in these years by $3.2 billion[25] between 1975 and 1982 by the South African decision to cut the number of Mozambican miners in South Africa, and the later decision to stop paying the miners in a price related directly to gold. Moreover, Mozambique suffered a drop of $250 million in fees between these years from South Africa's reduction in the level of commerce moving through the port of Maputo, which fell from 600 million to 100 million tons in the period.[26]

A combination of this, and all the other factors causing the decline of foreign currency earnings, not least of which was Frelimo's attempt to reduce the dependence of the Mozambican economy on exports, and spend massive quantities of foreign currency trying to boost domestic production, made Mozambique's development very difficult. For Mozambique was still dependent to a large degree on imports for economic growth. It was a vicious circle. Frelimo was trying to get Mozambique out of its economic problems by following a route which in the end exacerbated them. With all this, there was the problem of operating an already misguided policy in an intensely hostile context.

South African hostility was very costly for Mozambique. There is much discussion about the South African policy of destabilising its neighbours during the 1970s and 1980s. That there was such a policy, which set out with one hand to make its neighbours dependent on it, and with the other, to squeeze them tightly enough to establish South Africa's economic supremacy, is an established fact (see Chapter 3).

The problem that Mozambique faced in trying to be independent of its neighbour was, simply, that South Africa was stronger and hostile. This, together with the way that Mozambique's economy had been specifically structured by the colonists to be reliant on South Africa, greatly frustrated Mozambique's attempts to be self reliant. Mozambique's attempts to become self-reliant were in direct conflict with South Africa's policy of making it more dependent. Mozambique joined the Southern African Development Coordination Conference (SADCC) when it was formed in 1980, to try to create a southern African economy whose epicentre was not South Africa, and thereby to counteract South Africa's attempts to make southern Africa dependent on it. South Africa's destabilisation policy in turn became orientated to counteracting the effects of SADCC.

The hostility of the South Africans combined with the terrible droughts convinced Frelimo that the economic problems Mozambique was facing were to do not with their policies or their methods, but with external factors frustrating them. Frelimo's resolve hardened, and it simply implemented its policies with more force. Military men who had fought for eleven years to achieve independence were not going to give in easily. The harsh methods used in the policies were justified in a steady stream of propaganda blaming Mozambique's economic decline all on South African support for the Renamo rebels, and the lasting reaches of colonialism. The strength of Frelimo's attachment to the idea of being 'independent' from its neighbours, went beyond a sentimental aversion to the perceived exploitation in a relationship which benefited one more than the other, and was not to be undone.

Mozambique recognised, for example, the fact that having an economy dominated by one or two crops or minerals, as is the case with most African countries, resulted in an undesirable degree of vulnerability to fluctuations in world commodity markets. When a third world economy, teetering on the brink of survival, relies heavily on the favourable price of one or two unstable commodities, the people of that country are guaranteed little stability, and suffer immensely when prices decline. In Frelimo's eyes, autarky was preferable to vulnerability. It wanted Mozambique to be able to provide itself with all the basics, and only have to worry about the price of foreign goods if it had earned a surplus with which to buy luxuries. Frelimo had fought with the lives of its people to achieve the kind of political independence which such a system would bring, and was still determined to make it work.

Neighbouring Malawi, ruled by strong capitalist values was no place to be envious of in Frelimo's eyes, except that it had no war to deal with. Frelimo was right, in that the poor in capitalist Malawi really were poor. They had no access at all to consumables which were imported from South Africa and therefore extremely expensive. Places like neighbouring Zimbabwe, where supermarkets frequently post signs pleading with the customers to use as few plastic bags as possible since they have to be bought in precious foreign currency, did not seem so bad. Better for those who could afford luxuries to do without, Frelimo thought, than for the poor to starve to death. Frelimo did not mind making Mozambique suffer this kind of deprivation, because in every deprivation of a luxury it saw a less wasteful distribution of the country's economic wealth. Frelimo's blind faith that its cause was the only good and moral one, and that this was understood by the rest of the country who would therefore have the discipline required of the whole population to make it work, was the root of its misplaced confidence.

For most people, it was the problems that were on view, not the advantages which in comparison seemed so small. It was true that even the poorest had access to basic food requirements, where food was available, but the country's poverty was so desperate because of years of failed economic policies that food was frequently simply not around to be had, for rich or poor. 'Resting' had done no good, for there was nothing to buy with increased wages; nor had the massive injections of capital into the unpopular communal and state farms done any good. People today living in the Beira corridor of Mozambique, remember well the foodless days of the mid 1980s; the shelves were empty in the towns, the market places were deserted, and people died, as one man put it to me, like flies.

The government's inability to cope with the ravages of nature and the war was so limited that the low price of the basic subsidised foods was comparable to a very small ill-equipped life boat thrown to a shipload of drowning people. Many people didn't see some big 'cause' in Frelimo's policies, but instead, the reality of the situation, which was a now officious government, making impossible demands under impossible circumstances, and trying to coerce them into living their lives in ways that they did not want to. The people saw more clearly than anything else the government's mistakes.

In a sense this is not surprising. The droughts and the floods of the 1980s were the harshest in living memory, and affected the whole of southern Africa dramatically. Mozambique had to cope not just with this but with a war which was possibly more devastating than any in the continent. The war caused massive population movements which disrupted the entire economic and social fabric of the country.

Indeed, the war drew out in every way the negative aspects of Frelimo's policies, and also exacerbated the sting of the medicine. The fate of Frelimo's policies on health and education best illustrates the devastating and independent role played by the war on the failure of Frelimo's policies. Health and education are policy projects which, in spite of the negative aspects of Frelimo's policies, developed considerably, only to be targeted by Renamo and largely destroyed, as will be discussed later. They also demonstrate that in spite of the abhorrent and fatally forceful way that Frelimo's massive and statist approach was enacted, there are some ways in which the belief that the entire economy should be at least be restructured, should be respected.

If you consider that when Frelimo took over, the population was barely educated with adult illiteracy at 93 per cent, while health facilities were so poor that there was only one doctor per tens of thousands of people, it is quite reasonable to argue that a massive revamp of the structure of health and education in Mozambique was critical. Without a huge injection of investment into these areas, Mozambicans could never be part of their country's progress. If the building of health and education facilities had been left to itself to increase at the same rate as the growth of the economy, the availability of these facilities today would probably be below colonial levels.

Instead, there have been significant improvements in the availability of both health and education facilities. There are now over 300 doctors in the country,[27] compared to the 519 before independence, and the 86 immediately after independence. The number of health workers increased significantly too, from 2000 in 1975 to 3800 ten years later. Much well directed attention has been paid to setting up a sophisticated health service in Mozambique. Mozambique, in fact, was applauded for its speedy adoption of the World Health Organisation (WHO) approved drugs list. Many African countries are prepared to take short cuts with their medicine and, spurred on by profit motivated Westerners, the result is that Africans become the guinea pigs for the world's drugs.

Mozambique also managed, at an early stage, to break out of the vicious circle that health systems easily find themselves in, in which so much is spent on curative health care in order to try to catch up with the situation, that preventative care is ignored. Considering the prevalence of bilharzia, tuberculosis, tetanus, measles and hepatitis, mass immunisation programmes are essential. Coupled with the emphasis on preventative medicine is the concentration that has been put on family-planning education. With the prevalence and pervasiveness of Catholicism left over from the Portuguese influence, birth control was not condoned, and thus people knew very little about it.

The need for the large proportion of budget allocation to health care, and the drastic restructuring of the way it operated, is reinforced by the fact that, although health has improved, it still remains very bad, as will be discussed in detail later. Seventy-five per cent of total deaths are caused by infectious or parasitic diseases; half the population is affected by malaria. With all this there is still only one hospital bed per thousand in Mozambique.

The other problems remaining with health care, which require a pro-longed and far-sighted approach to solve, also point to the continuing need for governmental, as opposed to private, responsibility. The main barrier to accessing health units now is locational. Even with Frelimo's attempts to increase the accessibility of health care by restructuring it away from the cities where it has always been concentrated, a significant degree of urban bias still remains. The 17.5 per cent of the population living in urban areas in 1989 had access to 90 per cent of the doctors and to 66 per cent of all medical staff.[28]

The state of public health facilities in Mozambique would only be much worse without the government's massive investment and far-sighted attempt at rebuilding, as the scale of capital investment necessary would be unattractive to private investors. It is thanks to the statist approach, too, that educational facilities have improved dramatically since independence. Since 1975 it is estimated that one million people have participated in adult literacy courses. By 1980 illiteracy was down by 23 per cent. The numbers attending primary school almost doubled between 1975 and 1985, and numbers attending secondary schools increased even more dramatically in the same period. A programme initiated in 1975, which introduced teacher-training schools for primary school teachers helped the number of trained primary school teachers reach 10 000 by 1981.

Frelimo's goal of creating a country in which people produced food for themselves, were healthy and educated, and played a part in their own development has not been proven to be either misplaced or unattainable. It was only the lethal combination of using unexplained, forceful and eventually unpopular policies to achieve it, and trying to make such policies work within a hostile context, that led to the great economic decline of past years.

By 1983, only six years after its formal adoption of Marxism, the economic decline was severe enough for Frelimo's party leaders to begin to recognise that the failure of the policies was due partly to the policies themselves, and not just to external factors, and to consider radical changes to its methods of achieving its goal. True to its nationalist and pragmatic origins, Frelimo began to stage an about-turn as dramatic as any that took place in Eastern Europe in 1990, but more potent than many because it was staged from within the government, not from without.

That such changes were to come, not just to economic policy, but in the attitude to all the problems which were hindering Mozambique's development, was Mozambique's best ever kept secret. Machel's decision to negotiate with the South Africans, and sign the nKomati Accord, which was widely seen in southern Africa as collaboration with the enemy, was sprung on the unsuspecting with considerable panache. Even the diplomats had no inkling that such a move was imminent. nKomati was widely reported as Mozambique finally 'giving in' to the enemy, and when Machel signed the historic document in the white train astride the nKomati river, observers looked hard for signs of emotion.

But any such signs were well hidden. Perhaps the only evidence of Machel's feeling of insecurity and isolation on that day, was that he is said never to have forgotten the first congratulation on the signing of the accord, which came from the British Ambassador. The germ of the decision to compromise with forces working against his socialist principles had already begun to take root two years earlier, when, with the upswing of the war and downturn of the economy, and in spite of its harsh anti-Renamo rhetoric, Frelimo first attempted limited contact with the rebels.[29] In October 1983 on a visit to Western Europe, and in discussions with American foreign affairs officials, Machel asked for Western pressure on South Africa to sign an agreement along the lines of nKomati. Even before that, starting in 1975 and going on until 1978, Frelimo had had a tacit agreement with South Africa to mutual nonaggression.[30]

The compromise and change was not just a decision by Machel to go against what Frelimo had been, but a move in line with Frelimo's original goals. The structures for change had long been there. For a one-party state which alleged support to the dogma of Marxism for six years, Frelimo's five yearly party congresses have always allowed an unusual amount of open criticism. At the party's Third Congress of 1977 Frelimo made its commitment to Marxism, yet by the next congress in 1983,[31] severe criticisms of some of the ambitious projects which had been adopted were already being being voiced. Although the commitment to Marxism was reaffirmed in 1983, commitments were made to attack the problem of the over-centralisation of power which had been vehemently criticised.

The infamous agricultural policy was criticised so much that its core, the practice of putting emphasis on the huge state farms and communal villages, was scrapped in favour of a reversion to emphasis on the family as the main farming unit. In the same year Frelimo started talking to, and in 1984 joined, the IMF, decentralising power, and generally loosening the economy up. The most profound economic changes came in 1987 when Frelimo embarked on the IMF-backed ERP. In the 1989 congress references to Marxism were dropped altogether. In November 1990 a new democratic constitution was passed. Together the changes mean that free enterprise and free elections are not just allowed, but are now encouraged.

The economic decline that stalked Mozambique after 1980 coincided not just with Frelimo's most disciplinarian years, but with the dramatic increase in war activity in 1980. There had been some economic growth between 1975 and 1981, but thereafter the decline was chronic. Overall production fell by 30 per cent and consumption per capita by 45 per cent between 1981 and 1986. Yet in spite of all this, the changes towards an altogether looser, freer system were the direct result of Frelimo's conviction that its policies had failed to achieve their goals. As the Prime Minister Machungo said recently to the South African newspaper, *Business Day*, 'Central planning and nationalisation do not work. They fail to produce economic growth. I can tell you. We have tried them.'

Frelimo's emotional pain at what it knew it had to do was less well hidden at the passing of the new constitution in 1990 than it had been at nKomati. The feeling of nostalgia for the good old days of fighting off the world and enforcing their policies against all odds in the name of a revolution that never happened, was poignantly evidenced at the party's Fifth Congress in 1990. After the new constitution had been accepted, Marcelino dos Santos, the speaker of the assembly, led the leaders into a burst of revolutionary songs denouncing the bourgeoisie. But, the feeling was decisive and strong in the government that the changes had to be made for the sake of economic growth.

As George Rebelo, the Party Secretary for Ideology said, we must 'operate in the context of reality and not in a world of ideals'. The support of the entire Central Committee underpinned the dramatic changes that came about in the 1989 conference.[32] This fact is a tribute to Frelimo's commitment to a pragmatic approach to what is best for its nation. It was able to drop all its firmest beliefs in the way its goals should be achieved, and most cherished ideals when it was proven that another route had to be taken to promote economic growth.

Although internal criticism and economic failure contributed to the decision to enact the economic changes, the requirement by the IMF and the World Bank that liberalising measures be taken in exchange for loans, of course, added impetus. A formative part of Frelimo's new attitude to following IMF strictures was the knowledge that any other path would jeopardise continued donations of Western aid, particularly in the form of loans. Eastern bloc aid was becoming less of an alternative, given the economic and political decline of the bloc. Even in the past, Eastern Bloc aid had been largely military. Aid from the West was something that a country as poor as Mozambique simply could not afford to turn down. Added to the fact that more aid is invested in a country if Western policies are pursued, something which in itself is more likely to make the policies work, Western policies attract private foreign investment. Mozambique, with its new policies, now has the whole Western world behind it, supporting its new path to development; this makes the policies much more likely to succeed.

Frelimo has moved back into the real world, and abandoned its belief that economic independence from the world means true independence. It has seen instead, that foreign investment, cooperative trading and foreign aid are essential to Mozambique, if it is to achieve any economic growth at all. Without economic growth, Frelimo has come to realise, no economic development of any kind is possible.

The new method of achieving growth, and Frelimo's change of heart, has for many been very difficult to bear; for some it even means death. In the war situation, where even subsistence agriculture is often rendered impossible, the enormous price rises, in some cases of up to 200–300 per cent, caused by the withdrawal of subsidies in the freer market mean that basic food stuffs cannot be accessed by all. There are now about a million people in Maputo alone who have been forced to flee their land in other parts of Mozambique because of the war. These people no longer have access to the farm land which they had relied on for survival. The severity of the droughts of recent years, and the consequent crop failures, have also caused many to suffer; many thousands have survived thanks only to donations from emergency aid organisations, and many more only because of the governments policy of subsidising the foods essential for survival. Perhaps it was pure defiance against these hard facts of life that lead dos Santos to burst into defiant song as he and his colleagues passed the new constitution. Nevertheless, it has been admitted by all, him included, that these people must be the lambs sacrificed for the sake of Mozambique's economic growth.

There has been a political shift within Frelimo of a very serious kind. It has been away from seeing the reduction of poverty as the primary means of achieving development, instead seeing it now as simply a very important element of development, with the need for economic growth shifted into primary place. But Frelimo has not departed from itself or from its *raison d'être*.

Frelimo has come a long way since 1975, and has learned from its mistakes, but still remains faithful to its core motivation which Machel expressed in that year. He said 'We know very well what we do not want: the oppression, the exploitation, the humiliations. But as to what we want and how to get it, our ideas are by necessity still vague. They are born of practice, corrected by practice'.[33] Frelimo has proven that it is still the pragmatic organisation which Machel had fostered; the same organisation which recruited women to fight because it was practical, which tried to gain the support of the people during its war of independence because it was practical, and which begged whites to stay in Mozambique after independence because it was practical. In a sense Frelimo has come home.

It has been the same body since 1962; it has been made up of largely the same people. Through all its mistakes it has had the national interest at heart, and not those of its own; at its top ranks are earnest and rational people who are willing to criticize themselves in the final event, even fundamentally in order to keep sight of their goals. Frelimo is a body of a fundamentally different nature than Renamo: it is an organisation with deep roots in a political cause.

Moreover, though Frelimo is to be scorned for the harsh measures that it used to try to achieve its political cause, its political cause should not be scorned in the same breath. For Mozambique's poverty is so penetrating that if development is to be of a meaningful kind, and if a return to the kind of development that the Portuguese considered valid is to be avoided, special and considerable attention must be focussed on basic mass needs as health and education. As chapter four reveals, the fragments of Frelimo's success, hard as they are to see through the shadows cast by the past years of economic decline, would have been much greater without the activities of Renamo, as would the successes of any government trying to develop the people of Mozambique in the face of Renamo's war.

Frelimo failed because it lost sight of its goal for a time, and enacted its policies with haste and consequently with force. But in part this was a response to the difficulties of the circumstances, for Frelimo was also profoundly frustrated by a war that was being waged directly against the people of Mozambique on whom its whole development plan relied. Frelimo made some grave mistakes which its cannot be excused for, but its task, as will be seen, was never an easy one.

3   The 'Khmer Rouge' of Africa?

A war of liberation seeks to free the people and the land; a war of destabilisation, on the other hand, seeks to destroy the people and turn the land to wilderness.

Derek Knight

'It was war' said Ken Flower, the Head of the Rhodesian Central Intelligence Organisation, 'and in war all things are allowed'.[1] But even in the madness of war the world holds certain standards and norms of behaviour. Without these, war can no longer even hold the status of an event where human sanity is temporarily suspended while the ugly means to a higher end briefly takes precedence. When the minimum standards of behaviour are ignored, the end becomes obscured while the means, the destruction, becomes paramount, and seemingly an end in itself.

This is what happened in Nazi Germany, this is what is happening in Cambodia with the Khmer Rouge adopting mass slaughter as its main activity, and this is what is happening in Mozambique with Renamo: destruction, brutality and mass slaughter have all become its core and definitive activity. Renamo, until very recently, has advertised no coherent political agenda to Mozambicans and has likewise never, until the recent threat of democratic elections in Mozambique, sought real support from inside the country for itself as a genuine political movement.

Nobody knows with absolute certainty who, if anyone, the rebels represent, how organised they are, what they want or what their purposes are if they have any of their own. The rebels are not even called by one name. Some people call them by their Portuguese acronym RENAMO (hereafter Renamo), some call them the MNR (Mozambican National Resistance), some the 'Matsangas', (after their early leader André Matsangaissa) and some, who do not credit them with as much authenticity, refer to them simply as the Armed Bandits (Armados Bandidos).

What is known about them is what they do and how they go about it, and from this much can be gleaned. Their targets and tactics, their inauspicious origins, and the logistics of how they keep their operation running, are painfully clear, as are a host of other telling details which glue together to form an ugly collage representing the brutal face of a nation's tormentor. Even Renamo's self confessed founder, the very same Ken Flower, who had said that in war 'all' things were allowed, later said in his memoirs 'I began to wonder if we had created a monster that was now beyond control'.

He is not the only one who was slow to see Renamo for what it is. The world over politicians and the public, confused by the preponderance of liberation movements in Africa and unable to distinguish between them or even to remember which one is which, have simply dismissed Renamo as 'another one'. Yet on the slightest inspection every observer notices something different about Renamo. A proper look reveals an organisation without any apparent legitimacy as a liberation movement from the beginning of the story right up until the end.

Condemnations come flying from all corners. Javier Perez de Cuellar, the Secretary General of the United Nations, recently voiced his abomination of the 'campaign of terror being waged against the civilian population.' Chester Crocker, too, the former American Assistant Secretary of State for Africa to the Reagan administration, and architect of the Namibian independence accord, has repeatedly condemned Renamo. The U.S. State Department made it clear that it could not act as the figurehead in the 1989 peace negotiations between Renamo and Frelimo since it would be morally obliged to take Frelimo's side and could not take an unbiased stance even for the sake of peace.[2]

For the United States which openly supported UNITA (the organisation in Angola which the uninformed see as Renamo's counterpart),[3] and whose foreign policy is often so concerned with globalist East/West concerns, to come out so adamantly against Renamo says something very damning about the organisation. The United States' and many other countries' condemnation of Renamo is unequivocal. There is not one government in the world that openly supports Renamo, and with good reason.

Such criticism is directed at Renamo because the scale of its brutality seems to outweigh any possibility that it even thinks that its actions are concerned with the interests of its country. A belief in its own concern with the long-term welfare of its country is the most minimal qualification for a 'liberation movement'; without it one need look no further. However, one must first establish that Renamo does not have this minimal qualification, and perhaps try to explain what, if not some concern with the country's long term welfare, motivates it to fight.

Renamo was founded outside of Mozambique, in the rooms of the Rhodesian and South African Secret Services as a 'fake black liberation movement'[4] to disguise the regional concerns about Mozambique's independence. Renamo's real support is tenuous at best, and small compared to the amount of destruction it wreaks, and its logistical support and funding come largely from outside Mozambique and Mozambican interests. Its internal operational support is largely coerced, and the targets and methods of the war it conducts vile and inconsistent with an organisation which has plans for government. Compared to the way Frelimo conducted its far from pretty war of independence, or the way other liberation movements, like ZANLA[5] in Zimbabwe, for example, have conducted themselves in the past against much tougher odds, Renamo sticks out like a sore and bloody thumb.

The key to understanding Renamo today is understanding how, why and where it started. The fact that its origins were from interests outside of Mozambique is a profound indictment of its credibility. Even if it later gained some support from inside Mozambique, the fact that Renamo sprung from other interests which went out of their way to foster active discontent for their own purposes, and not from real Mozambican active discontent, means that it lacks authentic roots. Renamo supporters frequently distort this point by claiming that they are being criticised for having outside funding, and that it is hard to name one liberation movement which does not have outside funding.[6] This, of course, is not the point, but rather that outside interests actually founded Renamo, and were formative of its *raison d'être*.

This is how Renamo came to be formed. Mozambique's geographical position, amongst other things, had long made Rhodesia and South Africa reliant on it for economical import and export of goods. This, combined with the enormous political threat posed by the imminence of their mutual neighbour becoming black-ruled, stirred them into action. The threat of Frelimo's increasing advantage over Portuguese Mozambique in the early 1970s was a particular source of worry for the Rhodesians who were beginning to smell the smoulderings of their own imminent war of independence. The Rhodesians were quite aware that their own survival relied to a large extent on the survival of Portuguese rule in Mozambique. If the unthinkable happened and Frelimo became Mozambique's government, there was no doubt that Rhodesia's own black rebels would be provided with a massive and secure rear-base in Mozambique. Over one-third of Rhodesia's border was with Mozambique.

In South Africa the township walls began to dance with Frelimo slogans. The cooped-up energy behind black political consciousness was stirred to heights when Mozambican independence finally became a reality. The Africans of the rest of southern Africa began to realise that self-rule could for them too become a reality. For the whites too the reality was becoming unpleasantly vivid, and they responded with age old tactics. The

Afrikaners, not so long ago, in their famous trek northwards had learned how to secure themselves by positioning their wagons in a circle, creating a 'laager' which no intruder could penetrate. For South Africa and Rhodesia to protect their 'laager' of white rule, outside influences had to be subdued. For Rhodesia the threat became part reality when Northern Rhodesia gained its independence in 1964, becoming Zambia. Suddenly Rhodesia saw the possibility of being hemmed in by hostile forces on its eastern border and northern borders. Thanks to Zambia's cooperation, by 1968 Frelimo became considerably more active in the province of Tete, which directly bordered Rhodesia, and later in 1970 as Rhodesia had feared, south of the Zambezi on its eastern border. Thus, in the spiral of events that the Rhodesians had most dreaded, a larger and safer sanctuary for the ZANLA rebels in Mozambique opened up. Because Zimbabwean geurillas could now harbour more safely in Mozambique, this gave the Zimbabweans' war a new impetus. By 1975 the number of ZANLA recruits crossing the border into Mozambique was dramatic, at an estimated 1000 per week.[7]

Already the Rhodesians who had long ago learned that black disunity was the most effective weapon in any African war, were thinking of setting up a fake Mozambican black nationalist movement to counteract the threat that Frelimo was posing. They broached the idea with the Portuguese government as early as 1972, but until the eleventh hour of Portuguese rule the Rhodesians received only a hesitant response.[8]

At that eleventh hour, in March 1974, the Portuguese finally gave the idea their full support.[9] Even the South Africans claim part involvement with the formation of Renamo. As Gordon Winter, a previous South African Secret Service Agent, put it in his book *Inside Boss*: 'The best example of South African involvement in the affairs of other countries came in 1976 when Army Chief Magnus Malan and his military intelligence set up a fake black liberation movement in league with Rhodesian Intelligence. I know all about this movement because I was its number one propagandist from the start . . . its name was the Mozambican National Resistance and when I first started glorifying its exploits it existed in name only.'[10]

The Portuguese had agreed, the South Africans had agreed and Rhodesia had been ready for a long time to put this outrageous plan into action, and the time had finally arrived. It was the start of a war which was to carry on for years after the Rhodesians themselves had left the scene, and a war which was to ravage Mozambique to its very core.

Before any recruiting was done a radio station calling itself 'The Voice of Free Africa' was set up on 5 July, 1976. Broadcasting from what was then called Gwelo, and now Gweru, in Zimbabwe, the station raved about the exploits of the so far nonexistent MNR, and expounded anti-Frelimo propaganda. It had its listeners believe that it was broadcasting from within Mozambique to lend a mask of authenticity. An aura of jest rounded the station and its broadcasts. Listeners used to send in letters to the producers writing of how well the 'resistance' and its brave fighters were faring in Mozambique. One particularly humorous correspondent added the words 'Viva Resistência!' to the end of his letter, a joke intended to be taken, as it was, exceedingly well by the radio staff, who knew as well as he that there was no resistance on the ground.[11] Frelimo, who had become rather worried about the station after failing to silence it, began to put out anti-'Voice of Free Africa' propaganda dubbing it 'A Voz Da Quizumba' (voice of the hyena).

The point of creating Renamo now, and later when ex-Portuguese PIDE and defence-force members and the disaffected from within the Frelimo army had been recruited to support the movement, was twofold. It was a mixture of Rhodesia's goal of bringing down the Frelimo government so that its own position as a white-ruled capitalist country in southern Africa would not be threatened, and its goal of fighting of its own ZANLA rebels. Renamo's tactical value lay in the recruitment of Mozambicans to the movement. On the one hand it would appear as a Mozambican anti-Frelimo movement, and on the other the Mozambicans would be able to use their ethnicity to tap valuable local sources of information about the location of ZANLA fighters in Mozambique.

Moreover, having an 'African' movement at their disposal protected the secrecy of their attempts. For the Rhodesians the creation of Renamo was a stunning military move. Rhodesia's purposes and role in the formation of Renamo were spelled out in detail by not just by Ken Flower, but also by Renamo itself, in the form of Evo Fernandes, its one time Secretary General.[12]

Rhodesia was engaged in all-out war against Mozambique. In 1976 the new Frelimo government declared its border with Rhodesia shut, thus trapping Rhodesian trains inside Mozambique, and increasing land-locked Rhodesia's isolation by cutting off its access to Mozambican ports. Although Rhodesia was concerned with its own military intelligence ends, it never for a moment forgot that to bring down the Frelimo government was its long term aim, and through Renamo it blended its ends carefully. The Rhodesians taught the Renamo recruits, in the training camps established in Odizi (near Umtali), later in Bindura, and in Salisbury itself, that their job was to be a movement which would liberate Mozambique from Frelimo. When the recruits realised this, they would 'spontaneously' attack ZANLA bases since Frelimo and ZANLA were fighting together.

The Rhodesians in their formation of Renamo were hardly, as it was claimed, capitalising on existing mass anti-Frelimo feeling. Amongst other things, both the makeup and size of Renamo are witness to this. The role of ex-Portuguese security forces members, like Orlando Cristina[13] and Evo Fernandes,[14] in the top ranks of Renamo from early on, is evidence enough. Cristina, indeed, is the most central figure who originated from within Mozambique, to the Renamo that we know today. He had previously worked with the Flechas, a hard-core Portuguese 'crack squad' along the lines of the Rhodesians' Selous Scouts. As Ken Flower's original inspiration was to model Renamo on the Flechas, Cristina's past link presumably did not go unnoticed. Even before the involvement of the Rhodesians, however, Cristina, independently from any of the many opposition groups that sprung up at the time of independence, had taken it upon himself to produce an anti Frelimo pamphlet and distribute it Mozambique. The pamphlet, produced first in September 1975, was entitled *Magaia*.

When Cristina fled to Rhodesia after a month's detention in Malawi for allegedly selling confidential documents to a French magazine, he began to work on the radio station set up by the Rhodesians. Cristina, who recruited Evo Fernandes, and who fostered as his protégé Afonso Dhlakama because of his willingness to accept South Africa's role, was not only the first evidence of Renamo, but until his murder in 1983, played a crucial role in its identity. *Magaia* can thus be seen as the original Renamo document.

Magaia was printed very cheaply, as is clearly evident from its quality, out of Cristina's own pocket.[15] Yet, Cristina's reputation in Beira was that of a hard-headed mercenary, an unlikely candidate for such unselfish political activities. His image, presumably created by the popular knowledge of his involvement with the Flechas, was misplaced. He was, in fact, a strangely idealistic man, who had in his youth been a communist, and later a Frelimo supporter, holding peculiar and intense fantasies. One of these was a curious obsession with the gallant Lawrence of Arabia. He used to play the theme music to the feature film in the background during some broadcasts, and ultimately, because of his obsession, even married a woman of Arab extract.

Cristina's poor relationship with Ken Flower, was exacerbated by his difficulty in accepting the commands of his paymasters at the radio station. Taking orders, did not fit into his idealistic view of the world; indeed his colleagues claim that he eventually became 'power mad' and tried to dominate Renamo. This eventually lead to his death, probably at the hands of a group called REMO,[16] a Portuguese cell in South Africa whom he organised to raise funds for Renamo.[17] It was Cristina's bad relationship with the Rhodesians and his wish to dominate Renamo which eventually made him so willing to accept the transfer of Renamo's control to South Africa. It would appear that Cristina was not the only of Renamo's central figures whose political activities were unashamedly spurred on by and adorned with a keen fascination with the heroism and rewards that accompany power.

André Matsangaissa and Afonso Dhlakama too, who ventured over from Mozambique soon after Cristina, to ask the Rhodesians for money for them to fight Frelimo, had their peculiar histories. Both had been imprisoned by Frelimo for theft of property whilst in the army. The significance of their thieving, should not be missed. Although the conservative view that all political views start with small personal grievances or biases, and that this is what gives them their validity, carries considerable weight, this point becomes rather stretched when applied to Matsangaissa. Some Renamo insiders themselves admit that the leader was a man of 'limited political views', a view which reflects even less well on Dhlakama, whom the Rhodesians considered to be of a lower calibre than Matsangaissa. In the case of many Renamo members who defected from Frelimo, the main complaint was that they had personally not been accorded the power or paid the rewards for their efforts by Frelimo.

The main factor that transformed their discontent into such radical and destructive action was that the idea of a resistance movement had already been born far away from the Dhlakama's and Matsangaissa's of Mozambique, and even further from any latent mass anti-Frelimo feeling that might have existed at the time. Indeed, if such feeling did exist, and, as has been seen, there were strong grounds at the time for anti-Frelimo feeling, it played no part in the formation of the Renamo which Dhlakama, Matsangaissa, Cristina and the Rhodesians built. Their movement was indeed at this point to be no more than the fake black liberation movement that it was dubbed by its Rhodesian financiers and founders. Mass population movements away from zones held and harassed by Renamo in recent years, suggests that this is what it essentially remained.

Renamo, the Mozambican National Resistance, was given its name at some unspecified point in 1976/77 during meetings between Cristina and Matsangaissa; it was a name which 'popped up' because of the radio station's humorous usage of the slogan 'Viva Resistência!', taken from the letters of the listener mentioned. The formally called meeting of 1 May 1977 at Cristina's house in Salisbury, at which Renamo was supposed to have been named,[18] was actually called by Cristina to introduce radio announcers to students who had come down from Kenya. The announcers had insisted on the meeting after chastising Cristina for being 'secretive' about the students. Cristina, irritated by their nosiness, called everyone to meet as requested, waited for silence, and sarcastically inquired what they would like to talk about to each other.

Matsangaissa was sent and paid by the Rhodesians to recruit fighters for Renamo; they added some of their own recruits. For the bulk of these early Rhodesian days Renamo was only about two thousand strong. Since Renamo's goals, existence and sustenance up until 1979 were mainly Rhodesian,[19] the so-called rebels had good reason to be worried when the Rhodesian war ended and Zimbabwe was given its independence. The Rhodesians were in an urgent hurry to disassociate themselves from their operation in Mozambique whilst the Lancaster House talks were underway, and denied any involvement in such a project. But the two thousand had no need to fear for long, because Rhodesia in its last parting gift to southern Africa, the land on which it had fought a bitter fight and lost, was to provide for its pet very well. Renamo was offered to the South Africans, and as Ken Flower put it in his memoirs, it took them over 'lock, stock and barrel'.

Considering its size at the time of Zimbabwean independence Renamo surely would have faded out had the South Africans not come to its rescue. It went through a very rough period between 1979 and 1980 when there were massive internal upsets and power struggles. Matsangaissa was killed in a suicidal attack which he led on an enemy base whilst in a fury and, after a bloody internal battle, Dhlakama came to power. Dhlakama describes it as 'a disastrous period in which many soldiers and leaders were killed'. Faction fighting is perhaps inevitable in an organisation whose identity is as open to definition as Renamo's was at the time. For its identity was never in as much question as at the time of the hand over from Rhodesia to South Africa.

Renamo's very existence at this point was totally reliant on South Africa; Dhlakama's consolidation of his position as leader was largely thanks to his willingness to access South African resources, and he was thus very reliant on them for the maintenance of his position. South Africa had some very specific tasks in mind for its new acquisition. The South African goals fitted very nicely with what the goals of a black Mozambican liberation movement should be, except in one respect. South Africa's goals as they affected Mozambique were all destructive whereas a liberation movement is usually expected to have some constructive aspects to its make up, such as a coherent political agenda and an intention of converting the masses to its cause. Either Dhlakama was totally unconcerned with positive aspects of liberation movements, or the South Africans would not let him distract himself with such concerns. Whatever the case, South Africa's goals became Renamo's.

At this point Frelimo leaders were happily relaxing in Maputo in the expectation that Zimbabwean independence heralded the end of Renamo. They had every reason to hold this expectation. The Zimbabweans were friendly neighbours and the bulk of the Rhodesian army and secret service had fled the country. But their confidence was a fatal mistake. They let their defences down and began to concentrate on the daunting task of government with relish, as if they had not another care in the world. This gave Renamo the chance to expand.

The South Africans, whose resolve and instinct for self-preservation had been heightened by the recent events in Zimbabwe, were all set to pump Renamo up into a much more formidable force. By the end of 1980, it is believed, Renamo had grown to a force of about 5 000. By 1983 Western diplomats believed that it could be as big as 10 000, though this was far from Dhlakama's claims of running a 17 000-strong force.

For a time it was a matter of some dispute as to whether or not South Africa was backing Renamo in the years prior to 1984. Eventually, however, the evidence began to trickle out. Dhlakama, although denying the South African connection, rather gave the game away when he boasted to Portuguese journalists that South African Defence Minister Magnus Malan had made him a colonel with the reassuring words, 'your army is now part of the South African Defense Force'.[20] Numerous other reports confirmed the connection. Now even Renamo activists admit the massive role played by the South Africans.[21]

Plenty of physical evidence that the South African part in Renamo was not just financial but also logistical is available. South African weapons had been captured as early as 1979 at Renamo's Sitatonga base. A Durban registered boat, which was supposed to be a fishing boat but had no tackle on board, was captured off the Mozambican coast. Pilotless spy planes were spotted flying over Mozambique. In 1989 a former Recce[22] commander, Mervyn Malan, gave a public description of an élite SADF Recce unit operating with Renamo. He claimed that South Africa had been training MNR forces at Letaba Ranch near Phalaborwa in South Africa in 1983/84. What was not documented in the Garagua documents found at a captured Renamo base, or by the other barely concealed evidence about South Africa's involvement with Renamo, was testified to in the memoirs of Gordon Winter, the South African secret service insider.

The significance of South Africans' support for Renamo lies in their motives for supporting it, for, at least in these early days, they had total control over Renamo, and to the extent that they took part in the military side, they were Renamo; thus their goals were its. Renamo was no more than a potentially self-exploding branch of South Africa's foreign policy.

The poignant suggestion that South Africa had a specific policy of destabilising its neighbours is made by the wide evidence of actual destabilisation and the testimonies of South African government insiders, such as Eschel Rhoodie,[23] which leave no room for doubt. Skeptics may doubt nevertheless. That there was such a policy was confirmed to me personally in an interview with a professor at the University of South Africa, in Pretoria. The interviewee, André Thomashausen, presently a policy advisor to Renamo, and previously a specialist on Mozambique and Angola whom the South African government frequently called on, had frequently attended Ministry of Defence meetings in the past. His comment was that in many of those meetings, such a policy of destabilisation had been espoused; 'such a policy', said he, 'most certainly existed'.

He, Rhoodie and a plethora of established literature, point to the long-standing tensions between the Ministry of Foreign Affairs and that of Defence. The attitude of the former, epitomised by Pik Botha's diplomatic smiles, has always been that friendship with black southern Africa would bring South Africa the biggest rewards. The attitude of Malan's ministry of Defence, conversely, has been that neighbouring governments were unstable, and moreover, that they would always hate 'the white racists' and ultimately be undependable as friends and allies: destablisation was the answer to South Africa's security. Even without all the evidence, Malan's political proximity to P. W. Botha, and the fact that P.W. became President, is suggestion enough of which Department's attitude became policy.

The South Africans' objectives in applying this policy to Mozambique, appeared to be threefold. Their first goal, it would appear, was to destabilize their black-ruled and Marxist neighbour Mozambique so that it would look incapable of ruling itself properly. The world would think that black rule was an inevitable recipe for disaster. This was supposed to help justify continued white rule in South Africa.

Secondly, the wrecking of the Mozambican economy through Renamo activity was an attempt to let Mozambique know what it was up against when it harboured ANC members within its borders. This goal culminated successfully for South Africa in the signing of the nKomati Accord, in which Mozambique pledged to stop harbouring ANC activists. Thirdly, the economic destabilisation of Mozambique was an attempt to maintain South Africa's economic dominance in southern Africa by forcing transport business to circumvent the insecure Mozambican routes and use the ones leading to South African ports instead. Malawi's transport requirements are a case in point. An added bonus for South Africa was that the new economic dependence of its neighbours limited their ability to be politically hostile. All South Africa's goals required the destruction of Mozambique.

As time has progressed, how much political influence South Africa has over Renamo has become less clear. The murky waters of both South African and Renamo politics have obscured so many details, that much is left up to guess work. However, what has been clear from the way that Renamo organises its local support and its targets and practices, is that Renamo has continued to operate as if its goals were purely destructive. The possibility that it has developed into a rebel force with some of the positive aspects of a liberation movement, such as an idea of how it intends to govern or an authentic support basis, is strongly denied by the evidence. Accounts from refugees who are unable to collaborate on their stories because they live as far from each other as Malawi, South Africa and Zambia, build up an indisputable picture of how Renamo operates.

It may seem unlikely, if not impossible, that a rebel movement could exist in a country, affect as much destruction and grab as much international attention as Renamo does, without it having some kind of significant and authentic local support base to sustain and validate it. This is a total misconception. Renamo has proven it quite possible for a rebel movement to exist, and to exist effectively, without these prerequisites. Renamo does have a significant support base, but the majority of its supporters, and almost all its logistical backup and funding are not authentic. It is support which is either forced, manipulated, or comes from outside interests, and has nothing to do with the long-term welfare of Mozambique itself. This is how its works.

Refugee accounts describing Renamo camps throughout Zambezia, Tete and Nampula where the most extensive research has been done, are not disimilar in their descriptions.[24] Renamo appears to be a tightly disciplined force, not a group of bandits as it is sometimes made out to be. There are usually two areas to a Renamo camp: one for the soldiers, another for the captured population. One account says, 'The captives slept outside and were continuously guarded. There were about 600 people in the camp . . . meetings were held in the camp to warn them not to try to run away to their homes, and they were threatened with death'.[25] Renamo uses the captives as its work force: they provide the soldiers with food, they act as porters, and they help in the attacks.

William Minter, reporting the results of a set of interviews with a number of ex-participants in Renamo, says 'the author then asked 'And how did you come to be there in the bush with the Matsangas [Renamo]?' The replies were almost all very specific, almost all mentioning a specific month and many the day, most frequently saying 'I was *raptado* [kidnapped or abducted]'. Minter's research does little to establish that the majority of adults in the service of Renamo have been kidnapped, as his interviewees are all people who chose to take advantage of the amnesty· and defect to Frelimo and can thus be expected to denounce Renamo, but it does establish that kidnapping is one of Renamo's regular means of recruiting staff.

Reports of Renamo raids on towns and villages almost always report the killed, the injured and the kidnapped in the same breath; up to hundreds are kidnapped at a time. The Gorongosa documents captured by Frelimo in August 1985, which detailed Renamo operations, included a record of the 'Provincial Command' on April 14 instructing all sectors to begin a recruitment campaign. Each sector was to produce 500 recruits by 15 June. The wording ran, they should 'try to capture teachers, nurses, directors'. John Burleson, who was kept hostage by Renamo for several months, reported in 1982 having seen hundreds of forced Renamo recruits being kept under armed guard. These people too are kept loyal to Renamo through terror. If they are caught escaping they will be tortured and killed by Renamo, and, they are told, killed by Frelimo if found to be Renamo collaborators. Not just fear, but uncertainty of their future in a world which knows of atrocities that they are forced to commit keeps them loyal.

Aside from kidnapping, a certain amount of 'press-ganging' people into the service of Renamo also goes on. The South African elements that support Renamo, in this case particularly private elements such as Portuguese ex-Mozambicans living in South Africa near the Mozambique border, are especially helpful in this respect.

The South African newspaper, *The Weekly Mail*, published a report on March 22, 1990 saying that it held the names of two Portuguese men living in Komatipoort, one a farmer, the other a café owner, who were involved in, amongst other things, the press-ganging of Mozambican war refugees into Renamo's service. A simple tactic is used. If the refugees do not agree to become Renamo soldiers, their illegal presence in South Africa will be reported to the South African police. It has also been alleged that the South African security forces in trying to bolster up the size of Renamo when it was fully handed over to the South Africans in 1979/80 used the very same tactics on illegal Mozambican immigrants.

Probably the most common fate of the kidnapped is to be forced to act as porters for Renamo: another example of Renamo achieving the logistical back up that it needs by coercion. The fact that huge numbers of people are forced to act as porters for Renamo reinforces the point that a rebel force can exist forcefully with just a little bit of money and very few authentic supporters. It only takes a few guns to force a lot of people into doing things for you.

The porter issue is a nasty one. Men and women are taken from their villages in raids by Renamo, and forced to carry packs for Renamo soldiers. They are often kept underfed, partly to keep them too weak to think of escape, and partly because the food goes to the Renamo soldiers before it goes to the kidnapped porters. They are beaten if they do not walk fast enough, and sometimes flogged to death. Even very old men are taken as porters.

Many people die during their time as porters, and many take the opportunity to escape to neighboring countries. It is very common in Malawian refugee camps in particular, to come across escaped porters, who arrive in a wasted state, their skin clinging to their bones and their facial expressions telling a tale of horror. During the treks, which sometimes last only for a day but at other times last for weeks, the porters report that they are only allowed to drink when they come to streams or water sources. In many parts of Mozambique these are very rare.

Evidence from ex-captives and people who have been ambushed, indicates that Renamo puts great emphasis on the recruitment of children. Renamo's recruitment and abuse of children is one of the most horrifying of its tactics. The children, who range in age between eight and about fourteen, tell the story themselves from the rehabilitation centres and projects in Maputo to which some have escaped. All tell strikingly similar stories of the way they were captured and trained, regardless of which part of the country they have come from.

The pictures that small children who have escaped draw in their school books speak poignantly of the traumas that they have suffered. Pictures of mutilated people with missing limbs, of blood flowing through their village huts, and even of just severed limbs floating around on the child's page tell much.[26] The children, after being kidnapped, report that they are brought to Renamo camps and, if necessary, are initially subdued by beating, by being tied to trees for days, or just by being deprived of food. Then they are trained for between one and three weeks before they are sent out to inflict the killing and mutilation, which they had only recently witnessed in their own villages and on their own friends and relatives, on to others.

The training that they are put through is brutal but carefully thought out to be as effective and thorough as possible. Some Western psychologists who work with the children from the south of Mozambique who have escaped or been rescued from their tormentors say that the methods of training used to dehumanise the children to the point where they are as brutal as their masters, are not the usual or traditional methods found in

Africa, and appear to be the result of some outside advice. Initiation into the dehumanisation often comes in the form of the child being made to watch a close relative or friend being hacked to death or sexually abused at close range. After several days of the effects of drugs,[27] witchcraft, isolation, exhaustion, starvation, severe discipline and so on, the child is brought to the climax of his training. Here he is in one way or the other made to kill.

One child's account says 'The bandits told us to chose someone from among the civilians that they had kidnapped and kill him. They gave us an axe or machete to strike the person with until he died.'[28] Often the children are made to kill or mutilate their own relatives. Another account reads 'The bandits came at dawn . . . a man gave him matches and made him set his family's house ablaze. His mother ran out first, then his father. With scythes, as Firnice watched, the bandits cut their heads off. His five brothers and sisters were killed next. His parents heads were put on poles.'[29] If the children do not carry out the command, they themselves will be killed. After that they are taught how to assemble assault weapons.

Kok Nam, Mozambique's top war photographer describes the situation with this anecdote 'When I went to a rehabilitation centre for Renamo defectors in Maputo I met a young man named 'Fifteen'. I said to him 'Hey man, why do they call you Fifteen?' He didn't want to say anything but the other guys said to him 'Hey man, tell him why.' He said, 'I burned fifteen buses with people inside.' And he laughed just like that . . . But he had a crazy look on his face. Most of that group had no normal reactions.'

The discipline in the Renamo camps is severe; where attempts at escape bring death or mutilation, minor misdemeanors are punished by mutilation or by beatings. This and the psychological burden that the children carry by the time they have finished their training is enough to stop most of them from attempting escape. By the time they have personally killed their own relatives, or other people from their village, they are caught in the trap which Renamo has set for them. If they were to return they would probably be, if not killed, at least shunned and would have no means of survival. Their guilt is often too strong to make them think of facing their own people again. This, and the knowledge that if they escaped back to their villages it is likely that Renamo would attack their villages again, is enough to bind them to their tormentors.

Reports[30] of attacks by Renamo, where the 'men' have been children of eight, nine, ten and twelve years old, are frequent. From the reports it seems that the child attackers are almost more brutal than their masters. Wielding AK47s and machetes these children made beasts are extremely vicious. A Zimbabwean businessman who spent time in Renamo captivity said 'they were so highly motivated . . . it was frightening.'[31] It is often them that carry out beatings and other tortures.

In recent years children have made up a higher proportion of total Renamo recruits than previously. In the Gorongosa documents, a list of Renamo recruits, with their ages and other details, was found. Between 1978 and 1987 the average age of recruits fell from 25 to 16.93 years. If the average age was 16.93 in 1987, it is likely that large numbers of children of eleven and younger were being recruited. That this is the case is witnessed also in the reports of people who have escaped from Renamo captivity, and of the many people who have been ambushed by young children.

It is perhaps not surprising that Renamo finds it necessary to have such an established machinery for forcing support from locals, for even the uncoerced support given to Renamo's leaders appears to be largely manipulated and consequently fragile, or just tenuous by its nature. Although it a largely an unscientific business pinpointing the pockets from which Mozambican support for Renamo emanates, a collation of reports from Renamo supporters and defectors who have lived in Renamo areas, foreign anthropologists, and refugees, identifies three main groups who support Renamo out of choice. One sources of support is that of the 'Mambos', the traditional tribal chiefs. These people have a profound reason for discontent with Frelimo, as Frelimo stripped them of the political power that they held in the days of Portuguese colonialism, and replaced them with government-appointed administrators. The support of a Mambo entails the support of his entire community. Renamo uses the Mambos in Nampula province at least, as its 'tax collectors'. They provide Renamo with food and sometimes with fighters from amongst their people.[32]

A second, more negative, attraction of Renamo, as these leaders know, is that if they do not support Renamo their land will be repeatedly attacked and mined by Renamo, whereas a refusal of support for Frelimo would be unlikely to engender such basic and constant threats to life, limb and the ability to grow their food crops. The chief of any tribe's job is to provide for his people. Chiefs often feel that if they have to support Renamo in order to feed their people, then it is their responsibility to do so.

Renamo, though, is not always consistent in its support of specific tribal settlements. In the barren and desolate refugee camp of Mkwai, in Malawi, there were about ten thousand refugees. After fighting broke out among the refugees, between those who, in Mozambique, had lived in Renamo-held zones, and those who had come from Frelimo areas, half of the refugess were moved to a nearby camp. On interviewing residents of both camps, however, it emerged that both groups had in fact fled from Renamo attacks on their villages. A man explained the situation: 'we used to live peacefully with Renamo in our village, but now they have changed and they kill us'. This type of story is not uncommon.

A second pocket of voluntary and at times tremendously positive support for Renamo is that of people who wish to live in their traditional ways, something which is largely prohibited by Frelimo. Support from such people in any considerable numbers would appear from reports only to emanate from the north of the country.[33] Infuriated by Frelimo's disregard for their religious artifacts and traditional practices, these people support Renamo as if they were fighting for the Gods, creating their weapons in one instance with a 'deathly creativity',[34] and seeking vengeance on Frelimo.

Renamo has fostered this pocket of discontent, blaming the droughts and other natural disasters which have plagued Mozambique in recent years on the neglect by Frelimo supporters of their ancestors. Taking advantage of the deep rooted Mozambican belief in the ability of neglected ancestors to punish has not been difficult in recent years. The droughts of the mid-80s were worse than anyone had seen in their lives. It was easy for a already superstitious people to attribute this to the evils of the new 'modern' way of life that Frelimo made them live.

The widespread use of black magic in Mozambique, and a heavy reliance on witch doctors and spirit mediums has been taken advantage of by Renamo. Renamo's use of drugs to whip its fighters into the necessary frenzy before an attack, and to keep recruits loyal to Renamo, is a more striking example of the use of irrational forces to gain support. Support which is gained wholly by the exploitation of the irrational can safely be called manipulated.

It seems, incidentally, that the bulk of Renamo fighters are themselves as highly superstitious as the average rural Mozambican. This was evidenced by the recent emergence of a young man called Manuel Antonio in the Zambezia town of Alto Molocue. Antonio is a traditional healer and has a band of followers armed with sticks, stones and a healthy respect for superstition. The group calls itself Naprama; it is not the first group of its kind. With only sticks, stones, a few red handkerchiefs and incantations about Antonio's ability to turn his enemies into stone, Naprama has chased Renamo away from areas which the government, with their automatic weapons, have been unsuccessfully trying to recapture for years. Antonio, who believes he has a divine mission to rid Mozambique of war, conducts ceremonies in which he rises from the dead and stamps out bonfires with his bare feet. These lend him a fame that terrifies even the most hardy warrior.[35]

The people of Nampula, those who believed that they were engaged in a 'good and beautiful war' discovered, and voiced through the work of

Christine Geffray, that Renamo's encouragement of the traditional, and superstitious was encouraged for purely military reasons. It was not, as they had hoped, part of a broader political project. In the end the people considered themselves 'made fools of' by Renamo because they believed that it was no more than a skeletal military body. Research in the south of Mozambique, in Gaza, where Renamo has been found to be run by tribally chauvanistic war lords,[36] has revealed a similar failure of Renamo to gain popular support for leaders who seek only the power of their tribe, and fail to support anything broader and practical.

This research into Renamo's structure in southern Mozambique, together with the accounts of refugees in South Africa, indicates a third group that give Renamo voluntary support. This group is made up of alienated male youth, who support Renamo for what can offer in terms of looting, excitement and a meaning to life. This group would appear to be the best rewarded for its allegiance to Renamo, for villages are often looted for everything, including sometimes the clothes that people are wearing, and Renamo uses motor bikes to an extent as a means of transport, an obvious attraction. The state of spiritual frenzy that some attackers are reported to reach, the magical powers associated with the N'dau tribe and the vividly deep, though often obscure practices of traditional life, offers a cultist meaning to a life which might otherwise, in the context of today's destroyed Mozambique, be very dry.

How Renamo operates and organises itself varies tremendously over the country, and is enormously complex, wrapped up as it is in the infinitesimal subtleties of particular tribal and personal characteristics. Yet there are discernible patterns of its modus operandi, the central feature of which appears to be extraction on the part of Renamo. Robert Gersony, commissioned by the US State Department to gather and synthesise Mozambican refugee accounts, in a report[37] based on meticulous research methods, identified three broad ways in which Renamo organises itself across the country.

The first type of affected area which he calls a 'tax' area, is one in which Renamo just demands food, short term porters, and sexual favours from the women. In the second more severely affected area, which he calls 'control' areas, Renamo demands full time work from all the people whether it is as porters or in the fields. Families in these areas are split up into their service function, so that a woman will live with the other field workers near the fields and the children will live wherever their work is needed. The men are usually away being porters. A high percentage of Gersony's interviewees who had escaped from these areas had witnessed the flogging to death of weakened porters who could not keep up the pace with their load. One man reported that he had been taken to a clearing with a pile of decomposing bodies and told that was what happened to those that attempted escape. Fifteen percent of interviewees from these areas had witnessed the systematic rape of women and one third of them had seen their own houses being burnt down by the rebels.

The third type of area described by the refugees are areas containing sizeable villages which are attacked and destroyed by Renamo. It is not without reason that Gersony calls these 'destruction' areas. Renamo's priority for these regions seems to be to wipe them out, kill as many people as possible and take the rest as prisoners to the control areas.

That different areas with more or less these categories of attachment to Renamo, exist, has been confirmed by other people's interviews with refugees, including my own and the accounts of Christine Geffray, although one point that has arisen is that some of Renamo's bases are itinerant rather than stationary. Gersony's use of the term 'area' should be taken to mean functional rather than geographical space. One refugee from northern Tete[38] interviewed in a Zambian refugee camp is descriptive on the subject.

The refugee identifies three groups of people subject to varying degrees of Renamo control, apart from the relatively small number of Renamo soldiers themselves. They are the Juhbas and Majibhas,[39] lowly forms of Renamo soldiers; the captives, who were closely guarded and lived near but in the same camp as the Renamo soldiers and performed slave labour and also, in the case of women, sex for the Renamo soldiers; and the villagers who lived within the vicinity, who were not captives and from whom food and other material goods were extracted. The husband of this refugee gives an account of the areas subject to complete destruction, when he speaks of his village Mauera. It is clear from this account and those of the children's description of their training that Renamo is not a small group of gunslingers that somehow forces the masses into submission, but a force which co-opts the kidnapped into its game by a mixture of threats, negative incentives and false promises.

Although Renamo's system has proved highly successful in terms of destruction and military forcefulness, this does not correlate to how deeply committed its supporters and potential supporters are to it. Indeed, it has been shown irrefutably that the Mozambicans who run away from Mozambique to become refugees, almost all run from Renamo. Out of the 170 refugees that Robert Gersony interviewed, 91 per cent were 'very anti-Renamo' whereas only 5 per cent were negative about Frelimo, 72 per cent had no complaints at all about Frelimo.

I talked to thirty eight refugees in Malawi and South Africa, over a year and in ten different camps, about why they had fled their homes. All mentioned Renamo as at least part of the reason, food shortages being another reason given in every case but two. Twenty five of those who cited food shortages as a reason for leaving blamed the shortages on Renamo, and some said that they had also fled from Renamo violence. The other eleven were unspecific about the reasons for food shortages, but said that they had fled from Renamo violence. This, the accompanying stories of the traumas of escape, and Gersony's extensive research left no doubt in my mind as to what Mozambicans think of Renamo.

The evidence of how Renamo extracts military support from Mozambicans and that so many of them run away at given opportunities, is evidence enough that Renamo does not support a political project which it imparts to its supporters and shares with them. Credible reports of the existence of schools and hospitals in Renamo areas do not exist, where reports to the opposite effect do. Renamo's operation is an unreciprocal arrangement, through which it extracts the military and logistical support of the people, without returning them any favours.

Supporting the picture that emerges of Renamo, of a movement which exists solely to destroy and not to build, are the stark facts of the kind of damage which Renamo has wrought on Mozambique. It is true that all wars are about destruction, and that no army is kind to the country it is trying to conquer, but it is impossible not to see that Renamo's most attentive target is the country's long term welfare; and this it targets with a degree of brutality unknown to most of the world.

Renamo's main targets are civilians. There is relatively little targeting of the enemy forces. Renamo's aim appears to be to ruin the Mozambican economic and social structure as much as possible, to completely destabilise the country and to cause as much disruption and suffering as it can. The way to do this, in its eyes, is to kill as many people in as brutal a way as is possible. Indeed it is Renamo's readiness to commit atrocities on unarmed civilians on an unbelievable scale that has led to the comparisons between it and the perpetrators of the Nazi holocaust. Renamo's repulsive tactics remove it furthest from its claim to be a liberation movement.

The number of people estimated to have died as a direct result of Renamo activity is 700 000. This figure does not just represent deaths by direct murder, but also the number of extra[40] deaths caused in the droughts of the mid-1980s because of Renamo's sabotage of aid projects, and deaths resulting from their general destruction of even the most minimal levels of economic activity. The number of children estimated to have been abducted or orphaned by Renamo is 250 000. In addition the United Nations fund for children, UNICEF, estimated in their 1989 report, that 494 000 children 'could have survived' had it not been for Renamo activity.

Robert Gersony in his report estimates that on the basis of the 600 murders of unarmed civilians witnessed by the 170 refugee families that he interviewed, and taking into account that there are in total about 250 000 displaced or refugee families from Mozambique, 100 000 civilians may have been murdered in this way. If his interviews of the 170 families are totally representative, approximately 850 000 murders would have been witnessed by 1988 when he conducted his research, by Mozambican refugees and displaced people. Taking into account that there are are over half a million more refugees in Malawi alone, than when Gersony conducted his research, the figures both of how many have been killed and how many people have witnessed brutality, must be considerably higher by now. These morbid figures give some idea of both the scale and openness of the slaughter.

The scale of suffering is something that is difficult to quantify. Murder and abuse on such a large scale is difficult to imagine. The families that Gersony interviewed also reported hundreds if not thousands of cases of forced portering, beatings, rape, looting, burning of villages, abductions and mutilations. As he puts it, 'Conservative projections based on this data would yield extremely high levels of abuse'.

The total number of massacres carried out by Renamo has not been recorded, as many things go unreported in Mozambique, but the most infamous ones stick fast in people's memories: names like Manjacaze, Moamba, Guija, and Taninga ring like the toll of death bells to Mozambicans. The massacre on 18 July, 1987 at Homoine, however, was probably the most atrocious. 424 people were killed, almost all of them unarmed civilians. Out of the 386 identified 186 of them were men, 156 women, and 44 children. Another 298 people were taken hostage by Renamo. It was the usual dawn raid and the fighters were merciless. People were shot at close range, and 50 people were massacred whilst laying on their hospital beds, by bayonet, knife or machete.

The killings are accompanied by vile tortures and brutality. Renamo is guilty of uncountable atrocities. Nam, the war photographer, remembers a visit to a village in Gaza where the army had just ousted a group of rebels: 'The rebels lined the entrance to the village with the heads of men on top of poles. They each had their genitals cut off and stuck in their mouths. On the other side of the path were women's bodies. They were naked and had their heads and legs cut off.'

Renamo systematically cuts off noses, ears, lips and breasts, gouges out eyes, cuts off limbs and children's fingers as punishment or just for the sake of mutilation. One report says that 'these too are not traditional African practices', and suggests that they have been imported from overseas train- ers. Thousands, as Gersony's report conservatively estimates, have been subjected to this kind of abuse. *The Guardian* testified to the systemisation of the abuse in a report published in 1980 which said that missionaries along the Mozambique-Zimbabwean border near Espangabera in Manica had reported that Renamo had 'launched a campaign of beheading Machel loyalists, abducting girls, and press-ganging young men into service'.[41]

Apparently, anyone who carries out any economic activity is considered to be a Frelimo loyalist. Thus some 10 000 people in Mozambique have lost limbs due to having stepped on land mines. Many of the people are ordinary civilians who were out farming their fields. It appears to be Renamo's policy to mine the fields of ordinary peasants in order to deter them from planting their survival crops.

In order to terrify people out of being economically productive Renamo targets and makes examples of those who show any signs of even the most minimal economic wealth. For example, Renamo will kill those with shoes first. It will even go as far as to check the soles of people's feet to see whether they have been wearing shoes. Many people do not dare to own goats or cattle for fear of reprisals. If they stick out as any bit better off than the rest of the village, they are asking to be butchered. It is not worth their while. It is not just ironic, but very telling, that a group which purports to exist to fight communism should punish riches. The type of destruction strategy that Renamo engages in, which will be looked at more fully in the next chapter, although it points very clearly to an attempt to bring down Frelimo, grates harshly with the belief that over the last years Renamo has seriously entertained an idea of what it would want a post-Frelimo Mozambique to look like. If it had, it surely would not have embarked on such a wholesale destruction of Mozambique's social and economic infrastructure. After all, when the people are killed and traumatised beyond repair, when they have forgotten how to plant their survival plants because it as been forbidden for so long, when they have fled to foreign countries and when there is nothing left of the economy, not even its most basic infrastructure, what or who is there left for Renamo to govern? As Derek Knight from Christian Aid put it: 'A war of liberation seeks to free the people and the land; a war of destabilisation on the other hand destroys the people and turns the land to wilderness.'

All this leads to a clear understanding that Renamo is not concerned with a better Mozambique, but with destruction. Yet, although its origins have had a lasting impact on its nature, it would appear that it has developed into something more than just a wing of South African foreign policy. The type of support it attracts from traditionalists and tribal leaders who try to express their grievances through it, and its internal dynamics of superstition, power lusting, looting and fear, give it something distinct from South Africa. Its structures have developed into something with a life beyond the South Africans; it has become, to an extent, a self-propelling force, and indeed it is now estimated to be a force of some 20 000. Moreover, Dhlakama has asserted his leadership of Renamo to the displeasure of South Africa on occasion, such as during the Pretoria Declaration talks of 1984.[42] More recently South Africa has been seen to need to negotiate with Renamo in order to achieve its ends. Eskom, the South African state electricity company, has had to send a representative, via a committee set up for the purpose, to negotiate with Renamo to stop attacks on the Cahora Bassa power lines.

If Renamo is not just a branch of South African foreign policy any more, it must be asked what motivates it to continue destroying Mozambique. Why has Renamo not developed the deeper political element which helps the credibility of other rebel groups? The answer to both questions lies deep in Renamo's roots, and in the type of people who form the Renamo that we know today, and it must be concluded that the Renamo that we know today is engaged purely in a bid for power, and one which is wholly unassociated with the support of a greater political goal, such as democracy.

From the beginning there has been a distinction in Renamo between the foreign backers, Renamo's 'external wing' (which began as the radio station) and the military Renamo. Broadly speaking the southern African foreign backers have always been concerned primarily with the destruction of Mozambique through Renamo. The South Africans and Rhodesians wanted Mozambique's destruction for the reasons given, and South Africa's Portuguese for either vengeance or as a desperate strategy to get back their property and positions of privilege within the pre-independence system. The external wing and the other foreign supporters (American and West German, amongst others, and eccentric Christian groups), which consists of a curiously idealistic and often eccentric selection individuals, has been concerned with Renamo as a right-wing pro-democracy movement, and has sought to imbue the rebel group with a political tag.

The military wing has never been concerned with such things. From the beginning the Mozambicans who came over to Rhodesia to be recruited by the Rhodesians, were motivated by the desire for personal power. The circumstances of the arrival of the two leaders, Dhlakama and Matsangaissa, after stealing goods from Frelimo, and of others who had been involved in Frelimo faction-fighting, is witness to this. The fact that there was no political organisation within Mozambique meant that it had to be fabricated. The concern of the Mozambicans in fighting for the Rhodesians was to create a situation in which they could fight for the personal power which they wanted or considered their due. But they were no more than toys in a Rhodesian game; Matsangaissa was only elevated to the leadership to give some credibility to the claim that Renamo was a black rebel movement.

The military wing has always, to varying extents, been at odds with the external wing. When Ken Flower said that he began to wonder if they had created a 'monster now beyond control' he had sensed already the growth of the divide. Even from the days of the radio station, Cristina tried to assert himself as leader, while his protégé Dhlakama was the leader on the ground. Later, Cristina's successor as Secretary General, Evo Fernandes, similar to Cristina with respect to his eccentricities and idealism (he used to habitually quote poetry in conversation, had a great obsession with his appearance, and was also a member of the communist party in his youth), played the same game. But the people who ran Renamo from inside, although they have never been educated people, nor apparently people with any great schemes of their own, have always had an intense dislike of being bossed around, either by their foreign funders or by their external wing. Thus, while they have taken the money, the arms, and heeded the necessary dictates of their external branch, they have never incorporated any of the motives of the external branch, preferring to stick to those they were born with. Eventually (in 1986, and then again in 1989) Dhlakama abolished the position of Secretary General entirely in an attempt to rid himself of the problem of an over-ambitious external wing.

With this move, Dhlakama abolished the only claim, however removed from Renamo's manoeuvres on the ground even before, that Renamo had a politically-motivated core. It was the external wing that wrote the political programme for Renamo which first appeared in 1979 in a document called 'Statutes', and later in two forms in 1982, the later of which forms the basis of its documents today. Cristina was involved in the writing of 'Statutes', and André Thomashausen, a German South African-based policy advisor to Renamo and a childhood friend of Evo Fernandes, with later documents. The 1988 programme was written by the Canada-based Renamo affiliate, Fransisco Nota Moises.[43]

The documents state, in skeleton form, 'Renamo's' commitment to democracy and free trade in Mozambique. But even if the authors' commitment to such political goals were separable from their materialistic fantasies, the documents were only a window-dressing for foreign money. The documents enabled the Americans and Portuguese to give to Renamo because they believed it was a pro-democracy movement, and enabled the

South Africans to pretend that it was a movement with a *raison d'être* independent from them. Actually the authors were very concerned with the continued flow of funds to Renamo, because in the case of Cristina, Fernandes and Tom Schaaf (the American representative) it was only the money that guaranteed their influence on Renamo.

Consequently Fernandes is described by his friends with mirth, as 'someone who would take money from anyone'. And indeed he and the rest of them did. Many funders stopped giving after the Gersony report was published, but other support continues to come from right wing groups in America like the Freedom Inc. and Friends of Mozambique amongst others, even in the face of the most vivid evidence of Renamo's brutality. Magazines such as Soldier of Fortune, and Conservative Digest, which is linked intimately with Freedom Inc., rave about Renamo's heroic exploits. Renamo has offices in both Lisbon and Washington, D.C. from where positive publicity is generated. Prominent figures, many very close to the CIA, like Ray Cline (previous CIA Operations Chief), Sibyl Cline (his daughter),[44] Daniel Graham (ex head of Defence Intelligence), and Senator Jesse Helms, contribute to Conservative Digest.[45] Other groups such as Free the Eagle (which Dan Quayle, before he was nominated for the vice-presidency, was very closely affiliated with), and the Heritage Foundation, whose offices were in the same building as those of America's Renamo representative's office, have at the very least given support to Renamo in the past.

The CIA is not the only intelligence service suspect of playing a supportative role in Renamo. The West German BPD supported Renamo with financial help, at least until the nKomati Accord or the death of Evo Fernandes, and may continue to do so through the Werner Kaltefleiter, who is a previous advisor to Chancellor Kohl.[46] Because of the allegations about Renamo's brutal methods, civilian targets and South African backing, and because Renamo has been so discredited, even the right wing organisations try to conceal their support for it. It is believed that some of these organisations in the United States set up imposter charities which not only allows them to raise funds for their cause, but to do so tax free.

Right-wing groups in Germany, Portugal and South Africa are believed to raise funds and channel them through imposter companies. Two of these companies were recently exposed in South Africa.[47] According to extensive investigations, one called Frama Intertrading and run by a former Mozambican called Arlindo Maia, for example, which supplied UNITA as a front for the SADF, was also deeply involved in the war against Mozambique. It had an old Dakota based at the Wonderboom civilian airport just outside of Johannesburg which used to make regular deliveries to Renamo bases inside Mozambique. Maia apparently owned another company too called General Trading Company (Gentra) which ordered supplies for Renamo. South African government interests too allegedly use these routes, using Portuguese export-import firms as conduits for supplying Renamo with weapons. Within South Africa there is a Portuguese network which still raises funds for Renamo. The network includes the core of the Cristina-organised REMO group.

Official South African support for Renamo continued well after nKomati, energetically violating the terms of the agreement. The main proof of South Africa's continued involvement was revealed, to South Africa and the world's horror, only a year after the nonaggression pact had been signed. It was when Renamo's central base at Gorongosa was overrun by Frelimo in 1985, that what have come to be known as the 'Gorongosa Documents' were found. They detailed dates, places and contents of arms drops from South Africa. They evidenced the training of Renamo men in South Africa, and they also evidenced the fact that white South African army staff were operating in Mozambique.

Other evidence of post nKomati support from South Africa abounded. A report from an ex-captive of Renamo detailed drops of weapons, food and uniforms at night, and the presence of white people in training roles in Renamo camps. The sophistication of some of the operations carried out by Renamo, and captured weaponry pointed to South Africa. In 1987 there was a parachute drop of supplies in Inhambane. In May 1987 one of the parachutes recovered by the Mozambican army was found to measure 29 metres across, and was known be a type previously supplied by the United States to South Africa. Evidence of a mobile Renamo base in the Ndumù game reserve, which is in South Africa on the southern Mozambican border, was found by a doctor who worked in the region. The Mozambican security forces said the indications from their end too were that this was a mobile base.[48] In March 1988 Paul Oliveira, a senior Renamo defector, told a press conference in Maputo that there was still a base near Pretoria. He also admitted that 90–95 per cent of Renamo's arms came from South Africa.

Only two years after the signing of the nKomati Accord, the most staggering event of all took place. Samora Machel, on his way back from Zambia died when his plane crashed in South African territory, less than a kilometer from the Mozambican border, in Mbuzini. Naturally, speculation about South African involvement in the plane crash followed. For some the 'coincidence' of the President of Mozambique crashing and dying just within South African territory reeked highly of sabotage. However, extensive investigations by the foreign and South

African press were inconclusive. The truth remains a matter of conjecture.

More interesting, is the question of whether or not support still continues to come in the post P. W. Botha era. The change from P. W.'s 'total onslaught', the policy which sought security of the nation before anything else, to F. W.'s policies of change and conciliation, has had a visible and dramatic affect on domestic policy. We can speculate that equally dramatic changes to clandestine foreign policy have been ordered from the top. Even if they have, however, it is another matter whether or not the orders have actually stopped the support coming from deep within the reaches of government and government affiliated bodies.

Evidence that has surfaced since de Klerk became President in Autumn 1989 does point to continued support coming from within South African governmental bodies, particularly the SADF, although de Klerk has denied it. There can be no doubt that members of the SADF have always been involved in operations with Renamo. Names such as Brigadier Cornelius van Niekerk, Brigadier van Tonder and Commandant John Forster have repeatedly come up in evidence relating to SADF involvement. The SADF has not been purged of some key figures, such as van Niekerk who remains in the same office that he held before.

Evidence came to light in Spring 1990 pointing clearly to the fact that the support from South Africa that continued after nKomati is still going on today. A journalist from South Africa's *Weekly Mail*[49] uncovered a telling story surrounding the continued existence of a base near Phalaborwa in South Africa. Renamo people had been living in a section of the Namakgale township called 'Skietog'; locals confirmed that Portuguese and Shona-speaking black soldiers lived there. There were SADF soldiers protecting the entrance to the base, and there had been tensions between the locals and the fighters. A one point hand grenades were thrown into the local *shebeen* (pub). Skietog was confirmed by an ex-SADF serviceman who used to serve there, to be the Fifth Recce Unit's base.

Strong suggestions of a further Renamo base in South Africa came to light in 1990 in the wake of the much publicised issue of the murder of David Webster. Webster was suspected to have been killed by the South African security forces because he had uncovered evidence of a Renamo network in the Natal's Kosi Bay area where he was working as an anthropologist. The base for these activities is believed to be located at Lake Sibaya, south of Kosi Bay.[50] David Webster's death has been linked with a recently exposed secret service unit called the Civil Co-operation Bureau (CCB). This unit, which carried out some of the nastier clandestine work for the SADF, is thought to have operated without the knowledge of the highest levels of the South African government. David Webster's interest in Renamo has led to speculation that it is a unit along the lines of the CCB which is at the centre of the SADF/Renamo link.

Finally, there was the sign of the continued existence of a link between Renamo and high level members of the South African government which came in June 1990. A South African family of four, the Muller family, were rescued from the clasp of Renamo by SAS Tafelberg which ploughed into the southern Mozambican Channel after 48 days of the family's captivity. Sandy Muller is said to have been a personal friend of President de Klerk's wife. Afonso Dhlakama himself gave the instruction that the family, who had been taken captive after their yacht had run aground in April, be released. Someone in the South African government not only had close enough links with Renamo to be worthy of such a favour, but to organise the rendezvous, and moreover, de Klerk knew it.

While the South African hard-liners have continued to support Renamo over the years for the ends of their own foreign policy, the Americans and the Germans believed, and still do, that they were giving money to a pro-democracy movement. Thanks to the image makers, who, because they gravely overestimated their own influence, believed that Renamo was such a movement, funders look no further. They do not look at Renamo itself, which is Dhlakama's Renamo in Mozambique.

In Mozambique, on the ground, people were not being gathered and told to support Renamo if they wanted free elections, they were not being recruited to support Renamo in the name of some goal as other rebel movements have recruited support. Until recently almost the only political meetings Renamo is reported to have held were during a campaign by the Rhodesians to recruit members to their embryonic rebel movement back in the late 1970s. Other reports of political meetings are sporadic and record, in one instance, an explanation only after a massacre. Not one refugee that I asked knew what I might be referring to when I asked if Renamo held political meetings. By contrast, when a selection of Zimbabweans from all over Zimbabwe was asked about experiences of their war, almost all mentioned that the rebels would hold all-night political meetings, *pungwes*, where political songs were sung and the motives and purpose of the war were explained as the rebels tried to gain the support and understanding of the people that they were fighting for.[51] It was this kind of thing which earned them voluntary support.

Renamo has developed into a body which is propelled by its own incentives, and the incentives of its leaders, which is to gain power; in this sense it has turned into a civil war, not just a war of Rhodesia and South Africa against Mozambique. Its logic, however, is of alien extraction

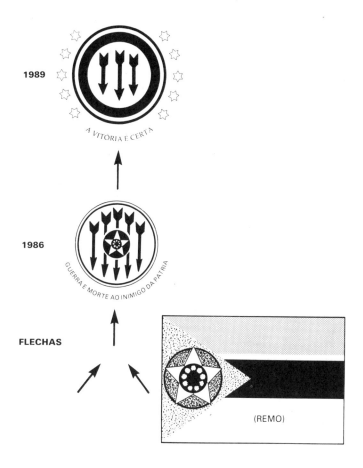

FIGURE 3.1   Evolution of Renamo Insignia
Adapted from Vines (1991)

and derives from its origins. It continues to function not because it has not achieved a political goal but, quite simply, because it is possible for it to do so. Its leaders have not yet been guaranteed any governmental power, and until they are sure that they will get it, the fighting will continue.

In the days leading to and following the December 1990 partial ceasefire agreement, Renamo demonstrated nervousness. With the threat of democratic elections following the government's changes towards multiparty democracy, and the possible demise of its South African backers, Dhlakama's Renamo was been forced to rethink its strategy. For money to keep flowing from the United States and other sources, it needed credibility as a pro-democracy movement. Yet, it was impossible for it to stand in elections because its support was so weak that it would not stand a chance of any success.

The consequence was a superficial attempt to revamp its image and hurriedly gain support amongst Mozambicans. Amongst other things, the Renamo emblem, which incorporated embarrassing symbols of its links with Rhodesian and Portuguese colonialism and Portuguese South Africans, was changed within months of Frelimo announcing that it was to pass a new Mozambican constitution (see Figure 3.1). It had as its symbol five arrows, a relic of Renamo's links with colonial Mozambique, and more specifically of Ken Flower's intention of establishing a group along the lines of the Flechas [arrows]. Arrows were commonly used as symbols of Portuguese Mozambique, and can be seen for example in the old Mozambican colonial crest which was used on coins and official documents. Renamo's emblem now only has three arrows. The star in the middle, which is associated with Cristina because it forms the flag of REMO (see page 73) has disappeared entirely.

In May 1990, following what Renamo called its 'First Congress' in June 1989 (actually its second, or even its third according to some accounts) Renamo started numbering its monthly catalogues from one, as if to erase what had gone before. By May 1991 Renamo was evidently receiving significant outside guidance on how to revamp its image. It adopted a new American-style constitution,[52] written by Bruce Fein (columnist for the right-wing newspaper *The Washington Times*). This calls for the establishment of a 'Congress' and a 'Senate' in Mozambique, the handing back of 'goods or the equivalent in money' to individuals who were 'robbbed, looted or despoiled by the marxist thieves of Frelimo', and, amongst other things, for the return of the death penalty. Journalists were approached and taken into Renamo bases on new Honda motorbikes to witness propaganda exercises in which Renamo soldiers donned brand new uniforms, embellished with new rank-indicating epaulettes.

Not until very recently, as it has become clear that a new route to political power is necessary, has Renamo begun trying to canvas support from Mozambicans.[53] In one political meeting in central Mozambique the Renamo speaker barely concealed a threat that if people did not support it, the fighting would have to continue, announcing to the audience that they should support Renamo because 'We, the Matsangas, are the ones to bring true peace'.[54] That inside Renamo is still a political vacuum, in spite of its recent attempts to market itself, was vividly portrayed in the admission of André Thomashausen (policy advisor to Renamo) in an interview, that Dhlakama is reluctant to accept democratic elections over guaranteed power as an exchange for peace. The press has blindly reported Renamo's new initiative as that of a fifteen year old pro-democracy movement which has been vindicated by Chissano's turn to democracy, and its hesitancy in accepting peace in exchange for democracy as a matter of 'politicking'.

Meanwhile the war continues to rage barely abated. Accredited commentators attribute varying amounts of blame to Renamo for the country's past ills. All of them, though, agree that Renamo has been the single most significant factor in causing the devastation in the country that exists today. All of them also agree that Renamo is the biggest problem that the country faces for the future and that without subduing it there can be no hope for the development of Mozambique. Some say it is already too late, and that Renamo has already created enough social and economic devastation to take generations to cure. In human terms this is nothing less than tragic. We must look more closely at the structure of the war which has brought this about.

4 Structure of the War – the Rape of a Country

> No passion so effectually robs the mind of all its powers of acting
> and reasoning as fear.
>
> Edmund Burke

Many facets of British life today are witness to the profound and lingering effects of six short years of war on a nation, on its way of life and its way of thinking. The years 1939–1945 – 'the war years' as they are called – changed everything.

In Mozambique, people do not refer to 'the war years' because most people have never experienced years of peace. Mozambique's population is very young. Few live beyond their early forties, and a large proportion of the population is made up of children. The short lives of Mozambicans have been dominated by war for the last twenty-seven years. If in Britain, ways of life are still being affected three generations later by six years of a war that was waged mostly across the Channel, it is likely that the effects of Mozambique's wars, whose physical violence has in recent years been felt directly by a huge section of the population, will reverberate at least half way through the next century.

The years of war in Mozambique are not entirely separable into distinct wars, nor can Mozambique's wars be seen as distinct from the goings on in the rest of southern Africa. This is a critical point, especially with regard to the war that has been conducted in recent years. In the early 1970s there emerged a pattern of war unlike any experienced by Mozambique before; it was sponsored by foreigners whose destructive motives have dominated aggression in Mozambique ever since. It is this same pattern that ravages Mozambique today. The pattern of war waged since the early 1970s has left Mozambique's normality in tatters. Disruption, upheaval and uncertainty now characterise the way of life for the millions of Mozambicans who do not live in the safety of the capital cities.

The story of how this pattern emerged started before Ken Flower's plan to form Renamo was put into action. Mozambique's tide of wars began in 1964. Whilst Americans were celebrating the wonders of flower power, and Britons were enjoying their years of economic boom, Mozambique

76

was embarking on the war that was to set the tone for at least the next two and a half decades: Frelimo's war of independence. Frelimo was challenging, as was much of Africa, the minority rule which had for so long dominated their lives. The tremors began. Vibrations from upheaval in Angola on the west coast of southern Africa, met with those from Mozambique, its eastern counterpart. The region in between became severely affected by the wars. In the face of the inevitable insecurity, hunger, economic and social destruction, and the other trappings of war, other disturbed nations began their fight. Zambia split off from the rest of Rhodesia, and the Zimbabweans began their long and bloody quest for independence. Southern Africa was crawling with refugees. Rhodesian refugees in Mozambique, Zambian refugees in Rhodesia, Angolan refugees in Zambia, and Mozambican refugees seemingly everywhere. The tide of change in the region raged across borders with impunity, spreading and multiplying its effects.

The war which started in Mozambique in 1964 may at first have been a simple war of independence, but it soon came to overlap with Zimbabwe's wars of independence, with South Africa's wish to remain white ruled, and even with Zambia's war. It was never really one war, or even two, but a collage of the region's distraught face. Rhodesia began its attacks on Mozambique in an attempt to protect its access to the sea via the Beira corridor, and to Malawi via the Tete corridor, which was being threatened by Frelimo activity; only later were the attacks primarily concerned with the rear base that Frelimo was providing for its own rebels. In 1969/70, with the first Rhodesians raids into Mozambique,[1] the beatings began, the massacres began, and Mozambicans got their first ugly glimpse of the way in which many of them would be forced to live out their remaining days. A report describing the operations reads: 'these operations . . . consist of speedy paratroop actions in specified areas and the liquidation of any human lives . . . and a return to their bases in Rhodesia'.[2] Eventually the Rhodesians carried out these attacks with and as Renamo. There was never an exact moment when Renamo 'took over', as joint attacks (called ComOps)[3] were the norm from when Renamo was first formed, up until 1979 when the Rhodesians stopped fighting their war.

The Rhodesian activity which went on in the late 1960s and early 1970s was of a very similar type to recent Renamo activity, marked as it was by its sheer destructiveness and stark brutality. A journalist who filed reports to the BBC, the *Guardian* and other major media media interests, was charged under the Rhodesian Official Secrets Act for exposing the activity in stories which detailed atrocities including the burning of bodies and the cutting off of hands and feet.

Some of the most bloody parts of Mozambique's two and a half decades of war occurred in the early seventies. One savage Rhodesian attack into Nyadzonia, Mozambique in August 1976 left 675 dead, some in mass graves full of children. Nyadzonia was a camp for unarmed Zimbabwean refugees. The Rhodesians soldiers had been told to kill them before they could become terrorists and arm themselves. The unit's white chaplain had blessed them first.[4]

By the time Mozambique's warring for independence came to an end ten years later in 1974, people's lives and perceptions of normality had been significantly altered. One moment they had been living predictable and stable lives, serving their Portuguese masters as was required of them, and taking punishment for any arrogance, but eating, surviving and living relatively quiet lives for the most part. The next moment Frelimo soldiers had demanded food, shelter and support which could only be given at great risk of being caught and tortured by the Portuguese. The people of Mozambique had suffered, yet there was no sudden peace that came with independence, no rewards for their traumas. Far from it.

Instead the garish face of war never averted its eyes from Mozambique. In its unflinching gaze Mozambique was to be raped, and its vitality ground into the dust. The Rhodesians had carried out an estimated 350 attacks into Mozambique between the years 1976–79 alone, but this was small compared to what was to come. The year 1980, far from heralding peace in a new and mostly independent southern Africa, marked the beginning of South Africa's onslaught. South Africa's quest for maintaining supremacy in the region, and thus the continued security of white rule, started with a bang.

The year 1980 was a landmark. Renamo, of course, did not just fade away as expected, but grew massively. The attacks did not stop but got worse, and the frequency did not subside. To some the point of the war seemed illusory without Rhodesia to lend it reason. Now that this was no longer a country to country war, what could the point possibly be in totally destroying a country's economic and social structure so violently and deliberately as to prevent its future development for years to come? This question must have preyed not least on the minds of the rural Mozambican people, the targets then and now of Renamo's war.

To the world and to the government the answer was obvious: this was still a war being fought as a country to country war. South Africa and interested Western parties, leading mercenaries and others, were now taking Rhodesia's place in helping Renamo fight Mozambique. Renamo's quest, as Rhodesia's and South Africa's, was to destroy the attempt being made at a new Mozambique, or indeed at any Mozambique at all. In truth, they were rebels with a goal, but without a cause, for although much destruction was targeted against government projects, it did not stop there, but targeted Mozambique as a whole. After South Africa took over Renamo, massive movements of population took place in Mozambique, away from Renamo areas and towards Frelimo safe havens. The direction that the millions of people run in has little to do with political ideology or any such fantasy, but with a much more practical concern: survival.

The kind of war which first emerged in the early 1970s, sharply accelerated in the 1980s, and which continues today in Mozambique, is a very different kind of war than most. It is not a conventional war, not a war of liberation being waged by guerrillas, and not a tribal war. It is not a war between two factions who are fighting for something, where one day one side will win and the other lose. The difference about this war is that it is not a fight for a country, but against a country. It is a war of constant destabilisation, a relentless and menacing pursuit to destroy everything which makes Mozambique function economically and cohere socially. It is an attempt to destroy the very fabric of a country.

Even after independence, after almost a decade of Rhodesian aggression and despite the ravages of the country's history, Mozambique was not a chaotic place, nor a place devoid of culture and life-force. On the contrary, Mozambique, in spite of the stripping effects of slavery, and of the imposition of Portuguese culture onto its own, was full of traditions, social culture, self-supporting economic activity and all the other expressions of human life which lend to existence identity and meaning.

Life, until Renamo grew so rapidly in 1980, was still relatively liveable. It was liveable enough at least that self-supporting activity could be carried out, some predictability of life maintained, and expression of thought continued. The wiry, grotesque sculptures of thin people with sunken eyes that Mozambican Makonde craftsmen create may not be expressive of joy, but they are at least an art form which survived the terrible times. Perhaps Mozambicans had become sufficiently used to war to live a semi-stable pattern of life in spite of it. Families were at least units, and it was still possible to sleep in your own home at night.

After 1980, when South African and Western interests combined to render Renamo a force which could gnaw more viciously at Mozambique, even the adapted patterns of life became impossible. For Mozambicans, adaptation had meant in many cases to survive by subsistence farming, to adapt to various fighter groups occupying their villages and to live side by side with them; to live quiet lives which could not implicate them for collaboration with somebody's enemy. With the larger Renamo, even this became impossible.

Renamo prohibits the growth of agricultural crops where it can, looting or burning what crops it finds, thus sabotaging attempts at subsistence survival. When Renamo rebels control a village or town, they are dubious allies to have. While forcing the population to grow food for them, they frequently turn to physically assaulting the villagers, and the villages in which they have settled. There is little security for the villagers, and little hope for a peaceful life whatever they do.

The Gorongosa documents revealed more about Renamo than anything else that has emerged in recent years. Most importantly the orders tabled in the documents revealed a deliberate strategy. The core feature of Renamo's destruction was embodied in the instruction recorded in the documents for Renamo fighters to 'destroy the rural economy'. The simple words of this brutal order have had a profound impact on rural Mozambique. They words have meant in reality, just as they imply, not the 'liberation' or takeover of the rural economy, but its destruction. Eighty-four per cent of Mozambicans are involved in the rural economy, mostly through small-scale farming. The rural economy is totally reliant on the productivity of these people. Thus, in order to destroy it, 84 per cent of Mozambicans must be the target of their attacks. This, surely, constitutes a war against the people.

It is this policy of destroying the rural economy which is the centrepiece of Mozambique's suffering. For Renamo's purposes, the rural population must be rendered incapable of producing, and the actual production, the remaining fragment of Mozambicans' ability to support themselves, must be disallowed. In practical terms this has meant the destruction of the market and of the infrastructure, the outright slaughter of thousands of people, the mutilation of thousands more, and the destruction of Mozambique's social cohesion. This cohesion has been torn apart on the national level, by the wrecking of all the vital social services such as health and educational facilities; on the family level, by the tearing apart of families, and on the individual level, by the traumatising of so many people. Much of the mental and social traumatising of Renamo's attacks has been focused on the family unit.

The family is the basic social unit around which production, the division of labour, and social organisation revolve. Village life revolves around the existence of families. A mother without a husband is often labelled a whore by Mozambicans, regardless of why she is alone. She can only escape this stigma by attaching herself to another man, be it her father, brother or new husband. A child without a family has no means of support and becomes a waif. Without a family a person is an outcast.

The mother is central to Mozambican families. Without her the children are not brought up, the water is not carried, the maize is not pounded, and basic agricultural survival products are not produced. She is bound to these tasks as she has often been paid for by her husband in bride price. The father brings in money for the purchase of goods that cannot be self produced. The children play their part, looking after any of their parents' cattle. They rely totally on their parents for their survival. Families are systematically broken up by Renamo, and all this falls apart. In areas which Renamo controls, families are split up into service areas, so that their normal work pattern is disrupted as they are made to produce for Renamo instead of themselves. Breaking up the family unit serves the added purpose of destroying the basic unit around which the government revolves its policies. In the many areas which Renamo sporadically attacks, people are separated from their families by being taken hostage. Other people lose their family in the panic that ensues during or after a raid when people scatter in all directions. In rural Mozambique it is almost impossible to relocate lost family members without outside help. There are no telephones, and no addresses to write to. Usually all the links would have been within the attacked village, and the villages are too dangerous to return to.

The 1.9 million displaced people in Mozambique and the 1.4 million external refugees combine to create a total of 3.3 million people who have been either totally separated from their families, or have been separated from one or more family member. The combination of the refugees, the displaced, the kidnapped, the killed and those within Renamo controlled areas, the majority of whom have become separated from at least some of their family, constitutes a huge scale of devastation to the family unit.

It is plain to any observer that the effects of social dislocation have penetrated deeply into Mozambique's character. Walking through a black township in South Africa, something strange soon became apparent to me. Some of the huts had no windows. The ground was arid and dusty, the sky grey but the heat fierce the day that I was there. There was no sign of life and no feel of energy, and the air was still. I asked a local priest why people would build solid unbroken walls to their hot, smoke-filled and unlit huts. He replied simply that they were Mozambicans. On questioning the inhabitants it transpired not that it was a tradition of some kind, but quite the opposite. They had built their huts like this in their village in Mozambique so as to provide extra security from Renamo attacks.

They had become accustomed to living this way, and, once refugees, continued living this way out of habit. It also made them feel safer from the hostile South African officialdom. As a security measure, having no windows on huts which are sometimes made out of cardboard or mud, with pieces of plastic or corrugated iron filling in gaps, and which cannot even stand the trials of the rainy season let alone armed attacks, is a pathetic gesture. It represents the everyday terror with which these people live. Knowing how powerless they are to create any real security for themselves, they resort to desperate and ridiculous measures. They shut their eyes hoping only that if they cannot see the enemy, it cannot see them. They do not seem to realise that it is their fear that makes them so conspicuous. Mozambicans live now like hunted animals. Villages have look-outs posted everywhere; at night Mozambicans in heavily war torn zones sleep out in the bush. They dig themselves holes in the ground, crawl into them and sleep, with half an ear open for any hostile sounds. During the day they return to their villages and tend to their crops. If Renamo was to attack their village their crops would all be taken or burnt. At least if the attack came at night they would have a better chance of escaping with their lives.

There is no better word to describe what is happening to so much of Mozambique's population than dehumanisation. Living with Renamo constantly on their doorsteps they must voluntarily turn to an animalistic life. Like the Renamo 'recruits' who have been taken and put through the kind of training described earlier, or who have voluntarily opted for the life of barbarism, those who have lived the life of the hunted for so long will also find it hard to ever adjust to strange and safe new circumstances. Certainly those who have taken refuge in South Africa have found it difficult to adjust to the relatively safe conditions. Fear is an instinct, and instincts take over when life is threatened.

Some head for the massive camps for dislocated people, others head for the cities. All the provincial capitals, and of course Maputo, are controlled by Frelimo, and people are safe there from murder, kidnapping or mutilation, if not from disease and the most despicable poverty. The government's efforts to abate the poverty are swallowed up in the huge vacuum of need, and its ability to cope constantly undermined.

As a critical part of its strategy to destroy the rural economy and any chance of development, Renamo has made special targets of health and educational facilities and personnel all over the country. Reflecting the high priority that Renamo accords to the targeting of health and education, the destruction has been widespread and severe. The development of both health and educational services, until the recent IMF-backed changes to economic policy, alongside agriculture, were the corner-stones of Frelimo's entire economic programme. Frelimo sacrificed much for the sake of developing these two areas, limiting spending on other areas of the economy so that these could be developed fully, in the belief that the universal provision of health an education to the country's capital base, its people, was the key to development.

Given that they were such priorities, if Frelimo achieved anything in the post-independence years it should have been apparent in the improvement of health and educational facilities and levels. The achievements made in these areas were significant, yet, as Renamo has partially destroyed them, the government's main success since independence has been undermined, and remains unrecognised by most. Many look at Mozambique and see the economic devastation as if it were simple policy failure. Yet until 1980 when Renamo began its major attack, Frelimo had enjoyed substantial success in the development of the areas which it considered fundamental to any further development. Notwithstanding the many economic policy mistakes which were made, the devastation wrought on these corner-stones of Frelimo's whole development policy to an extent caused its downfall.

It was not, of course, just Frelimo which suffered. The cost of attacks on health facilities to Mozambique and its development, in terms of loss of life and decreased standards of living, has been great. The Economist Intelligence Unit's country report for Mozambique estimates that approximately one million people died as a direct result of the disruption of the health services in Mozambique between 1980 and 1989. This is not difficult to believe. In spite of the Article II of the Geneva Convention in which it is stipulated that 'Medical Units shall be respected and protected at all times and shall not be the object of attack', Renamo has destroyed enough facilities, and killed or scared off enough health staff to make medical facilities inaccessible to about two million people who had previously had access.[5]

By 1988, 46 per cent of the entire primary health care network had been sabotaged, either by outright destruction or by looting. Mozambique's few hospitals have also come under attack. The government, now desperate to protect the remaining fragments of its efforts, has erected electrified fences around some hospitals. The Chinavanie Hospital, which was completely destroyed but has now been rebuilt with the help of the Swiss Mission, is one such hospital. Plans to wire the Manicha Hospital in Maputo province have also been formulated.

Altogether, by the end of 1988, at least 40, and probably far more, health workers had been killed in cold blood because of their profession; 43 more had been kidnapped and 700 stripped of all their possessions. Given the small number of health workers operating in Mozambique anyway, these figures are very high. These figures do not take account of those who left their posts because of the destruction of their premises, or simply out of fear, of those recently trained workers reluctant to take up rural posts, or of the drop in the number who are unwilling to train in the first place because of the hazards of the job.[6]

The number of health workers and medical facilities increased between independence and the early 1980s, but by the mid 1980s both had declined drastically. At independence there were only 86 doctors in the entire country. There was a long way to go, and Mozambique had started the journey. But it proved to be an uphill struggle. Between 1982 and 1986 the ratio of doctors to rural people decreased from one doctor to 161 000 people to one doctor to 443 000 people. In Zambezia province, a microcosm of Mozambique's war, there were 13 doctors in the 17 districts in 1982. Four years later, however, in 1986, only two districts had doctors. In the whole country in 1982, and 42 per cent of the districts had a doctor, but by 1987 this had declined to only 18 per cent.

Likewise, the number of rural health units and other health posts available had been increasing until 1986, only then to embark upon a course of drastic decline. For in that year the rate of Renamo destruction finally overtook the rate of rebuilding and building. Between 1980 and 1986 the rate of health service improvement slowed as Renamo learned its trade. 1983 was perhaps the quietest year since Renamo was handed over to South Africa, with only about 50 health posts destroyed compared to the 232 reopened and 397 new ones built. 1983 marked the year when the number of health posts had increased from only 426 before independence to 1171. But 1983 also marked the end of such progress in the face of adversity; at the end of the year the adversity became much more severe. In 1984 about 135 health posts were destroyed; the trend had been set. Between 1982 and 1985 over 450 were destroyed altogether. From 1986 it was all downhill.[7]

Some analysts have tried to estimate the rate at which the growth of health services could have continued had it not been for Renamo activity. They have done this by comparing the situation in Mozambique with that of neighbouring Tanzania. Tanzania is used as a comparison because there are so many similarities in both the colonial legacies of Tanzania and Mozambique, and in the policies that they have tried to pursue since independence. Arguably, the only significant difference between the two countries is that Tanzania has not had a war on its hands.[8]

According to this estimation, if the progress in the development of social services in Mozambique had continued at the same pace in the last ten years as it did in the first five years of independence when Renamo was less forceful, the social services would by now be very well developed. Frelimo's dream of making primary health care and schooling accessible to a huge percentage of the population, might actually have been realised. For example, between 1986 and 1988 the number of peripheral health units fell from 1326 to 1143. Without Renamo raids it is estimated that there would have been 2097 such units by 1987.

Instead, the destruction of the services, combined with the dangers presented by travelling to the nearest post and the fear of being seen as collaborating with the system, have reduced accessibility to very low levels. The dangers of travel presented by the war have had a major impact on other aspects of health care too. It has meant not only that drugs must be airlifted at great cost to some areas, but that the distribution of the drugs is at times impossible. In 1983 a shortage of anti-tuberculosis drugs was overcome by a foreign donation. The foreign donors might as well have saved their money: the drugs could not be distributed because of the dangers and unavailability of transport. Many areas are not accessible at all due to war activity. The decreased accessibility of primary health care has been accompanied by the increased health care needs which are a part of any war.

Though significant, it is not just mutilations caused by direct attacks or anti-personnel mines which cause the increase in health care needs. The war's adverse affects on the operation of preventative medicine has also been great. Mozambique had previously taken pride in the extensive network of preventative medicine which it had built. Now the efforts of the past are being wasted. Vaccination programmes face massive challenges: travel to many parts is not possible, the foreign doctors who often administer the programmes are specifically targeted by Renamo, and there is a shortage of gas to keep the vaccination refrigerators running.

These problems combine to limit the number of vaccination programmes which can function. Because the country is so prone to diseases such as cholera, polio, and malaria, diseases which are frequently fatal or permanently debilitating, the decrease in preventative medicine has taken a severe toll on the nation's health. The number of people contracting easily preventable and contagious diseases has escalated, and the need for health care with it. Major outbreaks of cholera in southern Mozambique in 1983 and of poliomyelitis in 1984 in Inhambane were directly related to the decrease in vaccination programmes.

The reduction in the number of women receiving ante-natal assistance, is said to have caused the death of 1000 women annually. Combined with the lack of vaccinations against neonatal tetanus, it is estimated to also cause the death of 800 children a year. In Zambezia alone the number of women attending the ante-natal clinics fell from 37 per cent of the population in 1982 to only 24 per cent three years later. In Tete and Sofala provinces, both heavily war torn, the percentage of people vaccinated fell sharply between 1983 and 1986.

The war has also taken a toll on the accessibility and cleanliness of water, reversing progress that was being made. Renamo has put dead bodies down wells purposely to soil the water, and often sabotages the electricity pylons which supply the water cleansing plants; the resultant polluted water has been a major source of disease. The overcrowding of camps, and other small areas of safety to which people have fled, has added to the water problem because a great strain is put on the water facilities available. In the entire country only 17 per cent of the people had access to safe drinking water in 1989/90.

The circle of injustice is cruel. Lack of clean water causes the spread of diseases. The diseases could easily be prevented by vaccination programmes, yet are not because Renamo activity makes the programmes impracticable. To cap it all, the health care which is now so badly needed, is not available because it has been the specific purpose of the rebels to completely destroy it. It is a three-pronged attack, and civilians are the targets.

All this destruction, needless to say, has been expensive for Mozambique. The cost in US dollars of the damage to health buildings alone by 1985 was $16.5 million, and the loss of the contents of the buildings through looting, a further $2.75 million. The cost of destruction to health buildings is a small indicator of how great the direct costs of the war are in total. In addition to the direct costs of the war which make health care and other areas so much more expensive for the government to maintain and virtually impossible to expand, funds that would have been spent on them have had to be diverted to defence spending.

Being forced to reduce spending on health care is in itself a major defeat for the government. In 1974, the year before independence, health expenditure only represented 3.3 per cent of the budget. By 1982 the government had increased it to 11.2 per cent of the budget. However, by 1985 the regression back to the low colonial levels had already begun. Health expenditure was reduced to only 8.1 per cent of the budget. This was equivalent to $4 per head per annum. In a country with appalling health conditions to start with, and with a war exacerbating the conditions, $4 per head is minuscule.

The cost of all this destruction to health care must be measured in human terms to give it any meaning. The human toll has been very high. Apart from the deaths which have resulted directly from the devastation wrought on the health services, primary health statistics have worsened. Not least the life expectancy of Mozambicans has fallen dramatically, to take its place as one of the lowest in Africa.

Primary health figures tell a familiar story. Improvements were made on the colonial levels of health up until 1980. Thereafter severe regression ensued erasing the achievements of the past. In 1960 Mozambicans were expected at birth to live to the average ages of somewhere between 25 and 33, with one third expected to die at birth. By 1980 life expectancy had risen dramatically to 45 years. The downward slide which followed left it at 43 by 1989/90.

Unsurprisingly, as with almost every other indicator of Mozambique's welfare, the slip backwards from the 1976–80 infant mortality figures was marked. Infant (under fives) mortality in Mozambique, amongst the highest in the world now, was so high that in 1987 one child was dying every four minutes. In 1980, 270 out of every thousand children were dying. This continued to rise so much that today 325 children out of every thousand are dying. Had Mozambique followed Tanzania's pattern, which, again, is likely without the war, the figure would have fallen to about 185 in a thousand by 1988, rather than risen. In human or any other terms, the destruction to Mozambique's health service has been severe. Tragically for Mozambique, the destruction was, of course, taking place at the worst possible time. For in the early eighties the droughts came.[9]

Renamo seemed to consider the monster of drought just another weapon in its hands. It sabotaged transport lines and aid on its way to feeding the starving, it specifically targeted expatriate aid workers and it continued its campaign of terror more violently than ever before, ransacking, looting, killing and mutilating. The destruction of the health services and buildings continued not only unabated, but at an even faster pace. Thousands died as a result of the famines, and for this Renamo must take a large portion of the blame. Without Renamo the droughts would have caused severe hardship, and some loss of life, but not the wholesale famine which occurred.

The droughts coincided not only with the general escalation of the war which followed the handing over of Renamo to South African control, but with its spread. The severity of the war situation built up steadily after the power handover of 1979/80. Although the only relatively quiet year in the decade was 1983, even the devastation wrought in that year was horrifying. It seems unbelievable that, despite all the destruction of the years following 1980, even in 1984 with the shadow of famine still stalking, the war had not yet reached its height. Until that year Renamo continued to concentrate its war more in the south and centre than in the north of the country. With 1984 came a war with new scope.

The war had slowly and steadily been working its way up north since 1980. The relative quiet of 1983 was a only a screen hiding the footsteps of the war towards Nampula and Zambezia provinces and much of Tete; by late 1984 the war had reached the remote northerly provinces of Cabo Delgado and Niassa.[10] This marked a propaganda victory for Renamo as it could now say that it was operating in all ten of Mozambique's provinces. The minds of only a few are unscarred by those years of the mid 1980s when the war's developments were mixed with the venom of drought. Not until 1986/87 did the rains slowly come to all Mozambique, driving the droughts back to their place of hibernation from where they appeared only sporadically in the years following.

The early 1980s, when regional political events and those of nature conspired to allow Renamo to pursue more effectively the goal for which it was born, presented opportunities for destruction that were not wasted by Renamo. Of this, Renamo's destruction of education, as well as of social cohesion and health services in those years, was proof. Education, like health, was one of Frelimo's great successes, but its success represented hopes for the development of Mozambicans which were never realised.

Before Renamo's interference, the development of education was on track. At independence 95 per cent of the population was illiterate, while 70 per cent had no access to educational facilities at all. By 1980 illiteracy had fallen to 72.2 per cent, and in the 15–24 year old age group it was low as 57 per cent.[11] In fact, despite the continued destruction of educational infrastructure the total figure for illiteracy fell a further 2 per cent afterwards, settling at 68 per cent in 1989. However, a 2 per cent fall over nine years is very slow progress compared to a 25 per cent fall over the first six years after independence. Tanzania, whose government also put significant stress on educational development, but whose progress was not limited by a war, sported 90 per cent literacy when compared to 30 per cent in Mozambique, despite Mozambique's equally, if not more, active attempts to increase it.

Mozambique had good reason to be proud of its educational system in 1980, for during the first five years after independence significant achievements were made. Post-independence figures showed a vast improvement on pre-independence education levels. The quality of teaching suffered, especially in the more élite schools whose Portuguese teachers fled, but the increased numbers of those receiving an education more than made up for it. The number of children enrolled in primary schools doubled between 1974 and 1982, rising from about 672 000 to 1 330 000. The numbers enrolled in secondary schools also more than doubled during these years, and reached 90 000 by 1980. By 1980 one child in every ten was receiving some kind of education. This represented a 39 per cent increase from pre-independence years. By 1981, 49 per cent of the population was studying.

After 1980/1 the post-independence surge halted. Between 1982 and 1985 alone, 300 000 would-be primary school children lost access to an education because of the war. The primary school enrolment rate was held to the 46 per cent that it had been in 1980, for the next five years. Renamo's policy of making education a priority military target has meant the loss of education for 20 per cent of Mozambicans who have been forced out of their schools by one means or another.

Such destruction is carried out in many different ways. Schools are burnt down or looted, books and school equipment are destroyed, teacher training centres are attacked, teachers are killed, mutilated, kidnapped or terrorised, and students are attacked. In 1989/90 some districts were left with 50–70 per cent of their schools closed. In marked contrast to the excited leaps of progress that were being taken immediately after independence, the development of education now is at a near standstill. In 1986 Zambezia province suffered worse than any other province, suffering the destruction of 82 per cent of its schools. Tete province came a close second at 74 per cent, Sofala 60 per cent, Niassa 56 per cent and Maputo province 56 per cent.

Raging by 1985, the destruction steadily became worse leaving few remnants today of an educational system which was once growing so rapidly that it had brought down illiteracy by 23 per cent in only a few short years. By 1985 1863 schools had been destroyed leaving 314 000 pupils without schools. By 1987 35 per cent of schools nation wide were out of operation. In 1988 20 secondary schools and 2655 primary schools were out of operation leaving five million children in total without education.[12] In 1990 at least 3000 schools were destroyed. The loss of a total of 3000 schools in, for example, the American state of Virginia, with a similar population to that of Mozambique, would cause a massive disruption to the educational system and to everyday life. But in Mozambique, an underdeveloped country, the loss of 3000 schools represents nearly the complete undermining of the country's educational system.

Teachers have not had an easy time. In 193 known cases teachers have been murdered by the rebels. This represents a large proportion of the small number of teachers in Mozambique: 185 more are known to have been kidnapped, 1,153 have been stripped of all their possessions, and a further 618 are known to be missing. Altogether 400 teachers are known to have been mutilated, killed or kidnapped; 3224 teachers are known to have been displaced within Mozambique, and a further 300 at least to have fled to neighbouring countries as war refugees. In total some 7000 teachers are known to have been affected by the war. The real figures are bound to be even higher than these, as much of what goes on in the war is undocumented.

Mapinda was a man who lived and taught in the village of Zavane. Zavane, as one of the government's communal villages, was a particular target for Renamo. One day Renamo came looking for Mapinda because he was the teacher. On entering the village he was identified. The rebels, after looting the village for all it was worth, gathered up about one hundred villagers to witness his fate. He was bound head and foot with cloth, and the Renamo leader called out to the villagers asking if they knew Mapinda. Mapinda intervened pointing out to the rebels that they were not speaking the local dialect and that villagers would not be able to understand. At this point the leader called on two of his men successively to 'cut' Mapinda for his arrogance. Both the men claimed to be without a knife, so the leader drew his own. He sliced off Mapinda's nose and ears in front of the villagers. When the bloody spectacle was over the teacher was left bleeding on the ground as an example. He managed to crawl to his hut after passing out several times, but when he got there he found that all his possessions had been pillaged, and his wife taken by the rebels. Only a little salt was left, and with this he treated what was left of his bloody face. With horrors like this the rebels achieve their target: Zavane used to be a village of some 329 households with a school of 125 pupils. After the attack the village became a pathetic settlement of only 19 households, with a school which never again reopened.[13] The pupils frequently suffer the same traumas as their teachers.

Thus education in Mozambique has been totally disrupted. Schools have been destroyed and the teachers and pupils dispersed. In addition to the 500 000 children in Mozambique who have no access to schooling, there are 1.4 million war refugees in neighbouring countries for many of whom education is not available. All in all Renamo's attack on education has destroyed mass education in Mozambique and almost brought it back to the tragic state that it was in at independence. Again Mozambique's future has been jeopardised.

The scale and structure of the war, together with its destruction of social cohesion and hope for development, has wrought untold damage on the economy. The kind of damage inflicted on the economy, like that inflicted on Mozambique's social structures and infrastructure, is of a type that cannot easily be overcome. The most far reaching problem that Renamo has created for the economy, perhaps, is embodied in the breakdown of small-scale production and of the marketing structure. The displacement of so many people within the country and into neighbouring countries has meant that huge numbers of people have lost their land, and thus their ability to be self sufficient. Instead now, they reluctantly rely on aid. The breaking up of families has meant the loss of traditional divisions of labour. There is no new pattern of labour division that is replacing the ones that are being destroyed. The labour, which is the country's main productive resource, is simply being lost.

Renamo policy of burning crops and punishing wealth adds to the effects of the dislocation of families and the destruction of health and education, to reduce the country's productive capacity. Even many those who are not displaced are too frightened to grow anything. Mr. Komo, living in the central Mozambican province of Inhambane, said 'we are frightened to plant anything. The Amachangas (Renamo) might come back'.[14]

He is not the only one with this attitude. The fields are heavily mined making it very precarious to plant. The roads are mined too, and the trains are frequently attacked, which often makes carrying produce to the nearest market nearly impossible, or at least not worth the risks. Even if, against the odds, excess food is produced and does get as far as a shop, the shops are likely to be looted. Because both ends of the trading structure are ruined, the incentive to produce excess is almost dead.

Thus it is that Mozambicans who have traditionally been self sufficient and wealth producing have been reduced to a state of dependence. The latest appeal for food aid in Zambezia, the most agriculturally rich province and the bread basket of the country, was for 429 000 people. Even this represented only about half the number who really needed it. In 1990/91 the need for emergency food aid is was so acute that over half the population were in need of it.[15]

Re-establishing Mozambique's productive base will be a long and complex task. The time being lost is more than just the immediate, for the future too is at stake. While people become dependent on aid they lose their initiative and forget their skills; they become apathetic and disheartened with life, and this is what their children learn.

The loss of Mozambique's productive capacity is further exacerbated by Renamo's physical attacks on infrastructure. Some 1300 motor vehicles have been destroyed, and about 310 miles of high tension power lines destroyed or damaged. A team is employed full time just to repair the electricity pylons that Renamo destroys. Out of 4000 electricity pylons 1400 were destroyed by Renamo in 1988 alone. This destruction and the destruction, for example, of Beira's oil storage tanks, has the dual purpose of slowing down production and causing Frelimo to spend precious foreign currency on either imported electricity from South Africa, buying oil for the oil fired electricity station outside of Maputo, or replacing the destroyed tanks.

The Chimavara electricity substation was also blown up, ruining plans for Cahora Bassa electricity to reach the north of Mozambique where it was to help run a textile factory at Mocuba. 503 shops have been looted or destroyed, as have 58 000 head of cattle. Thirteen bridges too have been destroyed. Suffering the most from this outright destruction has been train and transport infrastructure.

There are five main railway lines running through Mozambique, acting as links between the ports and the neighbouring countries. Transport earnings used to be higher than earnings from any other sector of the economy but this is now far from the case. Every one of the five lines has been heavily sabotaged by Renamo on a frequent but unpredictable basis. The sabotage started on the southerly lines running from Maputo to South Africa and Swaziland, but later in 1982/83 moved up to affect the Beira-Zimbabwe, and Nacala-Malawi lines. Between 1982 and 1985, 93 locomotives and 250 freight cars were destroyed. Trains are attacked almost every week.

Not just infrastructure but production plants themselves are being destroyed. Two major sugar factories, for example, have been ruined. One of the sugar plantations was at Luambo on the banks of the Zambezi River. In addition three cotton plantations have been attacked, and four copra producing plants destroyed. As foreigners are a particular 'threat' to Renamo's successful destabilisation of Mozambique, particularly since the recent increase in interested foreign investors, they and their projects are frequently attacked.[16] Some 195 'sequestrations' of foreigners took place between 1990–91 alone.[17] The April 1990 attack on the Corumane Dam in Moamba district, which was built by Coboco, an Italian consortium, is just one example. Other major production facilities which are targeted are tea estates, mines, cement plants.

It is not surprising then that the total cost of the war in hard financial terms was estimated to be in the region of $15 billion between 1975 and 1988, at 1988 prices. This is equivalent to four times Mozambique's 1988 GDP. This figure includes not just all the destruction and loss of potential earnings but also the very high defence expenditure, of which a large proportion goes on imports. At approximately 40 per cent of the national budget the defence expenditure of Mozambique is, relatively, one of the highest in the world. With the war costing the country so much in other terms one can see why this has to be.

The financial cost of the war can be catalogued in numerous ways. Mozambique's per capita income of approximately $210 in 1984, had dropped to $200 by 1985, and to $150–$175 by 1988. In 1988 Mozambique lost half of its potential GDP through the conflict. These losses are not just static figures, but are cumulative: the losses cannot just be counted in terms of the cost of damaged infrastructure. To this must be added the skills of the people who are no longer working or being trained, and who then have to rely on aid. The highest estimates say that 80 per cent of the fault for the economic devastation that Mozambique faces belongs to the war, while 10 per cent is attributable to policy failures, and another 10 per cent to natural disasters such as drought and flooding, but it is a very difficult thing to quantify accurately.

Whatever the appropriate figures, it is evident that the war has caused a level and type of destruction that reversed the chances of not just Frelimo's, but any development policy succeeding. Moreover it is apparent that the destruction has been wrought deliberately as part of a strategy of destruction. With the loss of productive capacity enhanced by social destruction, the loss of productive facilities and infrastructure, and the relentless destruction of all the major foreign currency earners, Mozambique is truly being raped. Even without all this, the sheer carnage it has suffered would be almost impossible for the economy to bear. The loss of hundreds of thousands of people has a massive effect on the physical strength of a country and on its mental integrity.

No country can live unaffected by this scale of devastation, least of all Mozambique which was underdeveloped and underpopulated to start with. Mozambique's physical and mental integrity has been shaken to its roots. Wholesale destruction like this is not wrought by people who are fighting for a better Mozambique, or by those who seriously entertain an idea of government. It is being wrought by interests which have no concern for the present or future lives of Mozambicans.

This is a very simple truth.

5   A War against the People

The Grizzly bear is huge and wild
He has devoured the infant child.
The infant child is not aware
He has been eaten by the bear.

A. E. Houseman, 'Infant Innocence'

In a Maputo church, light streams down from the broken stained glass windows at the back, blinding the congregation. As birds flap in and out of the high Portuguese vaults, squawking through the cool architecture, the Mozambican churchgoers sing quietly, as if exhausted.

The day before, the same people and several thousand others had gathered outside the same church for Nelson Mandela's rally. The party officials stood on the bandstand singing with lonely enthusiasm the rallying lines of the Frelimo anthem. The replies were so feeble that, as a stranger, I was embarrassed for the official. When he cried out Frelimo's revolutionary war cry *A Luta Continua* (the struggle continues) – a cry which is supposed to herald thousands of clenched fists breaking the air with the explosive reply *Continua* – the audience merely mumbled the obligatory. Better than anyone, Mozambican people know about the never-ending struggle.

In this war it is the people who suffer. The toll that the war has taken is counted by ordinary Mozambicans, not by soldiers or anyone else. In order to understand Mozambique as it is today, and the difficulties it faces on the road to recovery, the state of the country's most important resource and ingredient must be understood.

The physical uprooting and unsettling of so many millions has been the most devastating impact of all Renamo's strategies of waging war against ordinary Mozambicans. The disettlement of recent years has been exacerbated by the government's agricultural policy which has moved often unwilling people from their traditional farm lands to government farms. Displacement is something that Mozambicans have undergone for hundreds of years, from the days of running inland from slave traders, to the period of colonialism and mass plantation labour. Renamo's war, as is pointed out by observor, 'is a further event in a long standing process of incessant moving.'[1] Yet its effects have surely been the most dramatic.

It is only possible to spend a few hours in Mozambique before hearing talk of *deslocados* and *afetados*, classifications made for the purposes of aid. The former are Mozambicans who have fled their homes through terror of Renamo, according to the evidence revealed by interviews, and settled without land or possessions in other parts of the country. They presently number 1.9 million.[2] In addition there are some 1.4 million refugees who have fled for the same reasons to neighbouring countries, whose particular plights will be discussed later. The latter, who number about 2.4 million, are those who are seriously affected by the war, but for whatever reason, perhaps fear, have remained in their homes hoping that help will somehow come to them. All of these 5.7 million people are in need of emergency aid. Many of them are already in receipt of some degree of assistance.

The refugees, *deslocados* and *afetados* within Mozambique make up some 37 per cent of the country's total population. This third of the population is in need of relatively urgent emergency aid. All in all, about half the population is in need of some level of aid. While 90 per cent of the population is said to live below the poverty line, 60 per cent of the population, according to UNICEF, live in absolute poverty.[3] The UN estimated that 6.6 million were in danger of starvation in 1989, and that to avert disaster, some 726 000 tonnes of food was required. The situation is not getting any better.

The *deslocados* situation has wrought havoc on the country. They come almost entirely from rural areas, and end up living from somebody else's generosity on land that is not theirs to farm. They have sometimes fled hundreds and even thousands of kilometers and have usually left behind all their possessions. Arriving with nothing, with no roots or means of supporting themselves, leaving behind land that is no longer farmed, creating massive burdens in their huge numbers on the areas in which they settle, they are the devastation of their country.

The consequences of extreme poverty are particularly severe when combined with insecurity of life style. *Deslocados* suffer the the full severity of these consequences. Perhaps the most striking consequence of poverty, one that is usually ignored, is the intense humiliation suffered by people who have been reduced to such a state. That profound humiliation can be overcome in a lifetime should not be assumed.

A man whom I glimpsed in the Manica town of Chimoio, vividly told the tale. Standing in the market place wrapped only in the fragments of an old rough brown maize sack, with his genitals exposed, his legs and body uncovered, his face wore a look of numbness. Still, and staring into the space of his blank life, he was a testament to life at its barest; he could not even afford his dignity. Nudity is a widespread problem in Mozambique. It is not uncommon to see people who have fled from war-ravaged villages, from which the rebels have taken everything including their clothes, enter the cities without a scrap of clothing to hide their desperation. The strong African belief that poverty is equivalent to incompetence grips adults. In Malawi, child refugees from Mozambique refuse to attend school out of embarrassment at their lack of clothes.

Nudity is only one example of the extent to which psychological normality has suffered in Mozambique as a result of the war. A sense of psychological and social normality is desirable both as a means to economic production and in itself. As described in the previous chapter, lack of economic security and the destruction of social cohesion have upset life at it deepest roots. Villages caught in the crossfire of the war live in constant fear. Villagers cannot travel out of their village safely, and constantly look at each other with suspicious eyes. In Nhambonda, a Manica village, one man, asked if there were any Renamo supporters in the village, said 'there are informers'. When asked who they were, or if he knew, he replied that 'people are watching, people know'. Suspicion, one gathers, plays an important part in village life in times of such uncertainty.

Grown men who are not in the army are in a particularly bad situation. When Renamo attacks their villages and they flee, the women and children often flee to camps and places of refuge without their husbands. The men, afraid of being suspected of collaboration with one side or the other if found unattached to a definite village, often hide out on their own and fend for themselves, sometimes too scared even to show their faces at food distribution centres. If they are able-bodied, male and not in uniform, they are suspect. With many young males doomed to a life of hiding, family life is abandoned, saved perhaps for better years.

The widespread disappearance of men from the family unit is a significant and very negative factor. The assumption often made that men play a very minor role in African families, is only superficially true. It is true that women do the bulk of the unpleasant and daily work, and the men the extra work, but in a time of war it is exactly this which makes the man all the more vital to the continuing function of the unit. If the man is not there to provide the extra labour needed to produce food during a time of hardship, then there will simply be a shortage.[4]

Vestiges of normality are few in rural Mozambique, and much cherished. One fairly predictable fact about the war is that it is for many areas a war only waged at night. As long as you know which areas are which, and as long as you do not travel on trains or buses or on most roads, it is quite safe to be around during the day. The restrictions are severe, but after dusk they seem like unadulterated freedom.

Take as an example the town of Chimoio, a town often called Mozambique's most beautiful, situated about half way along the Beira corridor in the province of Manica. Here, night and day bear very different tidings. During the daylight hours the atmosphere in this town of quaint Portuguese architecture, smattered with elaborate balconies and broad verandahs, is of a quite normal and even increasingly prosperous town. As the capital of Manica province, it is the safest place for miles around. This becomes increasingly obvious as the day draws to a close.

As dusk falls the town is transformed. Droves of people are visible in long lines, like ants, with all their possessions piled high on their heads, filing into the town for the night. In the town they crowd the streets and pavements, sleeping wherever there is a space rather than risk the night in their village huts outside the town. They are reminded sometimes of the wisdom of their ways when firing can be heard only five kilometers out of town, and tracers are seen streaking the skies. The people of Manica are not alone in their habits, as the same pattern is followed over much of the country. Those not so fortunate as to live in the vicinity of a safe haven, either take their possessions at night and wander out into the bush, or stay in their villages and often suffer the consequences.

But these scraps of predictability apparent in some areas during the daylight hours, and the almost complete 'normality' apparent in Beira and Maputo, are thin disguises for the deep structural damage done by the upheaval of Mozambique's population. Some may be able to live with their dislocation, and, with what is left for them, may manage to save some sanity for another day when they can put it to productive use, but for the majority, today's misery is likely to mean tomorrow's.

Mozambique has two distinct types of area: the provincial capitals, and the districts, home to the villages. The provincial capitals are towns ranging in size from a few thousand inhabitants to a million and, all under the control of Frelimo, are safe havens for those fleeing the war. They all have airstrips, and now they all have food and water (at least at certain times of day). Although firing can be heard right outside some of these capitals at night often, they are rarely directly hit. It is the district and village level at which the war is waged. The districts are made up of very small towns, with perhaps one shop, a row of decaying Portuguese houses, and a number of villages, from which the vast majority of the population originate.

In normal times, of course, this section of the population would live in the villages from which they originate, but because of the war, a large number of people have fled to urban areas for safety. The dislocated live either in the slums of the cities or towns, in massive 'refugee type' camps which resemble sprawling urban slums, or in villages other than their own, which may sometimes grow to house so many *deslocados* that they are called, not villages but, more appropriately, *deslocado* settlements. Some of the camps are enormous, such as one called Pembane in Zambezia province, the biggest camp in the country with some 170 000 residents. Food arrives here by sea and consequently malnutrition levels are under control at below 5 per cent. This is in stark contrast to nearby Magulama where malnutrition levels are at about 50 per cent. Zambezia province has the largest number of dislocated people in the country with over 429 000. Even some districts, such as Lugela with 47 000 displaced, are like big camps.

Like the millions who have fled from their war torn areas into the cities, those in camps are undergoing the massive shock of learning to live in an urban context. Suddenly they are faced with the problems of disease and squalor which come from living in close quarters with thousands of others. The difficulties of adjustment to an urban living context, where ablutions must be organised, water kept clean and so on, present major problems for both the inhabitants and the aid workers who are trying to improve the situation. The problem of turning a rural population into an urban one literally overnight is not a small one.

Dislocated Mozambicans who have ended up in the 'reed cities' as they are called, the slums of the bigger cities, have the advantage of being in areas where food is at least around, even if they cannot access it legally or properly. Most of the food aid in the countryside is given out not just because people are too poor to afford food, but because in many rural areas the food is not available. The rural peasant economy has long been a subsistence economy for the majority, and when the peasants can no longer produce their own food because they are separated from their land, it simply is not there to be had. The sudden massive need for food in concentrated areas exacerbates the already existing problem of food shortages. Mozambique is reliant on other countries for 90 per cent of its market and relief cereal needs. 600 000 tonnes of maize, for example, are provided on commercial arrangements from overseas, 200 000 tonnes are received as donations, and only 110 000–120 000 tonnes are produced internally. Although the *deslocados* in the urban areas are largely ignored by aid agencies, some 2.6 million people in urban areas totally rely on food aid for their survival. According to the League of the Red Cross, some 5000 000–600 000 people have moved into the environs of Maputo alone in recent years. Others put it closer to a million.

The mass urbanisation that has taken place in Mozambique over the last few years is amongst the most severe of the long term implications of the *deslocado* situation. In terms of what Mozambicans produce for themselves, the farmers, who make up so large a section of the population, are the country's most important asset. Yet this asset is diminishing, as tens of thousands flee to the cities for shelter. Once in the cities, with no skills to sell, they are practically useless to the economy and become reliant on aid.

Mass urbanisation is a problem that many African countries have suffered as a result of independence. At its barest, this is frequently blamed on the colonial example that has left the impression in people's minds that 'big is beautiful'. Because the colonists developed their cities, it is said, access to wealth is now perceived to reside in the cities. Once everyone starts thinking this way, of course, it resides nowhere. Although Mozambique is going through mass urbanisation for very different reasons, the long term effects are similar. Unpleasant though the conditions might be in the reed cities, many stay there even once their villages become safe from the war. Like Mozambique's immigrant miners who first went to South Africa for the need of money, but who on their return have had problems re-adjusting to village life after the buzz of Soweto and Johannesburg, the thousands who have moved to the cities in Mozambique because of the war are likely to be reluctant to leave.

Maputo is now home to about 10 per cent of Mozambique's population. Not so long ago, in 1970, only 5.7 per cent of the entire population lived in cities. By 1990, almost 20 per cent of the population was urbanised. In 1985 when the war was at its peak, urbanisation was increasing at 5.3 per cent per annum. Beira, Mozambique's second city, has suffered too. Its population had increased since the mid 1980s from 400 000 to over one million. The strain on the infrastructure suffered by all Mozambique's cities, and even more its *deslocado* camps, is aptly summed up by the pompous piece by the literary editor of London's *Daily Express* on the demise of Beira, where he had grown up, published in *The Spectator*.[5]

The piece was entitled 'The Sewer of Africa' and described Beira as such. Bemoaning the demise of British economic colonialism and the last 'fifteen years of incompetent black independence', as he calls it, betraying his ignorance of the racial background of Renamo's founders and financiers, he describes Beira's once Grande Hotel as it is today. 'Now a blackened slum' he calls it 'with trees growing in the walls and squatters' laundry draping the balconies. The parquet tiles have been ripped up for kindling and sewage lies stagnant behind the ballroom where once the bemedalled President of Portugal entertained fine ladies in lace under the chandeliers.'

It is true that the cities are in a state of severe disrepair. The description above is of the centre of town, but the slums are much worse, for it is in them that most urban *deslocados* live. Disease, lack of adequate basic facilities such as water, cardboard shacks which fall down in the rain, and bits of broken-down Hungarian buses as roofs, characterise these pits of disgrace. Never mind the parquet tiles and chandeliers. Mozambique thus far, perhaps only because its people are exhausted by war, has avoided the worst of the pitfalls of urbanisation, such as high crime rates, and mass discontent with unemployment. However, though it is uncanny how safe the streets of Maputo are today, this is no guarantee for the future. Already as food and goods become available in the shops a little crime is becoming visible, and urban discontent, due to poor conditions and overcrowding is starting to gently simmer.[6] How many more dramatic price rises – such as those recently imposed in line with the IMF Economic Rehabilitation Programme – will be stood without major protest, is a timely question.

Even those who have become 'urbanised' through their time in *deslocado* camps will have problems readjusting to ordinary farming life again, if that time ever comes. They are forgetting their skills, forgetting how to look after themselves, and forgetting how important they are to the economy. The combination of the urbanisation and dependency of so many of Mozambique's farmers is a very dangerous one.

The structural difficulties posed by having so many people concentrated in small areas and trying to survive there, are that the whole economic balance of the country, the production and marketing structure, the transport network, the reliance on family for provision, is thrown into disarray. The problem is not just how the economy should deal with the imbalance now, but how it will ever be achieved again. Thus the migrations that Mozambique is suffering, both to the cities and to the camps, is a devastating blow in the short and long term.

The long term problems presented by the upheaval and random scattering of tens of thousands of people around the country do not end here. Another and perhaps the most disturbing aspect of the dissettlement caused by the massive population movements, is the effect that dislocation and upheaval has had on the mental and physical stability of Mozambique's children. The importance of children to Mozambique's future cannot be underestimated, as a staggering 46 per cent of the population are under the age of 14 years.[7] By the year 2000, it is estimated that it will still be as high as 44 per cent of the population. Even if the state of Mozambique's children was a healthy one, the high proportion of them in the population would be structurally disadvantageous for the economy. But of course, they are not in a healthy state.

Children always suffer more from the same problems than adults do. If disease is around, children will catch it; if family life gets upset, children feel it more; if relations are lost, children cannot look after themselves; if limbs are lost or violence, murder and mutilation are witnessed, the horror is all the more vivid and scarring for children. Mozambique's children have suffered all these things and more, and thus magnify the horrors of the war. If the future of the country is in their hands, the promise that it holds is precariously balanced. The effects of dislocation on Mozambique's children, and the implications for tomorrow's generation, deserve detailed mention.

Children, as has already been seen in passing, suffer abduction and experiences of extreme violence, as well as health problems as a consequence of the war. On top of this, they frequently suffer the effects of separation from their parents, which both exacerbates the other effects of the war, and has a separate and debilitatingly long term effect of its own. The huge number of children who have died as a result of the war, either because they have been killed or, indirectly, through disease, has already been mentioned. The figures for abduction are almost as overwhelming. UNICEF estimated that by 1987, about 200 000 children had become either separated from their parents, orphaned or abducted by Renamo. Their 1989 estimate was 250 000.

Excessive and widespread malnutrition amongst Mozambican children has been linked to a possible decline in their mental health. Without the proper food, their physical and mental growth is stunted, often beyond repair. Some 1.5 million Mozambican children have been noted to have suffered severe physical stunting because of lack of the appropriate foods. Health problems are exacerbated in children who have been separated from their parents, particularly malnutrition, as there is no one to provide for them.

As is slowly becoming apparent both infant and child malnutrition rates are extremely high in Mozambique, even compared to other third world countries. A limited survey done in 1987 found that 13 per cent of Mozambique's children were suffering from acute malnutrition. A more extensive survey carried out over several provinces in 1989 by the UN found that there was 57 per cent chronic malnutrition amongst children with 8 per cent acute malnutrition. According to UNICEF 1989 figures, children are receiving only 68 per cent of the necessary calorie intake, compared to 100 per cent in both Lesotho and Tanzania. The percentage of children found to be below the average weight was also found to be very high at 27 per cent. Not surprisingly, a survey done in 1987 found the overwhelming causes of all child deaths to be malnutrition and malaria. The problem of child health is certainly linked directly to the problem of dislocation, as parents find themselves unable to produce food whilst in *deslocado* camps, and children separated from their parents have no access to food.

There are a number of other needs associated with the family, in addition to health, which children must satisfy if they are to grow up whole and productive parts of the community. There are many more family-associated needs in Mozambican society than in the Western society, as the Mozambican family plays roles which in the West are played by a host of specialised institutions.[8] In Mozambique the family trains children to the household and productive duties, such as collecting the right wood for fires, house building, and taking care of illnesses; where in the West you simply switch on the stove, call the builders and go to the doctor. Without the family the Mozambican child does not learn the survival strategies learned by his/her countrymen over the centuries.

The emotional loss suffered, and the stress placed on the child by separation from the family, can also be dramatic. Jovito Nunes, who has studied the effects of displacement in Zambezia province, writes of the emotional comfort and understanding normally given by the extended family, which is lost: 'The baby too received the best attention. All her weeping was rocked by a cheerful group of grandmothers, aunts and sisters, who sang and danced'.[9] It is a poignant indication of the long term emotional effects of familial loss and other types of uncomforted traumatisation, that most Mozambican children are reported to respond to their circumstances with silence: the most traumatised talk only reluctantly and often suffer great problems of concentration.[10]

Concentration problems caused by the war exacerbate the effects that the war has had on education.[11] Half a million children in Mozambique do not go to school at all, thanks to the war. It is estimated that there are some 2.8 million children who are crucial to the development of the country and who, in order to fulfil their role, should be getting some kind of educational assistance. Only one per cent of them, however, is. Another problem attached to the educational drawbacks and difficulties for children of the war, is that children are more adversely affected by reliance on aid than adults, as the aid workers cannot work with them, as they try to with the adults, but only for them. The dangers of inducing a physical and mental state of dependency from an early age are considerable.

Displaced children in Mozambique either end up with the rebels, roaming the streets of the cities, in a *deslocado* camp with a strange family, or in an orphanage. Children who find their way to orphanages or foster homes can consider themselves relatively lucky. Orphanages are deliberately few in number in Mozambique, for fear that the families looking after other people's children, but who cannot afford to care for them properly, or families who cannot even afford to look after their own children, would inundate the orphanages. This is considered a real possibility, although Mozambicans, in contrast to many third world countries, are often noted for their tendency to give priority to the survival of even their very youngest children during times of drought and difficulty.

Conditions in orphanages are poor though through no lack of effort on the part of the usually inadequate staff. In an orphanage that I visited in Manica province fifty children, most of them scarcely even waist height, were all under the care of one man. Two women carried out the necessary breast feeding. Some of the children were under six months old. The young age of the children made me wonder how many children must die abandoned when they lose their parents. Witnesses confirm that a certain number do. A driver for a Maputo based aid agency told me that he had found a live child lying on the dead body of its mother. Another woman told me that when she was abducted by Renamo to act as a porter, she was instructed to abandon her baby so that she could carry more of their baggage.

This particular orphanage outside of Chimoio had recently moved premises from another site 12 kilometers down the road. When I asked the man in charge why they had moved, he replied that the 'bandidos came three times'. On their third visit to loot the orphanage, they had raped eighteen of the children. There were six older orphans who I did not see on my visit because they were at school; none of the others, as I have said, came above waist height.

Almost always, the children who suffer some kind of trauma from the war, such as witnessing extreme violence, being subjected to it or being made to participate in it, are also victims of familial loss. A high proportion of the children recruited by Renamo are put into active service. In research[12] done by a group of three specialists, a child psychologist, a psychiatrist and a health specialist, at least 20 out of the 35 children between 10 and 16 years at a Maputo centre for traumatised children, Llanguene, had witnessed killings, often of large groups. Most had suffered some form of extreme brutality, including beatings, hackings and starvation. The methods of recruitment and training mentioned, and the atrocities the children are required to carry out, are traumatic enough to permanently upset the child's mind.

The fact that some escape, at great risk to their lives, to find help is testimony in itself to Renamo's bad treatment of them. In fact, relatively few do manage to escape from captivity, and few are lucky enough to find help. The stories they tell indicate both why they take such risks to escape, and that after the ordeal of being made to participate in violence against friends and family, the fear and punishments associated with escape possibly have the most damaging effects of all. For, once they have escaped they have to deal with what has happened to them in the world of their future; too often they cannot.

The combination of the ordeals of not having family to explain and comfort, and the experience of violence and sometimes extreme guilt, often makes children develop their own strategies for coping. This may be the common reaction of not talking, or of adopting a preoccupied frame of mind. Other strategies, noticed by Nunes which in his study were adopted by adults,[13] but equally are adopted by some children,[14] are to take up beliefs in absurd fantasies, lying or exaggerating about themselves, affecting, or giving in to, madness, and in some cases, becoming deliberately subservient, perhaps to the authorities, as a means of estranging themselves further from their peers. None of these strategies or ways of coping are means of reversing what has happened and erasing it from their minds, but of adapting themselves to live with it painfully for the rest of their lives. None of the strategies adopted lead the afflicted back into the community, but further away from it.

One boy of six, called Franisse, told his story to a journalist, 'Son of peasants in the province of Gaza, Franisse was kidnapped by Renamo during a dawn raid. They set fire to all the houses in the small community. As the villagers fled their burning homes they were shot. Their bodies were then cut into pieces to be cooked. Francisse, the only one left alive. was forced to collect the remains of his relatives and put them in the drumns the family used for storing water'. Another. Ernesto Alfredo, told his story direct: 'When they came for the first time they stole food and killed my grandfather. First they tied him up then they killed him. Afterwards they hacked his body into pieces and laid it out behind our house. I was full of fear and anger. I felt so bad I wished I could die. But there was nothing I could do'.[15]

Another child had to watch his mother's head being severed from her body, and was then made to wrap it up in a cloth and carry it. The effect on that child, of having to deal with the head with his own hands, must have been insurmountable.[16] Yet another child, captured on a raid into Manica in January 1988, told of how he had been forced to kill twelve women with a bayonet as a punishment because they had tried to escape. Such stories give a better insight into the depth of the damage, than any examination of the effects. Tolls such as these, which are but concentrated drops in the great sea of the suffering of Mozambique's orphaned children, are hard to quantify. Suffice to say that for children like these, war has not become a way of life but just a torment.

Attempts are being made to deal with the vast spectrum of problems faced by the children of Mozambique, but the task is so daunting that the projects in operation do little more than dent its surface. One such attempt is a child tracing scheme which is run by the tiny government department of Social Welfare and the various Save the Children Funds present in Mozambique. Between 250 000–500 000 children in Mozambique are without parents or any relation to look after them. Out of these at least 2250 street children are living from scraps in cities.[17] Some estimates put the street children figure much higher. Some of the children have escaped from Renamo captivity, while others have simply lost their parents and families through the war, either because they have died or been killed, or because they have become separated from their children in the chaos after an attack.

Although few children are united with their families relative to the scale of the problem, the emotional response of aid workers to each successful case of a reunited child shows at once the massive significance of each child, and the small impact that their efforts are having on a problem associated with much bigger forces than they can muster. Indeed, their reactions indicate well the plight of aid to *deslocados* in Mozambique altogether, which, in the face of ongoing war and its devastating consequences, is wholly inadequate.

The problems, of poverty, urbanisation and child separation, presented by the mass dislocation that is taking place in Mozambique, are not getting any better. Instead as the war rages on the dislocation continues, constantly reinforcing as it does so the reliance of Mozambicans on aid, a problem in itself. With so large a section of the population affected by the war, the problems for Mozambique have become fundamental. Out of a random sample of 40 000 *deslocados* in 1989, 1900 were starving to death, yet the war goes on, and the population continues to move from war zone to war zone.

The true scale of dislocation in Mozambique is only just beginning to become apparent. Refugee accounts would indicate that dislocation extends further than than those who have fled from Renamo, to those who are dislocated within Renamo areas. In addition to the numbers mentioned, there are probably another half a million people in dire need of emergency aid who are inaccessible. These people live in Renamo held areas and it is not even possible to get in to count them accurately. The tens of thousands of dislocated who live in emergency camps or temporary settlements, though cramped and diseased, are at least fortunate that they can be reached by aid workers. Out of those reached by aid countrywide, only 29 per cent can be freely reached, 56 per cent by military convoy and 15 per cent by air only. It is in addition that there are those who cannot be reached at all. Only haunting stories told by aid workers, who every now and then chance upon an abandoned area, point to the real scale of the problem.

One such story is of the Niassa district of Nipepe. In June 1990, an Oxfam representative who was based in Lichinga, the capital of Niassa province, was reminded of Nipepe whose only airstrip had been shut down a year and a half previously after the rainy season's mud caused the near loss of a plane. Since then, because it is very hard hit by Renamo activity and is only accessible by air, no one has been able to get in to help or monitor the situation. After some effort, the aid worker managed to get hold of a plane with which she would be allowed to risk the unmaintained airstrip. On safely landing, the plane's passengers found a population totally without food, and dressed entirely in the bark of trees. The few roots and berries that could be scavenged were all that had been sustaining Nipepe's survivors. Such neglect is a grim demonstration of the importance of aid in cases of emergency.

As the true scale of the *deslocado* situation reveals itself, it further reveals the increasing inability of existing aid resources to cope with it. The run up to the peace process which began in late 1989, and the peace process itself, has proved to be a curse rather than a blessing. Not only has it contributed to the waning of donor enthusiasm by altering perceptions of Mozambique's needs, but it has also vastly increased the stress on the existing aid. With talk of peace, both Renamo and Frelimo forces have stepped up the war. Frelimo, in a run of good fortune, managed to free many districts from Renamo control, especially in the war-torn province of Zambezia. In Zambezia recently the situation has almost reversed.

From a situation where almost none of the districts were accessible freely by road, they are now almost all accessible. What this seemingly wonderful state of affairs has meant, is that thousands more people can now be reached. People who previously could not be helped because of their location within rebel held areas, are now coming out in their thousands. The needs amongst these populations are said by aid workers to be of almost unsurpassed severity. Aid, reduced in 1990 because of low donor morale, cannot cope with the increased need.

Observers have been given two glimpses at once of the true scale of the crisis that must be overcome before recovery can begin. For, in addition to the thousands of needy being revealed by the opening up of Renamo-held zones, the 1.4 million people who have taken refuge in neighbouring countries are beginning to return. If they all decide to return at once, which is likely, a full scale returnee emergency could emerge. Glimpses of this imminent scenario are already painfully visible. Even the mere talk of peace has led thousands to come flooding back across the borders. 154 000 were expected to return in 1990/91 alone.[18] Maputo province in 1989 had as many as 15 061 returnees in one year. 1989 was also a year of very poor rainfall in the area. Aid agencies are now concerned about the need for stockpiles in key areas to preempt the emergency situation which could well arise. Aid shortfalls however, have prevented the proper arrangements from being made.

Returnees, who were previously looked after by aid earmarked for the countries they had chosen for refuge, are suddenly finding themselves placing an unwanted burden on aid earmarked by international agencies for Mozambique. In the cumbersome world of aid it is not easy for funds to travel across borders with the speed and adeptness of the needy populations. Appeals have to be made for causes, people donate to certain causes, and if the causes change, the aid agency is faced with the moral dilemma of spending money given for a certain thing on another. In addition, the returnee situation in Mozambique is developing at the worst possible time. The United Nations High Commission for Refugees, just as the crisis is developing, is suffering budget cuts of up to $60 million, meaning that the agency which would normally deal with an emergency like this one is not far short of impotent.

The need for flexibility in aid is fundamental to the Mozambican situation, because the situation itself is in constant flux. Mozambique's emergency is not a short term burst of need, but a long term and fluctuating emergency. Needs in Mozambique, for example, as well as arising in time of severe year long famine and drought, are also seasonal. When the dry season comes and there is no food to be had, people come flooding down from the hills that they farm into the environs of the towns, so that they can survive another season on aid. Come the rainy season, many leave again.

Even without the seasonal fluctuations, the numbers of *deslocados*, refugees, returnees and their geographical location, is constantly changing. To stress the overlap and fluctuations of and between all these categories, take the example of a Mozambican living in Zambezia province who has fled her home and must find somewhere else to live. The safest route to neighbouring Tete province is through Malawi, as Malawi dips right in between the two provinces. She may not want to stay in Malawi, and so she continues through it, as many do, to Tete. For a week in Zambezia she is an uncounted *deslocado* because she has not settled anywhere yet; for however long she stays in Malawi she is a refugee; finally, when she arrives in Tete, she is counted as yet another *deslocado*. As well as giving a clear idea of how numbers can be exaggerated, this example demonstrates what constant flux the situation is in. Donors of aid, who give on impulse and are stirred by simplistic perceptions of disaster, do not cope very well with real complexities like these, as will be seen later.

One group of 3000 Mozambicans sheltering in Milange district of Zambezia at the end of October 1990 illustrates the complexities of dislocation well. This was the third time they had moved on. They had been evacuated to Milange from the Benga centre in Tete province, where in 1987 they had arrived from Malawi.[19] The emergency situation in Mozambique is not static but dynamic. Because people may become dislocated, then go back, then flee to some other *deslocado* camp, areas which are the worst affected are constantly changing, and numbers of needy fluctuate wildly, especially now that so many returnees are descending on Mozambique. Aid has a difficult task in keeping up with these changes. Strategic stockpiling is the most effective way of dealing with uncertainty and unpredictability, but it is, of course, very expensive, and unappealing to donors.

While the war continues, with talk of peace only hiding its state of flux and increasing unpredictability, the problems of dislocation and resettlement escalate. As they do so they increase the profound legacies that a future peaceful Mozambique will have to deal with. Aid is faced with serious difficulties at present, as shortfalls in funding coincide with both the huge numbers flooding back over the borders to a situation no better than the one they had fled in the first place, and the increased number of people accessible to aid because of recent government military wins. Yet aid bears massive responsibility.

Its responsibility is to try, for the sake of the people and in spite of all the difficult circumstances, to foster development instead of dependency. The biggest danger of all for internally displaced Mozambicans, for the children, the urbanised, and for those who have fled as refugees across the borders, is that their dependency will stifle their long term mental ability and initiative. If this happens to the people, the country's most important spark of hope will have been extinguished.

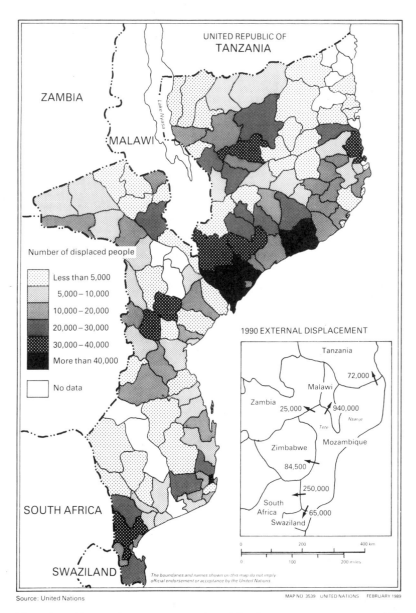

MAP   5.1   Mozambique: concentration of displaced people, February 1989
(Adapted from UN map no. 3539)

6 Refugees in South Africa – a Forgotten People

The days darken round me and the years,
Among new men, strange faces, other minds.
Alfred, Lord Tennyson, 1809–92

The movement of Mozambique's war into the the rest of southern Africa has been both forceful and menacing. Mozambicans, in an attempt to survive, and to escape the fear that plagues their daily lives, have scattered not just through Mozambique, but across the region, taking with them the ravages of their country's poverty. Mozambique's economy, depressed and inaccessible because of the war, hinders the development of the region. The increasing frequency of direct Renamo incursions into neighbouring countries has also taken its toll.

Southern African wars have traditionally ignored national boundaries. A century ago, when the region was carved up into shapes which ignored the tribal affiliations of the regions' people, tribes became divided by abstract borders. Some Chichewa were told they were Mozambican, some that they were Malawian; the Shangaan found themselves classified sometimes as Mozambican, sometimes as South African, and so on with many tribes.

Thus, in recent years, when wars have broken out in southern African countries, it has been natural for people to flee across invisible boundaries to live with their fellow tribes-people in safer zones. The 'export' of wars from one southern African country to another by the movement of people is widespread. Every country in southern Africa has at one time been affected in some way by the physical intrusion of neighbouring wars, and has also sent vibrations of its own wars across borders.

Mozambique's war is no different from other southern Africa wars in this respect. It has had a profound and lasting effect on the region's political and economic stability. The symbol and centre of the regional aspect of Mozambique's war is the refugee problem. The difference between Mozambique's war and other southern African wars is the sheer number of refugees in question. The 1.4 million Mozambicans who have become refugees in foreign countries, the vast majority of them since Renamo began its war, represent almost ten per cent of Mozambique's 15 million population. Just as the refugees have had a major effect on the countries in which they have taken refuge, so the type of hospitality offered to them has deeply effected them. How they are received is critical to them as people who are to take place in the building of Mozambique's future. The different ways in which they are received reflect various factors: how many other elements of Mozambique's war host countries are suffering which may influence how much they think they owe to war refugees, short term economic factors, and above all, short term political factors. The refugees are seldom welcomed with open arms and treated like nationals of their countries of refuge. What is common to all refugees in the world, and thus to Mozambican ones too, is that they are all balls in the batting game of politics. The Mozambican refugees suffer from, more than anything else, the lack of political and economic dexterity on the part of the international agencies and the host countries.

Complications and room for manoeuvre within the issue of accepting refugees in one's country are manifold. The primary issue, that which determines whether refugees are allowed into a country or not, is that of the definition of a 'refugee'. Definitions are of course great political tools. The semantic skirting around the definition of refugees, a subject of major debate, has severe human consequences. Even once a country decides who it will allow to be called a refugee, the problems have only just begun. The implications of the adopted definition, whether the international aid agencies should be let in to help, what status the refugees should be given and what rights, must be decided on. Should they be caged in fenced camps, or allowed to mingle as ordinary citizens and to work? Should they be sent back as soon as possible or left to make up their own minds? The questions are endless.

The phenomenon of a refugee is not a modern one, indeed the fact that people run away from persecution and seek refuge in neighbouring countries is age old. But the growth of the international aid structure, especially as developed after the Second World War, has heightened the debate about exactly to whom aid should go, and so the definition of a refugee has had to become more exact. Three general categories of refugees have developed: victims of natural disasters, economic refugees, and political refugees. Refugees who are victims of natural disasters are a fairly distinct category and there are a number of aid agencies which exist specifically to provide them with help. It is the distinction between economic and political refugees that is critical. Generally, a refugee who deserves the attention of international refugee aid organisations, such as the United Nations High Commission for Refugees (UNHCR), must be one who has run from his or her country because of political or social victimisation, rather than because of economic need. It is because a clear international commitment to political refugees has been established, which is not the case with economic refugees who are generally seen as part of domestic not international problems for which organisations like the IMF exist, that the definitional difference is of the utmost importance. The 1.4 million refugees in question are all political refugees.

There are about 72 000 of these Mozambican refugees in Tanzania, 25 000 in Zambia, 65 000 in Swaziland, 84 500 in Zimbabwe, 250 000 in South Africa, and, by far the largest number, 940 000 in Malawi. In each of these countries, except South Africa, the refugees are accepted as political refugees, but problems with their welfare are nevertheless manifold. To understand the state of this large section of Mozambique's population the way that they are received in some of the host countries must be examined.

Zambia, which despite its larger size, has the smallest number of Mozambican refugees, first noticed an increase in refugee influx in 1985. The situation developed in much the same way in Zambia as elsewhere, in that the refugees first settled spontaneously amongst their fellow clans-people or tribes-people, and were later put into special refugee settlements, or camps.

Zambia, a country which has been plagued by extreme poverty ever since independence, and whose attempts to solve its economic problems by various austerity programmes have led to political upheaval and food riots, decided early on that it wanted the help of UNHCR in sorting out the refugee situation. UNHCR came in 1986, and set up camps for the refugees far away from the border areas in which they had originally settled. The Zambian camps were considered model refugee camps. Everything that was supposed to happen in an ideal refugee world, happened, at least at first.

The refugees were given some land to work in order that they could eventually become self sufficient. Self sufficiency would not only reduce the burden on Zambia and the aid agencies, but also mean that the Mozambicans would not rot away during their time in exile, but keep busy and productive. Self sufficiency would keep the refugees from falling into the depressed state of mind, engendered by a feeling of hopelessness and of being stuck in a seemingly interminable rut, which is common amongst people reliant on aid. At first some of the refugees succeeded in producing a surplus of food, which the World Food Programme (WFP) bought from them to feed the newer arrivals to the camp. Unfortunately, due to insufficient funds for the self-sufficiency projects (which are quite expensive to maintain, but are supposed to ultimately reduce dependence and the long term level of aid) have fallen by the way-side, and the refugees are once again doomed to a state of full reliance.

In Swaziland, the set of problems is different, although as in the case of Zambia, they are bureaucratic rather than fundamental. In Swaziland, UNHCR, which exists specifically for the purpose of softening the effects of impersonal games of politics on refugees, in a sense caused for itself the very problems it usually seeks to prevent. The Mozambican refugees in Swaziland are mostly of the Mahlalela and Masilela Swazi clans, brothers and sisters to their fellow Swazis in Swaziland; Swaziland is relatively homogenous in tribal terms. Many Mozambicans have straddled the border of the two countries for years. When the Swazis on the Mozambican side started fleeing the war and settling permanently on the Swazi side, UNHCR had problems defining them as refugees, since they were Swazis in Swaziland. So they became, until UNHCR sorted out its semantic problems, caught in the definitional 'No Man's Land'. The definitional problems that the refugees in Swaziland have been subject to are more than matched by those faced by the Mozambican refugees in Zimbabwe. Until 1986, when the number of Mozambican refugees in Zimbabwe had reached about 45 000, the Zimbabweans would not allow UNHCR to help. The reason for Zimbabwe's stubbornness was wrapped up in intricate political complexities. Zimbabwe was friendly with Mozambique, and did not want to offend Frelimo in any way. Ironically the Zimbabweans believed, probably with good cause, that if they were to allow UNHCR into Zimbabwe, they would be tacitly admitting that the refugees were refugees in terms of the international definition.

To most this would not present problems, but it was believed by some that the international definition, as adopted by the United Nations 1951 Convention and 1969 Protocol, meant that a refugee was necessarily a person fleeing the persecution by the government of their country. The definition[1] as embodied in the conventions is in fact ambiguous. The later OAU[2] declaration on refugees more specifically included the definitional possibility that refugees were not running from their governments, but potentially from other hostile forces in their countries. This more progressive definition has been unofficially adopted by the UN now. Nevertheless the difficulties remained as the chance of causing offence lingered in Zimbabwe's mind.

Meanwhile, the refugees in Zimbabwe, uncatered for by official bodies, were settling in, just as refugees in Zambia and Swaziland had originally settled, amongst the local population. Many refugees in Zimbabwe are Shona by tribal affiliation and thus fit in culturally with the Shona tribes-people on the Zimbabwean side. As the war continued to escalate in Mozambique and the numbers of refugees with it, Zimbabwe finally decided that something had to be done, so UNHCR was 'called in'.

In fact, UNHCR had been in Zimbabwe for years, but until 1984 it had been dealing with returning Zimbabwean refugees from Mozambique. In 1984 it was given permission to set up refugee camps for the Mozambicans. It set up four camps, two in Mashonaland Central (Nyamatikiti with 2744 refugees and Mazoe River Bridge with 26 816) and two in Manica (Nyangombe with 15 150 and Tongorara with 30 732). Zimbabwe, very touchy about its sovereignty, insists on organising all the refugee affairs itself, and just takes UNHCR funding while allowing the UN agency only a nominal role in management.

The situation in Zimbabwe was very erratic at one time, with thousands being forcibly repatriated to Mozambique from where they had taken such risks to flee. Some say that about 8000 were forcibly repatriated in 1988 alone. This has more or less stopped now, and it is believed that any forced repatriation that goes on is the fault of individual Zimbabwean soldiers and not government policy. Certainly any continued forced repatriation victimises the estimated 100 000 refugees not in camps, rather than the 78 000 estimated to be in camps. Though the repatriation situation has improved, after the problems preventing an official UNHCR presence were solved, other definitional problems manage to frustrate the lives of the refugees in Zimbabwe.

It is their 'status' which is the problem. Zimbabwe is slightly unusual in having its own law about refugees.[3] It is a very liberal law which gives refugees status to work in Zimbabwe, as well as ensuring their long term ability to provide for themselves in Zimbabwe, and thus their long term welfare. The problem is that this law has not been applied to the vast majority of refugees in Zimbabwe, who are Mozambican.

The law was originally intended for the relatively few South African political refugees who crossed the border, and not for the enormous numbers of rural Mozambican refugees who arrived later. Thus the Mozambican refugees in Zimbabwe are treated as a special group. They are not allowed to work, or to have any land except that which is provided for them in the refugee camps. Zimbabwe, for the honourable sake of its own long term economic and political integrity, tries to keep the refugees in temporary circumstances so that they will one day return to Mozambique. However, it takes the jailor's approach, which does not help the refugees maintain productive or active minds.

The refugees are kept in fenced camps. Not surprisingly, this has become an issue of some significance. For days in a row, witnesses tell, the refugees pulled the fence down, only to have it resurrected. The voice of the Zimbabwe government, in the form of the District Commissioner, appeared and told them that the fences had been erected for their own sake and for their security from Renamo incursions into Zimbabwean territory.[4] Many still feel that it is to keep the refugees in. The refugees can walk in and out of the frequently guarded gates as they please, so the fences perform no formal caging function. But it is also true that Renamo, as yet, has never attacked a refugee camp, and it seems unlikely that it would do so. There are plenty of Mozambicans in Mozambique, and if Renamo takes the risk of going into Zimbabwean territory, it can make a bigger impact and create greater offence by attacking Zimbabweans. Nevertheless, the fences are there and they do have one very real effect, which is to create the sensation for the refugees of being imprisoned.

Generally the refugees, once settled in Zimbabwe, are not (thanks to foreign aid) totally destitute, although they are frequently malnourished, and their physical plight is generally well below local standards. Their mental plight is usually much worse, as is evidenced by the serious alcoholism problem in some of the better camps, and the general disposition of any refugees you choose to talk to. Their frame of mind adjusts itself to the depressing state of being permanently reliant on aid.

All the while the camps get more and more crowded, and even the few self-help projects that are underway are threatened by sheer pressure on space. The established camps all presently hold approximately four times their initially estimated capacity, and over six times the capacity at which it was estimated they could become agriculturally viable.[5] The possibility of opening even more camps is being discussed at a high level. But the root of the difficulties of accommodating refugees in both Zimbabwe and Malawi in a satisfactory way is land.

In Zimbabwe, land has long been a very touchy issue. The main issue of Zimbabwe's war of independence, still fresh in people's memories, was the question of land rights. Both tensions over the protection of white farmers' land, and inter-tribal tensions revolving around land rights, remain sensitive political issues today. Spare land which is not the subject of heated debate, is not easy to come by. Consequently, land for refugees is a subject that most politicians would rather not broach, and so they do not.

Most of the problems presented to Mozambican refugees by their host countries revolve around political and economic questions which could be overcome if there was a real commitment to the case of the refugees. However, refugees do present some very real problems to their host countries, and not least to the newly independent and mostly impoverished countries of southern Africa. Refugees cannot work, and yet they need land and food, while international agencies who offer help are seen as threats to newly attained sovereignty. In a sense, at least some of Mozambique's neighbours make an effort to help the refugees.

This is not the case in South Africa, a richer and more spacious country than any of its southern African counterparts. South Africa solves the refugee problem in a very simple way: it simply refuses to acknowledge their existence. South Africa chooses to forget about the refugees by not granting them status as refugees. They are given status only as illegal immigrants and, if found, are imprisoned or returned to Mozambique. Because of this, few know very much about them, least of all the international aid agencies, very few of whom operate in South Africa. The plight of Mozambican refugees is worse in South Africa, the very country which played a crucial hand in creating the war from which the refugees are fleeing, than anywhere else in southern Africa.

The elephants who plunder across the small Usutu River into the game reserve of Ndumu in northern Natal, driven by an innate sense of the dangers of the Mozambican side, are better off than the human refugees who flee across to the South African side. The elephants are given refugee status and looked after, since the South African park wardens know that they are very likely to be killed for their tusks or meat by Renamo if they are allowed to return to the Mozambican side. Often the elephants come over to South Africa with bullet wounds, or partially mauled tusk cavities. Nobody would like to see the inevitable happen to them again, and so out of sympathy and basic human dignity, they are looked after.

Not so with the human refugees. Sometimes they have come over fleeing Renamo attacks in droves of two and three thousand, as in July 1989 and May 1990, clinging to the edges of trains passing through Mozambique into the South African border town of Komatipoort. They are sent back to their imperilled Mozambican town as soon as it is feasible. Usually this is the next morning. Occasionally the South African police try to help the refugees by accommodating them for a few days or hours until it is safe for them to make the journey back to their homes. However, by law they can do no more than this.

The system which justifies this treatment of the refugees in South Africa is a very complicated one, and it affects the well-being of the refugees in many ways. A major effect of the denial of status to the Mozambicans is that they get very little aid from within or without South Africa, nor, as illegal immigrants, are they allowed to work to support themselves. Consequently, they are to be found, if you look, all over the place. Not in refugee 'camps' as such, but as hobos and down-and-outs in Johannesburg and Pretoria; in the squatter slums in which the South African victims of citizenship status problems sprawl their humanity, and in the 'independent' Homelands of South Africa.

Most of the refugees are to be found in the Homelands in the northern parts of South Africa, near the Mozambican borders. Estimates of the number of Mozambican refugees in South Africa vary tremendously, from about 150 000 to a quarter of a million and well over. The fact that the refugees are not put up in proper camps but are scattered wild, combined with the tendency for people classified as illegal immigrants to hide, makes it very difficult to estimate numbers accurately.

Compounding the problem of counting the refugees in South Africa is the large number of economic refugees from Mozambique, who must be distinguished from the political refugees. There are many Mozambicans who are blatantly in South Africa just to improve their economic situation, and have decided to take a calculated risk on entering South Africa illegally for this purpose. There are others who have come to South Africa as husbands and wives of people who are already legally or illegally employed in the mines or elsewhere. These people are all economic migrants. If these were counted as 'refugees' of some type, the figure would probably be increased by another two million. The people in question are those who have come over because their livelihood in Mozambique has been threatened fundamentally, perhaps because their villages were destroyed in an attack, because their fields were mined by Renamo, or for other reasons directly related to the war. They are political refugees, fleeing from the threat of the war to life and limb.

These people, who are forced to flee to South Africa, and undertake a life-threatening journey to get to a place where they never wanted to go in the first place, face enormous difficulties in crossing the border. They are kept out of South Africa with nothing less than wild animals and an electrified fence. On a journey down the length of the South Africa's border with Mozambique, I came across a small hut adjoining a fence, in which a young soldier sat. The hut boasted two switches: one marked 'lethal', the other 'non-lethal'. South Africa's border is very cleverly protected.

Ostensibly to keep the ANC (which is no longer banned in South Africa) out of South Africa, an electrified fence has been built along the South African border with Mozambique. The fence has been built only along the part that is not protected by the largest reserve of wild game in the world: the Kruger National Park. Only one very small section of the border, where Mozambique borders northern Natal, is protected by the army alone.[6]

Crossing Kruger Park by foot is no simple endeavour, but thousands do it. Walking is the main way of getting to South Africa and some refugees walk hundreds of miles. By the time they get to Kruger, the final frontier, they are in a state of near exhaustion, they are often nearly naked, and are surviving on roots and termites. In this state they make very easy prey for the park's famous predators, especially lions. Lions do not normally attack humans, but there is now at least one pride of lions in the Satara area of Kruger which has developed a taste for human flesh because of the sudden influx of easy human prey. Hyenas, who do not attack humans unless they are in a vulnerable or weakened state, have also been attacking the refugees.

All the refugees in KaNgwane, one of the Homelands, have been through Kruger: there is no other way to come, unless they skirt around half of South Africa, in which case they probably would not settle in KaNgwane. The very conservative assumption that roughly half of the 70 000 refugees in the Gazankulu and KaNgwane Homelands have travelled through Kruger leads to the conclusion that at least some 35 000 people have made the treacherous journey.

The only alternative route into the Transvaal is crossing the fence, which though also treacherous has been proved possible. Various methods are used. One is to throw logs over the fence, thus causing a short circuit and allowing time to scramble over makeshift bridges; another is to tunnel under the fence and hope your back doesn't scrape; alternatively, forked sticks can be used to prise the fence off the ground. Even a network of guides has sprung up, who claim to be experts at the lethal crossing and charging R100 ($40) a time. But the wooden structures which they create often collapse, and the primitive method of seeing if the fence is charged or not by throwing wet mud at it often fails. The consequence is that people are fried alive.

Rumours, perpetuated by the government, that the fence's electricity was switched off in February 1990 are spurious. For a time the electricity was turned down, which lead to a spate of severely deformed, rather than dead, refugees, whose body parts had 'stuck' to the fence on contacting it, and had melted. Even when the electricity was reduced for a time the SADF patrols retained the capacity to switch the voltage back up to the lethal voltage at any moment. Nevertheless so many refugees attempt the crossing that guards are forced to repair the fence every day from early morning until 10am, during which time the electricity is, of course, switched off. How many have been killed as a result of trying to cross the fence, is not certain. The official government figure for the number that have died on the fence since it was turned on in 1987, is 94. Other sources suggest that the figure is much higher than this. A hospital in the homeland of KaNgwane on the Mozambican border reported that 12 people had died on the fence in the month of December 1989 alone. All estimates from non governmental sources are similar. The South African Council of Churches Committee for Refugees, have estimate that 52 people were killed on the fence in the second half of 1988 alone, excluding those that found themselves at the other end of a bullet for trying to cross. The refugees themselves say that about ten a week get killed on the fence. No one can really know. All that is known is that many innocent victims of a war, instead of being offered refuge as they would be in most other places in the world, are being shamelessly murdered.

More people have been killed on the electrified fence running along the South African/Mozambican border in three short years than have been killed on the Berlin Wall since it was constructed, and yet the world has barely uttered a word of protest. Now, thanks to the world's focussed indignation, the Berlin Wall has been torn down, and yet the electrified fence remains, and it continues to kill political refugees. Why is it ignored? The answer is simple.[7] It is because the fence is in South Africa. The world's perspective frequently becomes obscured where South Africa is concerned.

Complaints about apartheid flood the world's press rooms and TV screens. To the world, white South Africa is bad; the issue is quite literally black and white. For all its good intentions the world punishes the victims of apartheid for the system under which they live, as much as its perpetrators. The world's concern about South Africa is so much with the 'issue' of apartheid, that the original priority which stimulated the concern, a sympathy with the people of South Africa, its victims, has been forgotten. The mesh of complex politics surrounding South Africa has obscured the original goals. Unfortunately, the Mozambican refugees who fled to South Africa have suffered the same fate as South Africa's own people at the hands of the world.

The behaviour of the UN is the prime manifestation of this. The UN protests against South Africa's domestic politics by isolating it and ignoring it, just as the international business community does through economic sanctions. The purpose of this is, ostensibly, to bring about a better quality of political life for non-white South Africans. Yet pretending that South Africa does not exist, does not just mean denying white South Africans and the government all the benefits of the world's co-operation, but also denying them to black South Africans, and with them Mozambican refugees in South Africa. The effect of this contorted method of protest is that UNHCR has no presence in South Africa, which means that few international aid agencies operate there, and that consequently there is very little aid for the refugees.

International aid agencies are reluctant to operate in a country with a refugee problem in which UNHCR is not present, as UNHCR is crucial to their smooth operation. Without UNHCR's presence it becomes very difficult, and sometimes impossible, for particularly the smaller agencies to operate. UNHCR is the 'official' body that represents international aid, and establishes a relationship and set of informal rules of conduct with the relevant government regarding the status of the refugees and how the aid agencies may operate to help them. Thus UNHCR is usually instrumental in bestowing refugee status on the refugees. In the case of South Africa, the UN has declared the Mozambican refugees merely 'persons of concern'.

South Africa, some believe, might think more favourably of giving the Mozambicans refugee status if it realised two things. First, how much more this would give it in international standing at a time when that is exactly what it needs; and secondly how little it would cost the country. With the international aid agencies that would without doubt come flooding into South Africa if UNHCR was allowed in, it is quite possible that South Africa, which does not have the same kind of land problem as somewhere like Malawi, would actually benefit from the situation. Locals are often included in aid packages for refugees when the refugees live amongst them, as so many in South Africa do.

With events leading to the slow decrease of South Africa's isolation from the world which began in early 1990, with de Klerk's February speech, the possibility of a UN presence in South Africa began to be discussed at a high level. Ironically the less complex pretext of wanting to help returning South African political exiles, not Mozambican refugees who are many thousands more in number, is the one being used. One of the main complexities which has presented such difficulties for UNHCR, and prevented it from establishing a presence in South Africa to help the Mozambicans is the set of issues surrounding South Africa's Homeland policy. The absurdity is, again, that international refugee aid, to which UNHCR is central, exists specifically to overcome the problems created by questions of borders. Its very purpose is to assist people who are victims of political problems alien to them. UNHCR, as far as South Africa is concerned, fails miserably in this task. Most refugees are in the Homelands because some Homelands accept them. But the international community, including of course the UN, has refused to recognise the existence of the Homelands. As UNHCR always operates on a governmental level, this makes it very difficult for them to operate without working with a Homeland government. It is also difficult for them to cooperate with the Homelands which give the refugees the status of 'refugees' while maintaining that Mozambican refugees are 'displaced persons' in South Africa, without tacitly acknowledging the independent existence of the Homelands.

The Homeland system and the way it relates to the Mozambican refugee issue is an area in which political wranglings get in the way of human need in more ways than one. The Homelands are, usually, fairly barren areas of South Africa which have been set aside for blacks to govern themselves in. The implication of the Homelands policy, which threw blacks who wanted to govern themselves into the most barren parts of South Africa with no infrastructure, no gold or diamond mines, and not much good agricultural land, was that it was a form of imprisonment for the rebellious. It was a snub, and a very cruel one which caused great domestic and international uproar.

The Homelands became semi-autonomous parts of South Africa, in which the leaders have total responsibility for all the problems of their land but not for its productivity, nor for the areas of policy, especially foreign policy, which affect South Africa. The issue of the status for refugees is, in some people's eyes, a matter of foreign affairs, and thus a South African matter.

The Homeland leaders have all taken different stances on the issue. Some, like KaNgwane and Gazankulu, have seen through the complexities and have simply taken the step of creating a truly independent foreign policy by declaring the refugees to be refugees and offering them refuge. Others, like KwaZulu, see all sorts of intrigues in the matter. They believe that if they were to declare the refugees 'refugees', that it would constitute an act of foreign policy that would make them look as if they thought they were truly independent from South Africa. Therefore, in order to appear as weak as they believe that they are, they have refused to take the independent step.

Thus the refugees get shunted around from South Africa to hostile Homeland, to friendly Homeland, to overcrowded Homeland and on and on until they are finally settled unsatisfactorily somewhere. The settlement is almost always unsatisfactory for Mozambican refugees in South Africa, because they are forced to take refuge in the very poorest and most overcrowded parts of the country. The Homelands are even worse off than the poorest countries in Africa (Malawi for example) for looking after the refugees, since, as they are part of South Africa, the aid that would normally be forthcoming for the local population or the refugees, is not.

The majority of Mozambican refugees will be an initial burden on their country when they return having suffered the conditions of involuntary exile; they will inevitably have lost their livelihood and their capital in Mozambique. Yet, the host countries are in a position to make a difference where their positive outlook, their initiative and their knowledge of how to provide for themselves is concerned. Status, the availability of land,

and especially conditions in the camps, all contribute to lessening the adverse effects of refugeedom on the refugee. Poor conditions in refugee settlements especially exacerbate the negative effects. The consequences of all the politics on Mozambique's refugees is nowhere more strikingly visible than it is in South Africa.

Walking through the refugee camps of the Homelands in South Africa is remarkably different from walking around those in Zimbabwe or Malawi. Though there are more imported cars on the streets of Johannesburg than in any other African city, there is not one to be seen in any of the refugee camps. The contrast with Zimbabwe, whose capital boasts few smart cars, and yet where the refugee camps swarm with aid agencies' cars, is stark. In the South African camps, usually only a few nuns or locals are in sight, a far cry from the plethora of professional aid workers in Malawi and Zimbabwe. The nuns distribute food for the refugees, 90 per cent of which comes from the same overstretched South African charity.[8] For the most part, the refugees in South Africa or in the South African Homelands are left to fend for themselves. Without papers, without land, without savings or belongings this is very difficult, and often impossible, for them.

Thirty-five kilometres from Giyani in the Homeland of Gazankulu, there is a place called Malamulele which is estimated to harbour some 30 000 permanently settled Mozambican refugees, and many more transient ones who pass through after finding it overcrowded. The 30 000 are settled in numerous settlements of several thousand. The settlements are informal, with shacks made out of cardboard, plastic, tires or any other available material.

Refugees in South Africa live in makeshift squattings. There are no committees organising habitable huts, sewage or rubbish areas. Nuns try to persuade the desperate residents of Malamulele at least to clean up the rubbish that is flung all over the place. But the refugees just nod their heads, or give them blank looks, as if, lost in their own desolation, they do not even hear. The refugees are totally uninterested in doing anything to improve their lives. These are people at the lowest ebb of their lives, in a rut of desperation that they cannot see themselves getting out of. They would rather live in complete squalor than waste their precious energy trying to raise their conditions to barely preferable semi-squalor.

The two nuns, looking after a thousand refugees, try to do what would normally be done by a large number of trained and efficient aid agencies. They try to organise the people into committees, to get them interested in their own well being, to help them financially and technically to build the basic needs of a settlement, like a water pump, a toilet and a rubbish pit. But in this settlement, the pit had been built and still people did not use it, the toilet was overflowing with sewage, and the water tap was surrounded by mud.

The apathy of the refugees in Malamulele is pathetic to witness. There is what is grandly called a 'reception centre' for new arrivals. It consists of a wall, three horizontal bricks high, running around a rectangular area of bare ground, but no roof, so when it rains its inhabitants get wet. The refugees were given the bricks to build walls around the structure, but the bricks sat untouched for three months while no one bothered. The nuns would have done it themselves, but as a matter of principle in this case, had not.

People lie in the 'shelter' surrounded by their total possessions. Usually these amount to a blanket and a pot, while some have nothing at all. Some of them have seen their relatives die on the journey over. Travel is very dangerous in Mozambique, and some have been shot. One woman watched her husband being mauled by a lion as she sat for hours shaking in a tree grasping her baby, and later crawled down to finish the trek across the Kruger. When they arrive they often do not have enough will left to build themselves a shack.

The exhaustion of these people who have been through so much is exacerbated when they arrive in a foreign land only to find more hostility. The only hospitality that they find is in very poor areas, where there is not a hope of them finding a job. The local chief will sometimes give them a small plot of land to settle on, but inevitably it is not cultivatable land. Those who take part in one of the few self-help projects going on in the area, run by a local priest, find that there is no one in the depressed local economy to buy the homemade pots and flower boxes that they produce. There is no medical aid available, while the squalor that they live in makes disease rampant. The story of neglect and squalor is similar in all the Homelands. In Lulekane, a township just outside Phalaborwa in the more southerly homeland of KaNgwane where about 6000 Mozambican refugees have settled, the attention given to the refugees is again totally inadequate, though not from lack of help from the locals. In late 1989, on a very hot and muggy day, I walked into Lulekane and was confronted with a mass of humanity sitting on the ground with babies crying amid the dust and flies.

Stepping over them, I headed for the blue and white striped tent. The smell from inside the tent was discernible from a distance away. Why so many people were sitting out in the sun instead of in the shade of the tent quickly became obvious. The strong and revolting smell inside the tent had been created by the fact that about 400 people were living and sleeping in there. To achieve this, some did, literally, have to lie on top of each other.

Each family or refugee had set up a cubicle within the tent for themselves, in a pitiful attempt to get some privacy. Some cubicles for a family of four or five were not as long as one person lying down, and about five foot wide.

The tent was a step up from those who, for lack of space, were forced to live outside. One seemingly impossible step further down the ladder of misery, these people had either built themselves makeshift shelters or were just sleeping on the ground. Some of the makeshift shacks were only a few feet high, and had been patched together with old pilchard cans and other rubbish, anything to fill in the gaps. In bad weather they fall down. It is estimated that there are 3078 children, 1920 women and far fewer adult male refugees in the small area.

The curious abundance of women and children refugees is matched in another area where refugees have settled, Winterveldt. Far from the friendly northerly Homelands of KaNgwane and Gazankulu, this settlement is in the Homeland of Boputhatswana. Boputhatswana is to be found spotted all over northern South Africa; this particular section is just north of Pretoria. Boputhatswana offers the refugees no hospitality at the moment. It is still in the process of deciding what stand it should take on the refugee issue, and whether or not it should grant them status. Boputhatswana is very sensitive to the political issues mentioned. Possibly if it were aware how many refugees there were in the area it would be even more reluctant to grant them status. Winterveldt takes much of the refugee overflow from KaNgwane and Gazankulu.

Winterveldt is already an infamous haven for black South African squatters; it is possibly the uncertainty about the Boputhatswana government's attitude to them and to the other squatters that attracts the refugees. Most of them walked the distance between Mozambique and Winterveldt, only to end up victims of both their own fate and apartheid.

Winterveldt is an embarrassment even to South Africa. Like a million people gathered in the same nightmare, the expanse of humanity is dramatic to behold. The numbers squatting on the land prevent even the hardened authorities from permanently removing them. Yet they are frequently moved on, and their tenure is permanently insecure. The people of Winterveldt do not live there out of an attachment to the place, but because they cannot get the necessary papers to allow them legally to live anywhere else. At night they are sometimes to be found, after being bulldozed off of the land they had been squatting on, wandering with gas lamps trying to find another suitable piece of land.

The situation is very bad for all concerned, and of course for the refugees it is worse. As illegal immigrants who are squatting, they must avoid the authorities on two fronts, they are unable to work legally, and usually cannot support themselves. Many seek refuge with fellow Mozambicans, sometimes people they knew from home, but this is not possible for all. Two children that I met were not so fortunate as to meet anyone they knew. They had lost their mother on the journey down; she had been shot by Renamo and they had managed to escape. On arrival in Winterveldt, the two children, one about four, the other about ten, had nothing. They had no food, no money, no blanket and no shelter. They managed to persuade someone to let them sleep in the pig sty behind their mud hut. At night they nestled up amongst the pigs to keep warm. South African nights on the highveldt can be bitterly cold in the winter, falling well below freezing.

Winterveldt, right outside the wealthiest business and industrial centres of the entire continent, is one of the worst refugee settlements in southern Africa. Malnutrition is rife, as is evidenced by the ubiquitous potbellies. Little research has been done on infant mortality and health statistics for fear of exposing the existence of the refugees. An informal estimate, by local church workers, puts infant mortality at 45 per cent.

Disease rages through the camps. With no clean water supplies, and barely any medical facilities, epidemics of cholera, tuberculosis and other fatal diseases are common. The health problems are exacerbated by the lack of medical facilities. One woman's experience demonstrated the difficulties. The night that her village in Mozambique was attacked by Renamo, the night she fled for South Africa, she was shot in the neck by Renamo. The bullet has now sunk deep into her breast. She dared not go to a doctor to have it removed because, like so many, she knew that he would ask for residency papers which she did not have. If caught she would be sent back to Mozambique where she could be shot again.

The problems of counting the number of refugees in Winterveldt reflects the fear inspired by the politics admirably. The Bishop of Pretoria estimates that there are around 10 000 Mozambican refugees in Winterveldt, local workers estimate that out of the total million people in Winterveldt, there are about 20 000–25 000 Mozambican refugees. Operation Hunger, in what is probably a purposely low estimate to avoid attracting too much attention to the illegal refugees, puts the figure at only 2000.

The refugees in the Homelands, miserable though they are having to live in these, the poorest areas of South Africa, with very little aid or attention, are no better off than the thousands of unaccounted for refugees living in South Africa 'proper', illegally resident, illegally employed in contract labour, and constantly in fear of being found and sent back to Mozambique which they had risked so much to flee. It is estimated that there are about 80 000–130 000 Mozambican refugees who are either in

places like Winterveldt where their welcome is very tenuous, or are trying to lose themselves somewhere in the rest of South Africa where they
will not be found.

Many of them stand in huddled groups at known street corners, warming
their hands over makeshift fires in the early mornings, waiting for a farmer
to come by and pick them up for a day's casual labour. They may pick up
odd jobs like this once a week if they are lucky. Sometimes they may be
picked up for a week's or a month's commission. But, without papers, they
are very vulnerable, and the farmers in the eastern Transvaal, used to seeing
large numbers of Mozambicans, have become wise to this.

Unscrupulous farmers exploit the refugees mercilessly. They contract
them for work offering a certain rate of pay, and then at the end of the
term, be it a month or a day, pay them less than was arranged. Sometimes
they do not pay them at all, threatening to turn them in to the authorities
if they complain.

One farmer employed a thirteen year-old Mozambican refugee to help
spray his fields with a poisonous insecticide. The boy was not given
any protective clothing, and was hospitalised for five days to treat the
severe rash resulting from his contact with the chemical. According to
the hospital workers, he should have been hospitalised for six weeks,
but instead he went straight back to work with the dangerous Organic
Phosphate chemical. For this kind of abuse, the Mozambicans are being
paid wages in the region of R3 ($1.50) a day, or R30 ($15) a month.
Sometimes they are just given food for the work they do. They are kept
alive, but no more.

The farmers go to the border areas purposely to pick up the refugees for
work, because they know that they can get away with paying them less,
and that they can abuse them without fear of reprisal. The farmers literally
hold the power of life and death over the refugees because they can have
them returned to Mozambique at their whim. Farmers buy and sell the
refugees amongst themselves. More politically motivated whites living in
the northern reaches of the Transvaal, it has recently been found,[9] take the
refugees to be trained for service in Renamo. The refugees in South Africa
are considered no more than illegal immigrants and are treated as such.

It is not just white farmers who exploit the refugees, South African
blacks play an equal, if not worse part. Recently two South African journalists[10] uncovered a highly organised exploitative trade in Mozambican
refugees,[11] similar to that operated by the farmers, operating in eastern
Transvaal and Reef black townships. The trade in these human beings
is extensive; the traders refer to the people being sold as 'stock', and
the people sold describe themselves as *izigcila*, a siTonga word which

translates directly as 'slave'. For about R200 ($100) a Mozambican can be bought as a concubine, a slave labourer, or for *muti* (body parts needed for ritual sacrifice). Others, who have not been trapped in the net of the slave trade, have made their way down to the big cities, especially Johannesburg. There are estimated to be thousands of Mozambican refugees in Soweto, where they have a good reputation for making do. They are to be seen selling fruits, potatoes or plastic bags on the side of the road. One man who walked half way across Mozambique and South Africa to get to Soweto has now set up his own hand crafted hardwood furniture business. But people like him are few. Mozambicans are more usually to be seen lying in the mornings, ashen faced, on the icy streets of Johannesburg with no clothes on their upper body, and just a grey blanket covering them; like so many they just beg for their existence. Some have children, some are wounded.

These are Mozambique's people, and this is what has happened to them. The tired and apathetic refugees of Malamulele who have lost their spirit, the diseased, the exploited are the fugitives running from the vile war raging in their country, only to find themselves fugitives in another land. It is these people who will one day have to rebuild Mozambique. The only positive sign is that, despite the fact that at present they are flooding into South Africa, most of them still consider Mozambique their home, and want to go back when times are better.

For the time being, however, despite how little they are being offered in South Africa, they go to the greatest risks to get there, because it is at least safe. They will even go back through Kruger, or through the fence, to get other relatives and bring them to safety. As if in total oblivion to the risks they take to get to the refuge of South Africa, the South African authorities continue to forcibly deport them to Mozambique at the rate of between 1500 and 3500 people per month,[12] where they must once again face the horrors that forced them to flee in the first place.

Meanwhile the world pours millions of dollars worth of aid into the development of Mozambique, and yet ignores a large section of Mozambique's people. The people of Mozambique should be their country's future jewel, but some of them have been forgotten.

7 Malawi – the Triangle of Discontent

Cure the disease and kill the patient.
> Francis Bacon, 'Of Friendship'

'The Warm Heart of the Real Africa' is how the Malawi tourist board describes it's country. It is an appropriate description. This land, which dips down deep into the most lush parts of Mozambique, whose steamy days are heralds to the nights of burning fields which gave Malawi its other title as 'the land of fire', truly suffers the problems of the real Africa.

In this small country of only eight million,[1] there are over 940 000 Mozambicans sheltering from the war being waged against them; they represent over eleven per cent of Malawi's population. Malawi, one of the smallest countries in Africa, has more refugees than any other country on the continent, even more than Ethiopia or Sudan. In fact in 1989 there were only two places in the world with more refugees than Malawi: Iran and Pakistan.[2] In contrast to those in South Africa, the refugees in Malawi have not been forgotten by the world. To their benefit, the entire international aid industry has descended on tiny Malawi, making them possibly the best looked after refugees in the world. More than one aid worker who has come down from the Horn of Africa to work in Malawi has commented that Malawi is the cream of refugee worlds. Yet, as the case of the Mozambican refugees in Malawi demonstrates, there are some problems that aid simply cannot solve; it is the condition of being a refugee, forced into a state of unwilling dependency and without the means of escaping the circumstances, that is the problem.

As well as being tragic for the refugees themselves, the Mozambican refugee problem is disastrous for the regional economy. The effects of Mozambique's war on the region are most dramatically illustrated by Malawi which suffers more than anywhere. These effects, of course, turn back again on Mozambique, affecting it as part of the region, while it suffers independently too from the loss of large sections of its population. Thus Mozambique suffers double punishment. The refugee situation, to say the least, is an unhappy one for all concerned.

Malawi, though a beautiful country, flat for the most part but smattered with imposing plateaus, is a poor one. Poorer even by some ways of measuring than Mozambique, it is one of the poorest countries in the world. From the top of Mulange, a cool mountain of mystery steeped in local superstition, it is possible to look out east over the barren plains below and see for miles over Mozambique's Zambezia and Nampula provinces into the Indian Ocean, and survey the miles of Mozambican unrest. If you are lucky enough not to be caught in one of the violent storms that come swinging in from Mozambique to rage over Mulange from time to time, you may see down south, past the barren plains to Malawi's green and rich tea growing area and from there south to the district of Nsanje. Nsanje is home to what an Amnesty report said was called the 'Nsanje treatment' involving various horrific tortures for domestic prisoners of the internationally respected regime of Hastings Kamuzu Banda. It is also home to the thousands of Mozambican refugees.

Banda, who is the self appointed Life President of Malawi, has been in power since 1964 when Malawi made the peaceful transition to independence from Britain. The world is prepared to ignore his shortcomings, and the dangers that will be presented by the vacancy of his powerful position when the old man dies. The world ignores much for the price of regular interest payments on debts, and for adherence to capitalist principles and compatibility with the IMF. But the world is happy with Malawi for another reason too.

Banda, and his countrymen, have the most extraordinarily hospitable attitude to the refugees from Mozambique who are all but sinking their country by sheer force of numbers. Perhaps on the part of Banda, who has at least in the past sanctioned the support of the Renamo (who are not just the perpetrators of his country's problem today, but also, by way of creating the refugee situation, the cause of all vast sums of international aid that come flowing into Malawi) it is an less an act of kindness long overdue than the sign of a man who knows how best to keep the international respect which he so much values. On the part of the Malawian people however, it is pure generosity and a reflection of their gentleness and immaculate courtesy. They have no choice about living with the refugees, but they do have choice over the degree of hospitality that they give. Malawians, a proud and dignified people who are often of the same tribe as refugees, offer complete hospitality, and do so with grace.

Banda has said 'We will assist the refugees using all our available resources'. But the truth is that Malawi does not have much to spare. In colonial times, because of it's proximity to Salisbury, the unofficial regional capital second only to Johannesburg, Malawi was seen by the

British administrators only as a subsection of the greater region rather than as a country that should try to be at all self contained. It was thus underdeveloped from the beginning, and remains so today. The assumption made by the colonists that Salisbury could act as its capital was based on its proximity to Malawi, which in turn relied on the free use of the road through Mozambique's Tete province. That road has been passable in recent years, but only under armed convoy, and sabotage is very frequent. Many, including trucks, prefer to use the 12 hour longer route through Zambia. The idea that Salisbury could be an effective regional capital was also based on its prosperity, but Harare today is not what Salisbury was.

Per Capita income in Malawi today is as low as $170 per annum. Wages for a night watchman, or a driver are between 40 and 80 Kwacha ($14–$28) per month. Like Mozambique, Malawi suffers malnutrition and infant mortality rates that are amongst the highest in the world, and the country suffers an enormous skills shortage. Malawi has suffered from the Mozambican war in more ways than one.

One devastating effect of the war on Malawi has been the increased transport bills that Malawi has been forced to suffer. Malawi's economy is heavily export orientated. The simplicity of the Malawian economy and its reliance on few export products is very visible. The roadsides of the entire country are lined with Malawi's three main exports: tobacco (60 per cent of Malawi's exports), sugar and tea. Malawi has long been forced to route the bulk of its exports through either the South African port of Durban or the Tanzanian port at Dar es Salaam rather than through the convenient Mozambican port of Nacala to which there is a direct railway line. Durban is three times further away than Nacala, and Dar es Salaam about twice as far. Vast proportions of Malawi's meagre earnings are being eaten up by one of the highest transport bills in the world. It was estimated in the late 1980s that the rerouting was costing Malawi a total of $100–$150 million extra per year, as Malawi was paying 40 cents of every dollar of its exports, a figure which was expected to drop to 16 cents once the Nacala line came back into full operation.

The Nacala line, the crucial link to Malawian economic success, has been shut since 1984. After extensive repairs a Malawian agreement was signed with Renamo in August 1989, in exchange for allowing Renamo free trading in Malawi in cashews, ivory and dug-out canoes,[3] which lead to the halting of direct Renamo attacks on the line, and its reopening. However, attacks continued in the areas through which the train was routed, and the trains were taking up to two weeks and more to complete the journey of about 550 kilometers. In January 1991[4] direct attacks on the line began again. The bulk of Malawi's exports have been rerouted since 1984.

Funding continues to be donated from foreign countries for repairs to the Nacala line, but its smooth operation continues to be sabotaged by the war. The Tanzanian option, closer than the South African one, has not been feasible because of the difficulty of the route. A new route to the Tanzanian capital is being designed in a $160 million project.[5] The goods will travel an inconvenient and arduous route, by road to Lake Malawi, across the lake by boat, by road to the Tanzanian border, and from there by train to Tanzanian capital. It is estimated that if the Nacala line through Mozambique comes back into full operation in the near future, Malawi's transport bill will be cut by two thirds.

Malawi tries feebly to protect the line with its own army and has stationed one fifth of the national army along the line. This, however, has a negligible effect as the Malawi's entire army is only 5 000 strong. Malawi's army is poor defence not only against attacks which hinder the operation of the Nacala line, but also against direct Renamo incursions. Its vulnerability to the kind of attacks that its more hardy neighbours, Zambia and Zimbabwe suffer,[6] has lead it to seek other means of self-defence.

Formal and semi-formal cooperation between Malawi and Renamo has been going on since 1982. For a time South Africa used Malawi as a point from which to supply northerly Renamo activity. This officially stopped in 1986, but direct links were re-established with Renamo in 1989 with the signing of the Nacala agreement. Non-governmental cooperative activity with Renamo, based in Malawi and often ignored by the government, has continued all along. The evangelistic missionaries Rodney and Ellie Hein, of Shekinah Ministries (Blantyre), who frequently cross into Renamo zones handing out bibles is one example of this type of activity. Other missionaries travel into Mozambique with clothes and other goods for Renamo, crossing the river which forms the border and travelling downstream for a way in dug-out canoes, using what would appear to be an established cross border transport network, and then by night walking to the Renamo zones.[7]

Thus it is that, although no physical boundary separates Malawi and Mozambique for the most part, the Malawian side is considered almost entirely safe from Renamo attacks. Only occasionally when the brutal war raging only metres outside the Malawian border overflows into Malawi, is Malawi's true vulnerability at the hands of Renamo glaring, such as when in November 1989 a single Mozambican battle sent 200 Frelimo troops, and 1000 Mozambicans into Malawi for refuge. For the most part Malawi lives in relative tranquility, and is only disturbed by the silent mass of humanity flooding its borders to join the peace.

In terms of the destruction it causes to the Malawian economy, the refugee problem arguably outweighs the transport problem. The stress on tiny Malawi of over an eleven percent increase in its population in only three years has been massive. Infrastructure in Malawi was already weak, even without the extra burden. The entire district of Nsanje, for example, whose population has more than doubled since the refugee influx gained pace there in 1987, increasing the size of the population from 150 000 to 390 000 people, had one doctor in 1989.[8] The 240 000 refugees entered the narrow Malawian district from both its eastern and western borders with Mozambique's most affected provinces, Tete and Zambezia. Nsanje was desperately short of medical staff even before the massive refugee influx, but the refugee inlux has made the situation critical.

Other services are in equally short supply. Water points, for example, whether in or out of refugee 'camps' are sometimes shared by up to 3000 people. This means long queues each day for everyone. The influx of refugees has obviously worsened the situation. Other infrastructure too, like roads, has come under severe stress in the last few years since massive quantities of food have had to be transported along them for the refugees who cannot provide their own because the farmland is not available.

Malawi's economic performance over the last few years clearly illustrates the effect that Mozambique's brutal war is having on its smaller neighbour both through the refugee problem and the attacks on the Nacala line. After independence in 1964 the economy continued, for a few years, to grow at the relatively healthy pace of 6 per cent per annum. Throughout most of the 1970s the economy grew at 6.6 per cent per annum but like most of its African counterparts, the export dependent economy suffered severe decline in the late 1970s as a result of the oil crises-induced fluctuation in commodity prices, and the growth period came to a sharp halt in 1980.

The economy began a recovery only a few years later following structural readjustments. Between 1982 and 1985 the economy was growing again, this time at 4.1 per cent per annum. In 1986, the economy took another dramatic downturn, due this time not to world events but to those in Mozambique. In 1986, the same year as the refugee population in Malawi increased from 70 000 to 279 000, economic growth fell to 2.8 per cent, and during this and the next year the economy was under crisis management.[9]

The downward spiral had begun. Massively increased transport costs because of the now inoperative Nacala line, and an unforeseen amount of public expenditure due to the refugee influx, coincided with a 15 per cent decline in export commodity prices. The debt service ratio running at 4 per cent of exports was an added torture. Imports were cut back by reducing foreign exchange allocations to government and industry, which led to a fall in production, with capacity in some industries falling to below 40 per cent because of a lack of the currency for new parts. In an attempt to save the day the Kwacha was devalued, but this only led to soaring inflation.

In 1987, while the refugee influx rocketed and transport expenditure reached $77 million, the economy contracted by 0.2 per cent. Due particularly to the transport costs, the fiscal deficit rose to 12.5 per cent of GDP. The effect of Malawi's economic decline on the region was significant as, in the years before 1986, it had been exporting up to 180 000 tonnes of maize to drought stricken countries. Exports decreased significantly with the economic downturn which coincided with a crop failure.

Since then, with all the help that international aid has brought in shouldering the refugee burden there has been a recovery. Economic growth for 1988 was at 3.6 per cent, almost even with the population growth of 3.7 per cent. The 1988/89 fiscal deficit was reduced to 7 per cent of GDP.[10] Under the current circumstances, the apparent recovery can only be sustained with a constant flow of aid. Even if aid continues to flow in at the same rate, which is by no means guaranteed, the increasing refugee influx rates mean that the economy will probably be lucky to stay afloat, never mind taking any great strides. Malawi cannot properly develop under the current constraints, as even its present recovery is a false one, reliant as it is on aid. The only solution to Malawi's problems, as for many, is an end to the Mozambican war.

Thus one unhappy side of the triangle is complete: Malawi is suffering tremendous hardship as a result of the war being waged in Mozambique. Both of the factors which hurt Malawi so much are also tremendously painful burdens on Mozambique. For the rerouting of Malawi's exports away from the Mozambican port costs Mozambique dearly too, and further, of course, Mozambique must endure the condition of being a country in exile and the consequences of this for its future integrity as a nation. Again, a glimpse into what these consequences might be is best gleaned by telling the tale of the refugees. The situation of the refugees in Malawi is different from that of their counterparts in Zimbabwe, Swaziland and South Africa, for the crucial reason that the main political obstacles to providing for the refugees have been overcome.

Nor are the political complications in Malawi small; indeed they are quite peculiar. Malawi fears the invasion of national sovereignty and the exposure of local markets to free foreign goods as does any nation which considers accepting huge quantities of foreign aid. The situation in Malawi, however, causes unique problems, in that the number of refugees coming in from Mozambique is so enormous compared to the total Malawian population, and they have had to be squeezed into a very small and overpopulated space. The situation in Malawi is also unusual because of the way that huge numbers of refugees are accepted in settlements within native Malawian settlements.

For obvious reasons aid cannot just be given to a refugee who is living with other Malawians, and living the same standard of life in the same villages. Nor can aid be given just to the thousands of refugees in, for example, Nsanje, who use the local facilities, if it is not given to the Malawians who are being negatively effected by the presence of the refugees. If aid was handed out to refugees just because they were refugees, a situation could result in which the Mozambicans were better off than the Malawians. This would not be popular with the Malawians and could jeopardise their hospitable attitude to the refugees, which is of such great importance.

Malawi's weak infrastructure, and the massive strain that the influx of Mozambicans and the transportation of aid to help them has put on it, adds to the political complexities of Malawi's situation. UNHCR and the government have cooperated to overcome these difficulties by an unusual alliance designed to match the unusual challenges faced by Malawi's situation. The main aspect of the alliance is that aid is funneled through the government and goes towards the upkeep and improvement of Malawi's infrastructure, as well as going directly to the mouths of the refugees. Thus the funds go towards road maintenance, the building and improvement of water facilities and paying refugees' hospital bills, as well as going towards essentials such as food, blankets, shelters and pots. The role of UNHCR in making it all work is fundamental. The importance of solving the political problems is well illustrated by the South African example.

On a macro scale the situation in Malawi is highly organised. Once the political problems were solved, the usual bandwagon effect took place as many foreign aid agencies jumped on the UN-driven train to Malawi. Now in Malawi's impoverished cities, Blantyre and Lilongwe, air-conditioned offices churn out statistics and registers of refugee conditions, charts and tables detail the administration of aid, and the restaurants, which a few years ago were almost empty, overflow with the Western staff. All this, of course, a far cry from South Africa where in one typical camp, there is only one nurse who has no telephone, speaks no English and could only give you a very rough idea of infant mortality rates or any other health statistics.

On the surface, life for the refugees in Malawi would appear to be fairly reasonable. The refugees are officially classified as 'refugees' and not as illegal immigrants; they have the same citizenship privileges as Malawians. They are allowed to work in theory, they can use the hospitals (aid agencies pay the bills for Mozambicans that the government pays for Malawians), they can settle in the villages and so on. The problem in Malawi is not legal or political, as it is in South Africa, but practical.

The country is overcrowded. Malawi has long suffered from a land shortage relative to the number of inhabitants; there is not enough land even for Malawians, and consequently there are not enough jobs. The refugees, as they are frequently not part of the local system whereby the tribal chief allocates some of his land to his people, often live on government land which has been set aside for them. On this land they are squashed. Areas and camps designed to hold three thousand now have twenty thousand living in them.

The refugees in Malawi are not, like those in Zimbabwe, forced into camps surrounded by wire with guards at the gates who check them in and out, nor are there any rules, except their huge numbers, which separate them from Malawians. In Malawi, the 'camps' are open pieces of land, varying in size from those with twenty five huts to those with twenty five thousand, which refugees have usually not been moved to, but have come to themselves. Nevertheless the land, uncultivateable from the start, is totally inadequate for them to make a living from. Thus refugees in Malawi remain reliant on food aid for their survival. It is the land shortage which lies at the root of Malawi's inability to cope successfully with the refugee problem that has developed dramatically since 1986.

Happily, a great number of the refugees do not live in the so-called camps, but these are largely refugees from Malawi's longer standing refugee problem, which goes back to the 1970s, and do not suffer from a lack of land as the newer and more numerous arrivals do. They are completely integrated with the Malawian population, and are usually given land on the strength of a tribal bond by the local chief, just like any ordinary Malawian. The number of these refugees is estimated to be about 58 000. They are not reliant on aid, and do not present a serious problem for either Malawi or Mozambique except in the sense that they over-populate the former and under-populate the latter. The number of integrated refugees is rapidly declining relative to the number in camps.[11]

There are three different types of Mozambican refugees in Malawi. The first two types of refugee from Mozambique are more likely to be fully integrated than the third. The first type are those who fled the war of independence in the early 1970s after seeing their country fall from one war into the next, and have not considered it to be worthwhile to return. The second, are the Mozambicans who never let the artificial boundaries between Mozambique and Malawi bother them in the first place. These are people who have always wandered back and forth across what is now called the border, mixing as easily with the Malawians of their tribe, as with the Mozambicans of their tribe. When the war broke out these people naturally started spending more time on the Malawian side.

The third type are those who have run from far afield to escape the war waged by Renamo countrywide and who have ended up living in the camps. They started running en masse in 1986 and by 1988 were flooding over the border at a rate of 20 000 per month. These refugees are less likely to be of the same tribal affiliations as the Malawians whose areas they settled in, as they had come from as far as hundreds of kilometers inside Mozambique.

The suddenness of their influx was startling, and contributed to their inability to integrate themselves slowly and their consequent need for established camps. In September 1986 there were only 70 000 refugees in Malawi. This number remained fairly stable until February 1987 and then increased rapidly to reach 227 000 by the end of May 1987. By 1988 they were coming over the border at the rate of 12 000 then 20 000 per month, meaning that by the end of that year there were some 359 000 of them in Malawi. The last few months of 1989, still saw an influx of about 12 000 a month. The tide of humanity sweeping into Malawi temporarily slowed down at the beginning of 1990 with only 6000 a month crossing over. Even 6000 a month, ten times the influx rate of refugees into South Africa, a much bigger country and Africa's wealthiest, was a massive burden for Malawi. It meant that by 1990 there were some 820 000 Mozambicans living as refugees in Malawi, and by the beginning of 1991, approximately 940 000.[12] It is significant, when considering why the refugees left Mozambique for Malawi, that it was in late 1987/88 that the influx of refugees began to accelerate most dramatically. For this period was not the peak of the famines or droughts, nor was it the height of the agricultural policy disaster in Tete and Zambezia provinces which neighbour Malawi, and from which most of the refugees came, but a time when the war was waged very heavily in these areas.

Their lives in the camps were to be very different than those of their integrated counterparts. It is the point of view of the refugees themselves that it is their state of dependency, caused by the fact that they have no land of their own, which is their greatest misery. With all the world's generosity piled on them, many feel not ungrateful, but extremely unhappy. The Mozambican refugees in Malawian camps whom I met and those whom I interviewed, were characterised by their despondency and sense of boredom.

Although aid which alleviated their physical suffering made a tremendous difference to those whom it reached, the refugees themselves repeatedly reinforced to me that they perceived the mental stagnation that affected them as refugees as almost as destructive in itself as the physical deprivation. Although many had run from Mozambique because they were suffering severe food shortages, they did so with great reservations about leaving their ability to produce for themselves and live in their own homes, only to become dependent in a foreign land. They did not flee to Malawi out of some fundamental disillusionment with the ability of their land to sustain them, nor because they trusted wholly that they would be fed in Malawi, but because they had no option: it was a matter of life and death. These refugees had been prevented by the war in Mozambique from either eating what they had produced, producing enough, or even producing at all. They desperately wanted to go back to Mozambique as soon as the war situation allowed, and to rebuild their lives.

On one side of the coin it is a positive sign for Mozambique that the refugees in Malawi have left for these temporary reasons, and look forward to returning. The negative and commonly expressed misperception that refugees want to go on living in the country that they are harbouring in, linked with the misperception that refugees enjoy being dependent, holds little truth in the Mozambican context. The misperceptions stem, perhaps, from the loose use of the word 'refugee' which allows it to be used for economic refugees as well as political ones. If 'refugee' is applied as here to mean strictly political refugees, it is rare, from my experience, for such people to want to stay in their country of refuge for any longer than they have to.

Worldwide, people argue that not too much aid should be given to refugees in case they become too comfortable in their state of dependency. Some feel that refugees should not be allowed to starve, nor to become diseased, but that the help should stop there for fear that it should be taken advantage of. Apart from the abhorrence of this view which expresses a willingness to keep a mass of humans, like animals, almost dead, but not quite, what is often ignored is that governments usually take care of these dangers anyway by prohibiting the building of permanent structures in the camps, prohibiting the refugees working, and taking other measures to ensure that the refugees do not become too settled. This, and in Malawi simply the lack of land, by ensuring complete dependency on the part of the refugee and in unpleasant surroundings, makes the unwilling victim of dependency even more certain that he cannot live like that permanently.

If it is a positive sign that refugees want to go back to Mozambique because of a hatred of their dependent circumstances, it also a sign of how deeply their circumstances are affecting them. Perhaps aid workers alone, and only the more experienced ones, are aware of the reality of need, and how destructive it is to the human spirit. They know that the refugees often have a dignity which is being damaged by their dependency, and that the last thing most refugees want is to stay in their present condition without being able to work for themselves, educate themselves, or have an ordinary family life. Many would be surprised to be told that a starving person will not necessarily eat what you give him, simply because he does not like the food, or because of a religious commitment. This has been witnessed in the Somali and Ethiopian as well as the Malawian refugee camps. This vestige of dignity, choosing for yourself, prevails with surprising frequency until the last.

My encounters with refugees who saw the need for mental progression, dignity and independence as of primary importance began in a camp in the district of Mulange. A Mozambican boy of about twelve was attending the water pump. A long line of women waited in order, with their buckets on their heads, for their turn. When we came up the boy worked at his job even more diligently, explaining to the women how they should properly use the pump so as not to ruin it. He then asked us quietly in Portuguese whether he should not be paid for the job he was doing. Talking to him for a short while revealed that, like all the other boys who gathered around, he wanted to go to school as he had in Mozambique. After that he wanted to become a driver. Our driver, a Malawian, looked at him with pity. The boy too knew that he would probably never go to school again, or be a driver, or for that matter ever get paid for attending the water pump. This desire for education and progression is a typical reaction amongst the Mozambican refugee children to their plight.

In another camp, this one in the district of Dedza, amongst some temporary huts built only knee high, I came across a larger hut that stood out as different. It was an elaborate hut for the barren surroundings, standing on a slight platform of baked mud, and with a small verandah about the width of a person fenced with a balcony of intricate lattice work made of woven sticks. Few refugees bothered to make their huts into anything but temporary shacks. Pausing outside it I greeted the man who was lying in the shade of the the verandah. He invited me in and, squatting on the verandah, we talked.

He had been a typist in one of Mozambique's largest sugar plantations just the other side of the border, until Renamo attacked. On his journey to the safety of Malawi, he had lost his two young children and had himself almost died from hunger. His wife, who was lurking in the hut, had survived the trip. With his education and fluent Portuguese he should have been usefully employed in the camps, perhaps as a teacher. The Portuguese-speaking aid worker whom I was with, myself, and he, all knew this, but no one broached the subject because we all knew that there were hundreds of people in the camps whose talents were wasted and who were seeking that kind of employment.

I asked what he did all day, and he looked at me blankly. 'In the mornings' he said 'I attend to my hut, because there is nothing else to do.' 'And in the afternoons?' I asked. 'I sleep and dream of the day I can leave this place.' He went on: 'Malawi is such a poor country'. Pulling out some pigeon nuts, part of his food aid ration, he said, 'these things we only eat in Mozambique when there is a famine or a time of great hardship.' The food rations in the camps, he said, were small and monotonous. Then, with the grace of a much more worthy host, he offered us lunch.

His story was a recurring one amongst the refugees in Malawi. They had left lives where they fended for themselves against unbelievable odds presented by the war, where their children went to school, where they had a life surrounded by people that they knew, they had standing and they had pride. Now, far from wanting to stay in the Malawi refugee camps, in spite of how well foreign aid looks after them, all they want to do is to go home. Perhaps it is not particularly surprising that those who are in better physical health, as these are, are so drowned by the tragedy of boredom and their closed horizons, and humiliated by their dependent circumstances. What is more striking is that there is evidence of a similar perception of the importance of mental as well as physical normality amongst refugees who are in extremely adverse economic circumstances. It is the stories in which this is demonstrated to be true that are the most poignant. Often, for example, people swap their small ration of maize for a beer or a cigarette. In some cases the importance accredited to the need for normality over physical health seems to be the consequence of sheer exhaustion from being helped. A stop at a small gathering of refugee huts in Dedza district one day, with a social health nurse, proved instructive in this respect.

After walking around some of the huts belonging to refugees whom the nurse knew, while she asked after broken water pumps and people's health, we came across a small hut with three young children with bloated bellies crying on the ground, a mother with her head hung low, and a girl of about twelve, a shadow of a human, leaning against the back of the hut. The girl's eyes were sunken and her arms as thin as sticks. Every bone in her body, it seemed, was visible. She would cough every now and then, the effort unbearably racking her body. She had tuberculosis, and with that was starving. People who are suffering from 'frank' starvation, unlike those suffering from kwashiorkor, surprisingly, suffer from a total aversion to food, along with an debilitating weakness and lethargy. While her mal-nourished brothers and sisters nosily cried for more of the protein-lacking maize, this girl was, like a sack of bones, slumped in exhaustion.

The nurse told her mother that the girl would have to go to hospital or she would die. The mother knew that this meant she would have to go too, as hospitals in Malawi do not feed their patients but leave it to relatives for whom fires and pots are provided. The mother also knew that this meant she would have to leave her other children alone for the villagers to look after. But even though villagers and relatives stood around, presumably expecting this outcome and encouraging her to go to hospital, the mother did not want to go. She told us that she would rather stay in her hut with her family, take care of them herself, and let the girl die if that was to be. The girl, through sheer weakness, did not want to go either. This was one of the many times that I saw people refuse help for imminent physical disaster in favour of attempted normality, peace and a scrap of dignity.

Any difficulties in imagining why refugees so often perceive their physical and mental problems as of at least equal importance, are soon overcome by a visit to two very different refugee camps, Mkwai, the Mulange district camp of 10 000, and Mankhokwe in Nsanje. Set on a vast and barren plain, surrounded in the distance by hills, the silence of Mkwai is oppressive. The physical desolation of the site seems to be endless. The huts, all identical and arranged in neat rows with wide roads running between them, each hut with a large number painted on it, are enough to bore you just looking at them. Sometimes in refugee camps, aid administrators make residents pull down their shacks and rebuild them in the orderly rows so as to give the place some semblance of order and to facilitate the administration of aid. Mkwai does not suffer from lack of order

If a foreigner drives through Mkwai, people come flooding out of their huts, stand up, wave, yell, do anything to stir the stale air that they have been breathing for the long months that they have lived there. Before the dust even settles, their brief excitement is over. The inhabitants slump back onto their doorsteps to concentrate on their main pastime of keeping out of the afternoon sun. The striking thing about Mkwai is that it is what is considered by aid workers to be 'not a bad place'.

Everyone receives their rations, malnutrition rates are not terrible, disease is relatively under control, the water pumps work and new ones are being built, there are medical units stationed in part of the camp, the huts are properly built on platforms so that they do not collapse during the rainy season and there is no rubbish on the ground. Yet the place is stifling and exhaustingly clinical. I felt sympathy with a woman who, as I drove away from the camp, was running down the dirt track with the flames of her burning hut leaping in the background, screaming and tearing at her hair as she watched her sanctity from the ubiquitous helpers disintegrate into a heap of black ash.

Not all camps are as comfortable as Mkwai. Malawi's biggest refugee camp, Mankhokwe, is packed to the brim. The official figures (which could be higher because the higher figures attract more aid) say that it has some 100 000 residents, the unofficial figures quote somewhere between 60 000 and 80 000. Either way it is massively over-inhabited for its size.

It would be difficult to find a starker contrast to Mkwai. One step into Mankhokwe is a step into chaos and life. The atmosphere is slightly crazed as people try to squeeze in between the huts to the market and back. The huts are built so close together that walking down the narrow tracks past all the people sitting on the door steps of their huts is like crawling through a snakepit of legs. The market is packed with noisy refugees selling everything from supposed hippo teeth to single leafs of spinach. Unlike Mkwai, the life force has not yet left this place and the extremely poor conditions are borne with spirit. Sanitation is the biggest problem,[13] with so many who are accustomed to living in the spacious rural areas of Mozambique crowded into an urban setting. Water is in short supply: instead of the twenty buckets a day, which is considered healthy, no more than five a day are available to residents. Because of the overcrowding, the available facilities have rapidly become inadequate. Aid workers believed that in November 1989 at least another 1500 pit latrines had to be built before the October rains, to relieve stress on existing latrine which caused unsanitary conditions. However, the latrines could not be built because of the high water table in the area.

Although in Malawi the crumpled shacks that the refugees in South Africa call home, or refugees sleeping out in the open because they have no shelter at all, are not to be found, even in Malawi, with so much aid, the physical conditions for some can be very poor. The scale of the problem in Malawi is simply so enormous that aid cannot always reach everybody, nor give much to those who it can reach. UNHCR had a budget of $22.89 million in 1988 when there were 359 000 refugees; its 1990 budget, with more than twice the number of refugees, was less, at an initial $22.5 million. The best that aid can do is to try to ensure that everyone has at one time received the basics. With the massive population movements and fluctuations, and the registration problems that these cause, this is a major challenge, and many slip through the system.

The brutality of aid, which lies in how crucial it is to the individual, how much control it has over his life, and yet how clumsy it is, is felt by many. To people who have left every possession behind in Mozambique, the basics which aid provide them with are like gold. In the temporary shelter of an Nsanje camp, called Tengani, a man stood with his deformed hands punching the air in angry despair. He looked an intelligent and dignified man.

He spoke with urgency and his teeth were gritted to stop his tears. He was a leper, and with his two brothers, was alone in the temporary shelter. Other refugees had merely passed through the shelter for a few days on their way to a hut in the camp. This man had been there for a year. 'Too long' he said, his voice rising. Perhaps he had been left in the shelter because of his disease, though contrary to popular perception, leprosy is only contagious after many months of extremely close contact with a person. But his isolation was not his main complaint; it was the fact that he had been forgotten, and that he had to rely entirely on those who had forgotten him. He begged and pleaded for help, like a man about to die of desperation, for a blanket. For a year he had been without a blanket. From the words that he used it was clear that not being able to get himself a blanket by his own means, was as frustrating to him as the physical problem of not having one.

The Red Cross has a policy of giving each refugee a blanket on arrival, so in theory more blankets are not needed. Yet, with the number of refugees in Malawi rapidly escalating towards one million, there are thousands who are out of reach. Aid administrators know this, but are overworked trying to cater for the masses, and better than anyone the refugees know this. There are some materials, for example, buckets, which no particular aid agency takes responsibility for, which there is a great shortage of. Life without a bucket is extremely difficult under refugee circumstances. The nearest water source is often several kilometers away, and without a means of carrying water to your hut, you would have to walk several kilometers or queue for several hours, every time you needed a drink.

It takes much to stir people to head off in search of this degree of poverty; many speak of their traumatic trips over to Malawi. Few regard their standard of living in Malawi as higher than the standard of their lives in Mozambique before they were forced to flee. Refugees often arrive in Malawi in a terrible state after traumatic journeys from Mozambique. Some, whose villages were raided for everything, arrive wearing only scraps of clothing, others arrive stark naked.

The aid workers who understand that much of the refugees' horror is that of humiliation, try to administer aid in an appropriately sympathetic way. They mobilise the recipients themselves into work groups which help to organise their people, and distribute the aid. It lends some dignity to the situation to be helped by your own people, rather than foreigners, though it does not solve the problem. The dependency and futility continue.

Aid to Mozambican refugees in Malawi is still largely concerned with trying to ensure that the basics are available to the refugees, and has little time or money for self-improvement and educational projects, although they do exist. The ones that exist have proved massively popular, demonstrating the cramped energy of many of the refugees. Between 1988 and 1989, 165 classrooms were constructed to be used as schools for the refugees. A total of 53 000 refugees now attend schools where they are taught the Mozambican curriculum in Portuguese. Even though it represents an improvement, however, it is not a very large percentage of the enormous number of child refugees.

The continued strength of UNHCR is not assured as the number of refugees continues to escalate in relation to the amount donors seem to be prepared to give. Yet even if it were, the relatively large quantity of aid coming into Malawi from overseas, the scale of its organisation, and the fact that the political obstacles have been overcome as they have not in South Africa, it only keeps the Mozambican refugees in Malawi from the brink of disaster. Being kept from the brink of disaster and death is appreciated by the refugees beyond belief, but the problem of their dependency on the continued flow of basic necessities, and their psychological discontent with their state of dependency will never be solved without sufficient land on which they can produce for themselves. As one aid worker said, 'We are in a permanent emergency situation'.[14]

Thus the only solution to Malawi's and the refugees' problem is mass voluntary and staggered repatriation, which can only come about as a result of the end of the war. The refugees cannot live an ordinary life in Malawi, and the Malawian economy cannot cope with the vast numbers of Mozambicans. Neither of them can live with a war that sends hundreds of thousands fleeing across the borders. Already so much damage has been done to Mozambicans by Renamo's war. Years of severe poverty and dependency will leave them scarred, and who knows what may have happened to the land they used to farm and the huts they used to live in when they go back. They will have to rebuild their lives and their country, and yet are in no fit condition to do so. They, like the internally dislocated Mozambicans, have reluctantly lost a generation of education into how to make a country grow, and gained a generation of education into how to run from life-threatening danger and survive like animals, to sit still in the sun all days shelter their eyes, to brush the flies from their face, and to depend on others for life.

In a hospital that I visited, the children who were sitting outside summed up the plight of their generation. They all had bloated bellies, and solemn faces. Not one was smiling. One boy of about three had deep gashes neatly arranged on every inch of his stomach. One of the many witch doctors had cut the stomach in an attempt to relieve the pressure that was causing the blotation. Other children were lying on their small beds, with no sheet because of the heat, but only holding onto the old toy animals sent over by their Western counterparts.

From outside the ward, as we walked towards the door, deep harmonies and the high and heart-piercing ululations of African women could be heard. The mothers, who were sitting around the kitchen area waiting for their fires to settle, and some in vain for their emaciated children to recover, were singing to us, with the spontaneity and rhythm that perhaps only Africans can muster, about how happy and thankful they were.

A Mozambican boy whom I caught sight of on my way out, while their tunes were still ringing in my ears, was preoccupied with deciding which hole in his T-shirt was the one for his arm, and then with carefully buttoning the cuff which was attached to the shoulder of the garment by a single thread. Like the women, he demonstrated the ability of his people to make do, and to preserve their dignity in the most adverse circumstances. Yet he must have wondered, like many others, why it had to be this way.

8 The Limits of Aid

The vice most fatal to the statesman is virtue.

Frank Johnson, 1981

The chasm between the solitary contemplations of this little boy and the vast world of aid, is a huge and unhappy one. For in Mozambique there are serious limits, some imposed by the war, and some by aid itself, to what aid can do to help.

Aid workers sit in their offices in Maputo, Blantyre, Harare and Lusaka punching computer buttons. In matters of seconds vast quantities of foreign money go shooting down the seemingly bottomless pit of relief. The administrators feel helpless; theirs is a comfortless job. They are the instruments of the massive machine that doles out the wages of Western workers to third world sufferers in an endless cycle of despair.

Many aid workers live with a deep guilt and disillusionment. They feel guilty because they are not feeding the mouths, but touching the computer buttons. The huge quantities of aid now being donated to the third world mean that large administrative staffs are required. They sit in the cities and live comfortable lives while people starve on their door steps. They are disillusioned because they are not giving out aid the old fashioned way, where the concept of charity has more meaning on an individual level. Instead they are operating an impersonal industry. Many feel that something is wrong.

The whole concept of international aid has changed dramatically in the past years. Giving enormous quantities of aid has become a normal part of Western governments' duties. Aid is expected: it is no longer charity, but duty. On the surface this would appear to be a positive change, a sign that the world's heart has taken a moral turn. Yet the disconcerted feeling that aid workers have about their new role is telling. Their discomfort, perhaps, stems from the aura of complacency and detachment surrounding the world's new attitude to aid.

Huge donations of hard-earned money to unending attempts at relieving suffering are such a norm now that relative to the greater amounts now donated, few ask where the money is going, if it really is making a difference, or if the need for it will ever end. Often people do not even know that they are giving the money, as it comes straight out of their taxes.

It is as if the systemisation of aid-giving represents an appeasing of Western consciences more than a true concern for the recipients. Some would say that the motives behind giving are incidental. So long as the money is given, who cares why? But aid has a major effect on the recipients, their countries and the donors alike. Questions about the role and inherent value of aid desperately need to be asked. More than anything it needs to be asked whether aid to Mozambicans is thwarting a never-ending disaster or solving a problem. Is the pit into which aid is poured bottomless?

There are two types of aid given by international donors directly to Mozambicans (I am not including bilateral aid given to macro-economic projects). One type is relief aid and the other development aid. The first, as the name implies, is purely for relief purposes: it is the disaster-thwarting aid given only in the cases of emergency, and exists primarily to thwart the emergency. Development aid on the other hand, is aid given for longer-term reasons. It is given primarily to foster the long term development of a country, and is not concerned with basics like survival food and medicine, water, shelter, clothes and blankets. Development aid is concerned with such things as educational projects, seed growing, preventative medicine, infrastructural improvement and macro-economic growth.

Simply put, in the sense that it never cures the problem, relief aid always goes down a bottomless pit. On the way down it saves millions of lives and does uncountable good. Yet, it does nothing to reduce the need for itself in the long term. One meal which keeps you alive until the next, does not reduce your need for the next meal; nor does it cure your poverty. The help that relief aid offers is comparable to that which the Malawian witch doctor, mentioned in the previous chapter, offered to his patient's Kwashiorkor. He cut gashes in the little boy's bloated stomach to relieve the pressure. Like relief aid, he may have saved the boy some considerable pain, for his method does in fact release some of the pressure on the stomach. He did not, though, reach the root of the problem, which was the protein deficiency causing the illness. Relief aid is very similar to primitive medicine in this respect: it does not attack the political or economic cause of the problem, but just seeks to relieve it.

Certainly relief aid can be given in various different ways, some of which exacerbate the problem that it is trying to cure less than others. Relief food aid, for example, can be administered by the needy themselves, so that the degree of their dependency is reduced. But the witch doctor too can make his cure less painful and more effective by sharpening and cleaning his knife. The result is not that the treatment gets any closer to curing the disease: it still only relieves it.

Unfortunately, a great number of Mozambicans are still reliant on aid, not for their development, but for their very survival and most basic needs. Their need to rely on relief aid renders the vast quantities of development aid in Mozambique both less relevant to them, and less effective in its task of bringing about development. Yet without effective development they are doomed to remain reliant on relief for an indefinite period.

This state of affairs has been brought about partly by the the scale and nature of the war in Mozambique. The scale of the war and other disasters in Mozambique has meant that the need for relief aid is so huge that donors often become demoralised with throwing money down the seemingly bottomless pit, and shortages of relief aid are usually suffered. The special nature of the war, meanwhile, dissuades development aid from operating with full effectiveness. The scale and nature of the war combine to make Mozambicans dependent on inadequate relief aid.

The scale of Mozambique's problem is massive. Everyone knows how bad Ethiopia's problem is, but few know that Mozambique's is almost as severe, and in some respects worse. Mozambique's infant mortality rates are 12 per cent higher than those in Ethiopia, only 1 per cent more people in Mozambique have access to clean water than they do in Ethiopia, and life expectancy rates in the two countries are fairly close. One third of Mozambique's population is threatened with starvation, and at least one half of the population is reliant to some extent on aid for its food requirements. Over one in fifteen have fled Mozambique as war refugees and are also reliant on or in need of aid.

Mozambique produces under 10 per cent of its own maize requirements, and its total self sufficiency in food is only 16 per cent of its total needs. Not even the huge quantities of aid that Mozambique is receiving can fulfill its food requirements. In 1988/89 out of the 916 000 tonnes of food deemed necessary and requested from the donors, only 295 000 were received. UNICEF in 1990/91 requested $13.5 million from donors in order to be able to continue carrying out its life saving projects, but only received $1 million of it. The 1990/91 UN Appeal resulted in 1.2 million Mozambicans being accepted as beneficiaries. Relief agencies, however, believe that there could be a million people in need of relief in Zambezia province alone.

Zambezia needs 3000 tonnes of supplies a month delivered by convoy. In 1988 when ten districts were inaccessible by road, the province had seventy trucks and appealed for twenty-two more. Since then all roads in all districts except one have been opened. Meanwhile Zambezia has only received eight trucks and lost 35 in sabotage attacks. At the same time donors are trying to cut the amount of airlifting of food because it is expensive [1] and inadequate. Thus provision for road transport is well below even the levels required before the army started opening up the roads.

Zambezia suffered terrible droughts in 1990/91. Even before Frelimo troops started opening up the province's districts making the residents accessible to aid, there was not enough aid to properly cope with Zambezia's hunger. Now, with cuts in aid coinciding with an increased need, provisions are even less adequate. Famine hit the Zambezian district of Ile in April 1990. Twenty-five people a day were dying in one small feeding centre. It was believed that as many as 96 000 people in the district were in need of food aid.

In Manica province in early 1991, signs of the worst drought in forty years appeared; a drought even worse than that of the mid 1980s. Of the 622 000 residents of the province, 560 000 lived in the areas where most of the maize and millet harvest was lost. A shortfall of 70 322 tonnes of food was suffered and the next season too looks bleak as seed stocks are now practically non-existent.[2]

The urgency of Mozambicans' need for aid is most aptly demonstrated when it is not forthcoming. This is demonstrated adequately by the state of the Mozambican refugees in South Africa compared to those in Malawi, but more dramatically by the case of a Mozambican district Memba. In early 1989 a famine hit the Nampula district of Memba before aid could respond properly to the food needs. Five thousand people died because aid was not forthcoming. In the mid 1980s thousands died because aid did not respond properly to the crisis.[3] This could happen again in 1991. Mozambicans' need for outside help, just in order to survive, is immense. There is not enough relief aid to spread around in Mozambique, nor is there an understanding on the part of the donors of the scale and ongoing nature of Mozambique's needs. Aid shortage in itself, by reducing the condition of Mozambicans, makes them even more reliant on relief aid.

While the scale of the problems in Mozambique keeps affected Mozambicans concerned with survival and not development, the nature of the problems in Mozambique, limits the possibility of effective development work, thus adding to the forces which confine Mozambicans to dependence on relief aid. It is partly because much of the disruption is ongoing and unpredictable that there is little potential for development.

The temporary and insecure nature of the affected areas, as well as limiting the amount of funds forthcoming because of unpredictability, directly limits the successful operation of development projects on the ground, such as education and the improvement of huts and styles of living. When such projects are embarked on in these areas, the fact that the camp is only a temporary and insecure shelter, frequently renders them ineffective or pointless. Hopes for development must often be suspended until the people are living in their own villages.

The insecurity of some camps, like Pembane in Zambezia for example, make the business of trying to develop education, through the building of schools, precarious. Pembane at times has been prone to frequent attacks from Renamo. Teaching the dislocated people how to grow crops more effectively is inappropriate if they are being taught how to grow alien crops in foreign soil. It might not even be possible if there was not enough land in the camps for people to grow any of their own food. Likewise it would be inappropriate to try to try to set up a healthy and developing village atmosphere in a camp of thousands who were ready at the slightest word to go back to their real homes. One widower who had been separated from his children by Renamo, had seen Renamo cutting people's throats for punishment, and who ended up in a deslocado camp, expressed the feelings of many: 'When you get taken away you never forget your homeland and you think of it until it makes you cry'.

In Pembane camp in Zambezia all the problems associated with the worst elements of the constancy of Renamo's destruction, which make development impossible, are on view. The poor soil and concentration of humanity in the coastal area make it impossible for people to produce for themselves. The constant fear of attack, aid workers say, undermines any sense of purpose or community. This is hardly surprising if you consider an account, given by residents, of a morning that is not unusual for dwellers of the camp. Hundreds were waiting around for food distribution when a mortar shot suddenly provoked screams and mass panic. A frenzy of half dressed people burst into movement, scrambling over each other to head for the jetty. Possessions were grabbed, and precariously thrown on heads. From the rescue ferry, the early morning light showed smudges of figures stampeding through the trees. Renamo was not visible, but the terror it inspired was. The ferry, only made for about 250 passengers, was weighed down with at least double that number, and others crashed through the water trying to jump on as the ferry left. Residents at Pembane talk of how, to them, anything but survival has become irrelevant.

Some might think that Pembane, as one of the largest deslocado camps in Mozambique, is an extreme example, yet conditions are hardly better in many other camps. In a settlement of deslocados in Maganja, the most secure town in its district, also in Zambezia province, similar problems limit the possibility of development work. Half of the town's 45 000 population is made up of deslocados. The pressure on land is intense. At least here, though, the residents are able to participate in the improvement of their own living conditions. Aid agencies have started pot making schemes, sewing ventures and so on. In addition, the teaching of efficient agricultural practices has made it possible for the deslocados to produce enough of their own food to halve the quantity of donations needed. Yet they are still dependent for their survival on aid, and though they are improving their conditions slightly, this is not development. At any moment all their improvements could be wrecked, because Maganja too is prone to Renamo attack.

The nature of a war which terrorises people also makes development difficult for the large section of the population who are refugees. Because they are refugees they are unable to settle permanently in the areas that they are living. Only the few who have become integrated with the local populations can develop; for the majority a better life is a hope suspended somewhere in the future.

Refugees are prevented from developing by the host of barriers which have been mentioned. In the case of Malawi, the severe land shortage caused by the influx of almost a million refugees serves as a barrier to development possibilities. In Zimbabwe the fact that the refugees are kept in the unnatural environment of a fenced camp, and in South Africa that they are not given legal status, keeps the possibility for the development of a normal life at bay. By dislocating people and making them move to places of temporary refuge, the destruction of the war has been very penetrating. There is not much that aid can do in these circumstances except keep people alive, and try to do it in as sensitive a way as possible.

The war also works against aid helping the Mozambicans to develop by severely curtailing the efficiency of the administration of aid to rural Mozambique. Many areas are not accessible at all, and some are only accessible at great expense, such as by airlifting the supplies in. Care, the aid agency which deals with the logistics of aid distribution in Mozambique, had seven drivers who drove over landmines, eleven ambushed and seven killed, in 1989 alone. Donors may give food, but not the money for airlifting it to the people.

It is not, however, just the scale and nature of the devastation being wrought on Mozambique that makes it nearly impossible for aid to concentrate on development rather than relief. There are also more general problems, problems with aid itself, which bring about this outcome.

In theory, and perhaps in the minds of those who are truly concerned with the welfare of the recipients, aid in its advanced stages is 'development aid'. Yet in reality, there are many obstacles to aid, which is donated in the belief that it is developmental, achieving this goal. Aid today, because of donors' motives, is self-limiting; it prevents itself from getting its recipients back onto the track of self development and into a situation in which aid is no longer required. This is because, in spite of the theory, donors generally do not give aid in a way which takes development to be its long term goal.

Globally there are some striking examples of this. East/West allegiances and other political issues, for example, distract aid from being efficient in terms of its theoretical goal. A country may receive food aid from an East bloc country, yet it of a kind that it does not really need, just because that is what the East bloc country happens to have to spare. A West bloc country may at the same time have a surplus of exactly the kind of food that it does need, and yet let political concerns stop it from donating it to the right country.

The American Food for Peace programme demonstrates admirably how political goals get in the way of the best allocation of world aid. The American Public Law 480 actually disallows the programme to give aid to countries of a communist persuasion. PL480 bans food aid to 'any country or area controlled by a world communist movement'. Many of its administrators have sought ways of circumventing this law, and have at times succeeded, yet the law still proves to be a major obstruction to aid reaching those who need it most. In 1988, for example, $39 million worth of food aid was being sent to El Salvador, a country which does not suffer major food shortages. Meanwhile Marxist Ethiopia in the same year, with its millions of starving people, received only $36 million. During the 1990/91 Gulf Crisis, relatively wealthy Egypt received $15 billion worth of debt write-offs because of the role it played in the war, while Mozambique languished in poverty.

Another factor interfering with the distribution of funds to places where they are most needed is that fashions, which have little to do with need, strike donors. The fact that donors are modish in their moods also has political roots. Whether donors are governments, companies or non-governmental charities they must keep their sponsors happy, and their sponsors (voters and shareholders) fall for fads.

Take Ethiopia in 1985 as an example. One journalist made a very compelling series of news stories on the famine there, and the world went berserk, determined as suddenly as a madman might become, to help Ethiopia. Ethiopia became the fashion, just as Cambodia had been a few years earlier. Suddenly tasteless jokes and wildly charitable attitudes were focussed on Ethiopia. Pop singers and celebrities started rallying the masses to their cause; red noses appeared on cars. If Ethiopia was indeed the most needy place in the world at the time, it was no reflection of the world's rationality where need is concerned. Ethiopia was dropped as quickly as it was picked up, yet the famines there continued. Uganda in the late 1980s was also picked from the lucky dip. Aid staff working in Uganda at the time, tell a story about a journalist who was at a dinner party in Kampala one night. The company at the party was fairly uninteresting and the journalist was not having a very good time until he struck up a conversation with a particular aid worker. The aid worker began to describe to him the atrocities going on in the country at that very moment. People were dying in their thousands only a few hours away, the journalist was told. The aid worker convinced the journalist that he should witness the horrors first hand, and they got in the car at that very moment, and drove. Thanks to nothing more than the dinner party's boring company, bad food or both, a massive human disaster was reported, and the world once again had the opportunity to demonstrate its over-excitable generosity. Now there is a new fad: Eastern Europe. People are considered 'with the times' if they talk about Eastern Europe and its aid needs. The third world has been discovered and forgotten: its needs are stale news.

Mozambique, like so many, is suffering from the world's irrational moods. The returning refugees and the opening up of Renamo controlled zones is increasing the demand for aid dramatically. Talk of peace, and peace itself in the short run, is only increasing the demand for aid, yet the world does not appear to understand this. With the increasing popularity of the Horn of Africa as a target for funds, and competition for funds from the newly liberated Eastern European countries, the future bodes ill for Mozambique.

The world's generosity does not go where it is most needed at the right times. This is the nature of generosity: the donor has the prerogative of choice. Mozambique is getting less aid instead of more, just as its needs are increasing dramatically. Ironically, the very same thing happened in 1983 during the famines. As now, plenty of warning was given to donors in advance of the impending famines of the 1983, and yet, for bureaucratic and political reasons, less aid was forthcoming than the previous year. This time with the prediction of needs so high, and the likelihood of getting enough aid limited, the government and sympathetic aid workers decided to employ the worn bag of 'Appeal' tricks.

The song and dance of the annual Appeal is an integral part of the world of aid. Every year UN-organised donors hold a conference, and the Appeal, a document detailing the emergency requirements for the relevant country, is presented. How much the donors pledge for that year depends largely on their mood. Even how much they pledge is not, in practice, the same as the quantities that ultimately appear on Mozambique's doorstep. This tempts the asking country to ask for more than its requirements in order to ensure that the actual deliveries satisfy their needs. This is one way of winning the game. The other trick to winning, employed by Mozambique in the 1990/91 Appeal, is to 'under-appeal', and ask for the absolute bare minimum in the hope that in advertising such an appeal, the shortfall between the amount requested and that pledged will be much smaller than it would otherwise have been. Mozambique was hoping that the amount pledged would actually be higher if it asked for less, because donors would respond to an honest request for the bare minimum. Unfortunately the trick did not work. $136 million was requested, and truly represented Mozambique's barest emergency needs, yet only $106m was pledged at the conference.

The requested $106 million was to cover the most essential needs of 429 000 people, about half the number who needed aid of some sort. It included requests for funds for limited stockpiling in strategic points to cope with the potential influx of huge numbers of returning refugees, or of people returning to zones previously held by Renamo. Even after extra bilateral donations were given to cover the shortfall, $11.6 million was still necessary to cover the basic needs of 1.5 million displaced people.[4] The funds raised during the donor conferences of 1987, 1988 and 1989, when there was only the usual war emergency to deal with, were $280 million, $270 million and $252 million respectively: each over double the amount donated for 1990/91.

Belying the supposition that the needs of the people are the central concern of aid, the 1990/91 shortfall was to do with all sorts of entirely unrelated factors. The shortfall was due to other events in the world leading to competition for funds mentioned, scandals of pilferage, and 'donor fatigue'. Mozambique's plight in 1990/91 is not an anomaly which is creeping into the otherwise quite rational world of aid. Rather, it is a prime example of how aid works. Donor fatigue, distracting world events and scandals, all move aid further away from its ability to respond efficiently to need. Yet such factors are the norm.

Some aid workers[5] have noted that donor fatigue is a cyclical phenomena, occurring randomly every few years because the endless flow of money into a particular cause suddenly becomes depressing to the donor. Donors start rationalising their generosity. The donor fatigue that has hit Mozambique's donors recently has harped on pilferage of aid supplies at docks and at distribution points by officials. Naturally it is unappealing for donors to give funds to countries whose administrators cannot even hand it out to the truly needy without siphoning off some for themselves. However, pilferage in Africa is rather like secretaries making personal calls on their firm's bill in the West: it is not a matter of stopping it altogether, but of keeping it in check. In Nigeria, aid staff estimate, pilferage at about 30 per cent is normal. Mozambique is relatively innocent. The 6 per cent pilferage which was noticed in early 1990 before the donor conference was small by world standards.[6] Yet the donors were suffering their usual lapse into fatigue, and let this add to justification of their reluctance to give.

Funding problems are manifold, and are an integral part of aid as it operates today. Aid raises money by pleading emergency. The bulk of regular annual funding to Mozambique comes because those in charge of the appeal have managed to convince the rest of the world that there is still a major emergency in the country. Aid agencies worldwide are faced with the problematic necessity of constantly having to brew up a sense of emergency. Yet Mozambique, and Malawi because of the Mozambican refugees, are in a state of permanent emergency. This does not have the same appeal to donors. An emergency, they apparently believe, must be an immediate thing. In spite of the fact that countries which are in a permanent emergency situation are frequently worse off than those suffering a one-off emergency, donors get bored of countries which year after year plead crisis.

Even with all the recent growth and modernisation of aid, the world of aid is not like the world of business. Aid organisations cannot get together to identify what they want to do and organise it exactly the way they want. Aid is not in charge of itself. It has to rely on the world's leftovers and moods and then make do. If the purpose of aid is to relieve or even cure world hunger, the world does not give aid rationally.

The paramount problem of aid shortages is compounded by the common feeling on the part of donors that it is enough that they give, and they should be able to give exactly how and what they like. It is their prerogative to feel this way, as they are not necessarily obliged to give anything at all, but it nevertheless makes aid horribly inflexible and seriously constrains efficiency, which in the end just means that more aid is needed for longer periods. The less efficiently funds are used the less chance there is of there being sufficient funds left over for development after relief supplies are bought and administered.

The tendency of donors to earmark funds or aid-in-kind for specific recipients and purposes is one manifestation of this tendency to donor-inspired inefficiency. One problem associated with this is that the aid given may be earmarked for a cause which is not particularly worthy or appropriate in the context. This may be because the information given to the donors is outdated, or just because they have a very limited idea of the extent and nature of the problems that they are hoping with their donations to solve.

For example, international donors at the annual conference may be told in April that it is projected that funds are needed in Mozambique for eight thousand blankets and half a million tonnes of grain for the year. Yet in December, when the funds have finally reached Mozambique and the administering agencies are about to order the grain and blankets, the situation may have changed. A famine may hit in an area of the country, refugees may start returning from neighbouring countries and the essential food requirements may escalate violently. But the agencies are tied to their original agreement of spending a specified part of the money on blankets. The donors would surely agree to a diversion of the funds to cope with the emergency if they were given the chance, but there is no time to go through the necessary bureaucratic procedures. Nor can the agencies go ahead and spend all the money on the blankets or they will have broken the trust of the donors, which may have severe consequences for donor enthusiasm in the next donor conference.

Emergency situations are constantly changing; it is part of their nature. Yet aid must go through long and tedious processes before it can be allocated: aid is as inflexible as emergency situations are flexible. One aid worker in the town of Chimoio told of how quickly changes in the scale and type of help needed happened. He worked at the district level, and was therefore the one who relayed messages down to Maputo detailing the most recent figures of the numbers of dislocated people in the area, and of the accompanying aid needs. Invariably, by the time his message got down to Maputo and the team in the capital had arranged for the aid which he had requested to be sent up to him in Chimoio, his figures had altered.

However, at least in the case of governmental donations it is theoretically possible to go back to the donors to ask them if the funds can be used for something else should the circumstances change. This is not so in the case of funds coming from non governmental organisations which raise their funds from the public to whom they are not accountable in retrospect. Often appeals are specific, and based on the need for a certain item. Oxfam or the Save the Children Fund, for example, may launch an appeal for funds for a million blankets, or three million pots, or for one hundred thousand tents. At the time of the appeal the item requested seemed to be the most needed. By the time the funds arrived, however, an emergency may have developed, and the funds would save thousands of lives if they were used on food. The administrators, in this case, are not faced with a practical dilemma, as it would be physically impossible to go back to every donor and it would probably not effect the level of future donations since the thousands of donors would probably never know, but with a moral one. Do they have the right to use other people's money for what they consider to be the best cause even if it was given for something very specific? This dilemma is not an easy one to resolve as it cannot be assumed that the donors gave with no more than general good intentions in mind, and that they would be more than happy for their money to be used for what others considered the most worthy cause. Too often this is not the case. A donor may have had a relation who died of meningitis, and may have donated ten dollars towards preventative meningitis injections in Mozambique due to a particular sympathy with meningitis sufferers, and not necessarily with Mozambicans in general. If they knew that someone else had taken a liberty with their donation and used it for some other cause, they would be displeased.

The tendency to earmark funds is increasing with the modernisation and growth of aid. In this new impersonal world of aid, where donating large quantities to Third World countries has become part of government and business, aid, like the system it has become part of, is now competitive. NGOs' fundraising staff are increasingly recruited from professional businesses. Fundraising departments have several divisions, including a special one for corporate fund raising. The days of charity coming largely from blanket squares knitted by grannies, and tiny donations from a world of sympathetic hearts, are fast fading. Instead, fund raising has become part of trade. Rather like it is modish to buy slimmers' bread, caffeine-free Coca Cola, free range eggs and not to buy veal in the supermarkets, it has become fashionable to buy the cereal packets, jam or baked beans which give five per cent of their cost to a named charity.

The amount of funds flowing from businesses to charities is now huge. Charity in a tin is the best sales gimmick since plastic toys in cereal packets. But everyone has caught on. Now it is not a question of whether a company is in vogue enough to have employed this gimmick, but of how worthy the charitable cause that they are selling is. The next link in the chain is that when the budget director of a firm decides which charitable cause is to be advertised on the back of his product, he has four or five corporate fund raisers sitting outside his office waiting for their hearing. They file in individually, each pleading that their cause is the most worthy and the most cost efficient, with the lowest administrative costs and so on. The budget managers give to the one they consider the most efficient and worthy. This represents earmarking at its most decisive.

On the surface of it, this competition for funds would appear to be a healthy thing. Assuming that budget directors listen carefully to each case presented to them, this new competitive aspect of aid means that the most worthy and cost efficient causes are the ones to receive the funds. However, in reality, the increase in the earmarking of funds just imposes more inflexibility on aid. Aid is something that needs to be as flexible as possible, and yet its administrators, who are most sensitive to changes in need, are the last one to have a say in the matter.

The problems associated with earmarking funds go even deeper: they limit how many funds can be raised. Sometimes aid agencies are forced into the dilemma of knowing that they can raise funds which otherwise would not be given at all, by launching an appeal for a relatively less worthy cause. If they can tap latent generosity which would otherwise lay dormant, the agencies wonder, should they do so even if the cause that they are raising it for is problematic?

This question arises with appeals for child sponsorship programmes, for example. Many people who would otherwise not give money are struck with the idea of sponsoring the development of one child. For many, it is a very meaningful way of giving charity. When the appeal for child sponsorship falls out of a Sunday magazine, the mournful picture pleads with great skill. The photos come of the child growing healthier and stronger because of the donor's tiny donation. When the child learns to read and write, he will perhaps start writing letters of thanks to his patron. One main attraction, apart from the personal touch of child sponsorship programmes, is the fact that the donors see exactly where their money is going.

Yet, there are such serious problems with child sponsorship programmes that many agencies do not run them even though they know that they could tap extra funds if they did. The core of the problem with such programmes is that the recipient children live in families with parents and brothers and sisters, and their families live in villages with neighbours. The aid agency can no more give to one child in a family and not the others, than it can to one family in the village and not the others. If one child had a particularly appealing face and was immediately picked by a sponsor for special treatment, how would the agency administer the extra food and attention to this child? Obviously it would have to be through its mother, but this is highly impractical, unfair and ridiculous. If the mother did give all the extra food to the favoured child, which is of course highly unlikely, the jealousy that it would stir up would be more destructive than constructive.

A similar problem sometimes applies to fund raising for refugees. If the refugees are all living in a camp together there is no problem with earmarking funds for them. If, however, the refugees have settled in villages and become integrated with the locals, as many have in Malawi and in South Africa, problems arise. The generosity of the locals which made them welcome the refugees in the first place might well turn sour if their guests, who were living at the same standard as them, began to get special treatment. The friendliness of locals to refugees is an asset whose value cannot be quantified in monetary forms. It is not worth upsetting their goodwill, even if it means that at least some people may have fuller stomachs than they would otherwise.

The same attitude of donors which causes them to earmark funds, the attitude that 'beggars can't be choosers', and that recipients should be happy to get what they are given, creates other problems which prevent the aid that is given from being used efficiently, or at all. A prime example of this is a container full of 10 000 pairs of shoes which after arriving in Maputo in June 1990, was being carted around from door to door unable to find anyone who would either store it or distribute the shoes. The donor had not specified whether they were all one size, or how many were of which size which caused complications about where to ship them to and who to distribute them amongst. In addition, no aid agency had sufficient storage space for ten thousand shoes. The cost of transporting them around the city, and eventually to an inappropriate distribution point in the country, and the time wasted on worrying about ill-packed shoes and what to do with them was probably more than the shoes themselves were worth.

The same sort of ignorance on the part of donors causes problems with food aid. Well-meaning Westerners may ship out food which either the recipients refuse to eat for religious or other reasons, and it goes to waste. Likewise it not unusual to hear of donors spending huge sums on buying and transporting aid-in-kind to opposite ends of the world when the goods were available much more cheaply locally, and the funds that the donors spent could have bought ten times more than they did and at the same time promoted the local economy. Often more thought on the part of donors would go a long way.

Aid, which is largely a reflection of donors motives, has lost touch with what used to be its central concern: the welfare of the recipients. Donors are concerned more with themselves and what satisfies them politically or personally than with what actually helps the situation in the country in question. There is a lack of coherence of purpose in the organisation of aid giving which prevents aid from achieving its ostensible goal: curing the problem of poverty. It might seem like madness that money is being donated to the other countries where it is not needed which, if it were diverted to Mozambique, could to begin to solve the country's problems. Yet an assessment of donors' motives reveals that it is not madness, but simply what aid is today.

What uncaring aid like this can achieve is limited. The problem is not just or always that the way aid is given leads to a lack of funds, but that it is given to places that are not necessarily the most needy, and that it is given in an inconsistent, counterproductive and unpredictable way. The recipients' psychological uncertainty of whether or not aid is going to come at all or be consistent, as well as the physical fact that it often is not consistent or in tune with the problems that it is ostensibly trying to cure, limits how far aid can bring about development. It is quite simply because donors give money without the long term view of abating Mozambique's crisis and enabling Mozambicans to take part in their own development, together with the frustrating effects of the war, that their development does not take place.

On a larger scale, because so many Mozambicans are starving and unable to develop on even a basic level, they are unable to participate in the economic restructuring of their country which is being undertaken as part of the IMF loans package. A huge number of Mozambicans remain affected by the war, confined to their camps in foreign countries or alien parts of Mozambique, underfed, uneducated, dependent and unhealthy. Imposed 'development', development achieved by others and not participated in by Mozambicans, is not truly development, but just, if it works, economic growth.

It is not just lamentable that Mozambicans must rely on others to jump start their economy, but potentially threatens the possibility that they may even one day play an active part in their country's continued development. Critics of dependency on aid have pointed to the danger of the recipient country's economy turning into an 'aid economy'. One symptom of an aid economy is large scale pilferage by officials and locals alike, and organised corruption. Mozambique thus far only shows the initial signs of falling into this trap of dependency, despite its great reliance on aid. Nevertheless the recent jailing of nine DPCCN[7] officials in the north of the country, and the pilferage scandals rife during the last Appeal, are ominous signs.

This together with the waste of aid that so obviously occurs as a direct result of the war, makes it very obvious that the root of the problem in Mozambique is not being attacked. Various bilateral donations which were made after the Appeal only raised the nomimal $106 million in 1990. Sweden, in August 1990, donated $4.5 million for relief projects in the northern provinces. Kuwait gave $3.6 million for the computerisation of the southern railway network. Spain gave a $10 million all-terrain vehicle assembly plant. The Paris Club in June approved lighter terms of servicing on $700 million of Mozambique's debt. The United States donated a further $10 million for railway repairs, and $12.5 million for development of the agricultural sector.

Yet the railways are still being sabotaged at the rate of almost one major attack per week. Cows are stolen and burnt in their thousands by the rebels. Crops are burnt, landmines prevent their planting in the first place, people who produce are terrorised, and foreign investors have to employ private armies to protect their projects. People continue to starve and die by their thousands, and more foreign funds are constantly needed to avert the climax of a disaster that will not go away.

The IMF sponsored Economic Rehabilitation Programme may succeed in partially lifting Mozambique out of the quagmire by encouraging foreign investment; if this happens it will be a happy event. But the people of Mozambique are not being allowed to play a part in the development of their country any more than they have been allowed to by years of Frelimo's imposition of its policies, or any more than they have been allowed to by the war that cripples them. Not just because the foreigners are the actors, nor because Mozambicans will have had yet another political solution imposed on them without their permission, but because they will continue to be vulnerable and dependent victims of the whims of the world of aid as well as of their own war.

The way aid operates now dictates that it cannot attack the roots of Mozambique's problem. At any moment the aid may stop, or decrease; it is given as a stop-gap measure because it depends on the donors' moods, and thus will remain a stop-gap measure. A more rational system under which donors give 'for' a country not 'at' one, accompanied by a systematic infrastructure for the filtration of the world's concern could be developed.

For the time being however, as Western companies continue to compete for charity credibility in the fashionable world of marketing, and labels on the back of baked bean tins advertise the world's complacency, the problems of the third world rage on. Today's system of aid-giving is not charity but a way of incorporating the third world's problems into the Western world's system, as if the third world was there to stay. If aid continues to operate in this complacent way, the third world *will* be here to stay.

A crucial aspect of the accidental, half-hearted and wasteful help being given to Mozambique is that while governmental and corporate bodies continue to provide aid, Renamo continues to be funded by independent foreign interests from the same countries, and Western arms companies continue to supply weapons which are now cheaply available all over Mozambique. Taxpayers in the West might well wonder why their money should be thrown at a problem which is partially perpetuated by their own countries which cannot muster enough energy to help stop the war in Mozambique by outlawing funding for the rebels. Certainly if the war in Mozambique cannot be seen for what it is, one initiated by foreigners, and one that has so obviously been waged by thugs, then there is little hope for other war racked countries where the questions are more complex. For this is a war of a type that aid in its present form cannot cure.

9 Mozambique's Future – the Dressing of a Skeleton?

From the people and for the people, all springs, and all, must exist.

Benjamin Disraeli, *Vivien Grey*, Bk VI

Samora Machel's optimism in calling the children of Mozambique 'the flowers that never wither' was tragically misplaced. Rhodesia's rebel group was supposed to have faded with with the slam of Lancaster House's front door, the wonders and good intentions of socialism were to have crashed the fences of dependency, and the glow of the nation's life force was to have shone forth in productivity. But it did not.

Instead the rebel group grew into a dangerous piece of machinery, and shredded the nation's inexperienced heart. The hopes for socialism were overrated and clumsily imposed. It was a like tea party doomed from the start; even the weather did not hold out, as drought raged after drought. Not just the children, but the entire country has suffered extreme poverty and misfortune.

A far cry from the high hopes of the early days, a vision of a Mozambican now is of a shrunken person, malnourished, dependent, unproductive and unhappy. Under the ground the rich minerals lie wasted and useless, while the fragments of the infrastructure which could have helped exploit them are blasted sky high with regularity; 3.3 million people of the country's small population, are in hiding from the war. Will the day ever come when millions of Mozambicans are productive and able, fulfilled, educated and healthy? What does Mozambique's future hold in the wake of all this devastation? In short, can anything be learned from the disasters that plague Mozambicans, or must they continue in Mozambique and perhaps be repeated again somewhere else at some other date?

The explanations of what has happened in Mozambique are not as simple as some would have them. Some analysts have simply said that Mozambique's entire ruin is due to the aggressive actions of the 'evil neighbour': South Africa. By funding the rebels, this critique goes, South Africa has prevented socialism from following its naturally successful course. Others have said, equally simply, that the opposite is the simple truth. They say that, like in the rest of Africa and Eastern Europe, socialism has failed; they imply that the rebels are an inevitable consequence of Africans trying to rule themselves, and believe perhaps that the dramatic improvements which have come about recently since the capitalistic IMF-backed economic reform package has come into effect, prove that a good dose of capitalism and foreign management was all the country ever needed.

But neither of these simple explanations encompass the whole story. These accounts do not count Frelimo's poor enactment of its policies of promoting health, education and agriculture as a fundamental element of the failure of its policies. Nor do they mention the power-lusting of Renamo fighters on the ground, as it exists on its own, independent from foreign enticements. Amongst other factors, such as the important role of Western, rather than just South African, support for the rebels, these stories ignore the element of Mozambican responsibility for the tragedies that the country has suffered; they treat the country as only a victim of greater forces.

That Renamo's roots, funding and methods are geographically foreign in origin and impetus, is of paramount importance, as it explains how the Mozambican rebel movement has come to hold values so alien to the good of the country, and to an extent how it has been able, physically, to pursue such unpopular goals. But, the significance of this element of Renamo does not lessen the responsibility of the Mozambicans who have ordered and taken part in the atrocities. Likewise the war does not lessen Frelimo's responsibility for mistakes that were its own.

The danger is that to ignore the Mozambican part played in the troubles of past years, is to ignore the potential ability of Mozambicans to propel their own futures. Ignoring the mistakes that Frelimo made in the enactment of its policies, for example, leads to the suggestion that policies which encourage primarily the development of health, education and agriculture as a means of development, are fundamentally mistaken, and that the mass of Mozambican people are incapable of playing a significant role in the development of their country. Ignoring the Mozambican element of Renamo entirely is simply unconvincing, as observers fail to see how a foreign force could impose its wishes on a country without some form of local logistical support. Without an adequate explanation of how Renamo works, skeptics might assume that in spite of reported atrocities it is indeed a political liberation movement, with significant local political support. This might lead to the belief that Mozambique, because of deeply held differences of political opinion held by large warring groups of the population, is a profoundly unstable country, and fundamentally difficult to govern.

Yet, it has not been shown that the bulk of Mozambicans are incapable of playing a significant part in the development of their own country, as it has not been shown that Frelimo's policies of concentrating on health, education and agriculture are incapable of working. Nor has it been shown that there are fundamental divisions within the country as to how it country should be run. Indeed the principles of democracy which Renamo claims is its political agenda, and must, if it is ever to have any credibility, eventually conform to, are little different than the principles that Frelimo has embodied in the reformed constitution.

Destruction caused by Renamo, has not shown that there are political divisions of this kind within the country, but only that there is a very forceful group who wants to run the country, and that they have manipulated the country into fighting for it, and in the process shattered much of the country's emotional and psychological stability. Only a full analysis of Renamo can understand how deeply its damage has penetrated. Nor have either Frelimo's policy failures or the continued need for vast quantities of aid, which, as has been seen has much to do with the way that aid itself operates and with the nature of the war, shown that the bulk of Mozambicans are incapable of producing for themselves and playing a part in their own futures. Indeed, to the contrary, there are many indications that the mass of Mozambicans are both crucial to the development of their country, and capable of playing a large part in it. So perhaps there can be great hope for Mozambique after all.

That 84 per cent of Mozambicans are rural farmers, is indication enough of the structural importance of agriculture to the Mozambican economy. That Mozambicans who are refugees want to go home, and want to provide for themselves, and their hatred of dependency is indication of their willingness to work and produce. That even children, who are threatened with horrendous punishment if they dare escape from Renamo, do so anyway for hatred of the destructive action which they are forced to partake in, shows commitment to their nation and the wish for a stable life. The positive response of children and adults alike to education programmes too promises much.

What is shown by the Mozambican example, far from the inability of Mozambicans to be productive and develop their country by producing, is merely the recurring ability of whims, ideals and intrigues of politics to work against rather than for the majority of the people, failing to give them a chance to produce for themselves and lead their own lives. The way that aid operates for Mozambique, the failure of UNHCR to establish a presence in South Africa, and the forceful way in which Frelimo enacted some of its policies, are examples of politics loosing sight of its goal of engaging people in their own future.

Frelimo became, for a time, more concerned with its belief in its cause than with the cause itself; UNHCR is more concerned with international diplomacy than with the Mozambican refugees in South Africa. Other respects of the politics that have effected Mozambique have simply never been concerned with the welfare of people. The South African government's treatment of the refugee problem, and the inability of the Western world, which spends so much trying to alleviate Mozambique's misery, to prevent the funding of Renamo, are witness to this.

More significantly for Mozambique, however, and the most poignant example of the unconcern of politics as it affects Mozambique, is the nature of the war waged against Mozambique by Renamo. Renamo's politics have little to do with trying to make Mozambique a better place now or in the future, but have to do simply with destruction and a quest for power. The war waged by Renamo against Mozambique has not lost sight of its original goal, which was to destabilise and destroy the country. Renamo, because of its origins and *raison d'être*, has always been an example of power-seeking politics acting deliberately to destroy Mozambique. The war has thrown people into a state of dependency and exile, out of which they cannot climb without an end to the war. It been shown very clearly that refugees in southern Africa are not able to develop until they have their own land from which to support themselves. It has also been seen how health, education and agriculture, the three corners of development in Mozambique, cannot develop properly until the rebels stop targeting them for destruction.

That the goal of the rebels remains now, as in the past, to destroy Mozambique until they gain power, and that they continue to lack an allegiance to democracy or any particular political system, has been demonstrated in the events surrounding the failure of the partial ceasefire agreement between Frelimo and Renamo signed in Rome on 1 December, 1990. In late December 1990, a month into the ceasefire and a month after Frelimo had passed its new democratic constitution, Dhlakama met secretly with the Zambian President, Kenneth Kaunda at State House, Lusaka. Kaunda telephoned Chissano to invite him to meet Dhlakama face to face. When Chissano declined, saying, in line with his new reforms, that he could not meet directly with Dhlakama without first consulting his central committee, Renamo denounced him as 'weak'. Kaunda gave the reaction characteristic of so many African dictators, and similar to Renamo's, saying, 'but you are President. You can do what you like.'

The formally written agreement between Renamo and Malawi signed in August 1989, was a potent demonstration of Renamo's ability to hold a ceasefire if it so wished. The agreement which specified that Renamo should stop direct attacks on the Nacala railway, although it did not mean that trains were able to run normally, held until January 1991. In the case of the Rome partial ceasefire agreement, it was apparent that Renamo was deliberately breaking the ceasefire. Attacks on the outskirts of the very towns in which the Joint Verification Committee (JVC) held its offices, Beira and Chimoio, had a particularly deliberate ring. Zimbabwean military intelligence said that it had intercepted Renamo radio messages in which specific instructions were given by Dhlakama to his men to break the ceasefire.[1] The decision to break the ceasefire characterised the uncertainty of the Renamo leadership of how to cope with Chissano's strategy of embarking on the very reforms that Renamo claims it has always demanded. Renamo is indeed in a difficult position. With the most meagre political past, limited support within Mozambique, the threat of democracy instead of guaranteed power as a reward for its fighting, and no independent political platform to stand on, Renamo sees its only immediate option as to keep fighting. What else is there for it to do but to continue fighting for power, either until the demand is satisfied in a ceasefire settlement, or until it has had time to win some support from the people, by whatever desperate methods necessary?

That confusion and the continued belief that gaining power is paramount dominates the feeling inside Renamo, is borne out by the report of an advisor to Dhlakama, who says that the leader is uncertain as to whether he should take the democratic route, or whether he should continue to fight.[2] Other reports confirm that the concern for guaranteed power is stronger than that for democracy. For example, the new level of brutality which followed in the months after the cease fire broke, marked by the re-emergence of castrations and the increased use of beheadings as a tactic.[3] Renamo's attitude to the other political groupings, amongst them UNAMO and PALMO[4] which have registered themselves as political parties in the wake of democratisations further evidences the feeling of discomfort within Renamo with the prospect of democratic elections. Raul Domingos, Renamo's Secretary for External Relations, has stressed that Renamo and Frelimo, and no one else, should be the ones to implement a new system, and said, 'we are the ones who fought for freedom for more than 14 years'.[5]

Certainly this was not the first time that attempts to achieve peace have failed. Contact between the rebels and the government has been going on since 1981. The attempts to achieve a settlement in 1984 at the Pretoria Declaration Talks failed, and were renewed by church leaders in 1989. It was in February 1991 with Renamo rejecting the partial ceasefire agreement, that they fell apart this time. Chissano announced in late March 1991 that elections would not be held until 1992, and Dhlakama responded with glee[6] suggesting that the fighting would not be likely to stop until then anyway. Nevertheless, hopes for peace are higher now than ever. The changing face of southern Africa, the growth of capitalism, democracy and peace in the region and, particularly the imminent decline of white South Africa, make the recent efforts to achieve a settlement more promising than ever before, in spite of the difficulties.

The paramount requirement for Mozambique's future development and success is that the war ends. However, although finding an immediate settlement which will stop the fighting that includes both Renamo and democracy at once is proving very difficult, it is not the only difficulty presented by the war. There are many longer term problems, other than the fighting itself, which the war has left with Mozambique. Like the fighting, they are problems which will have to be overcome if Mozambique is to grow and develop. The primary legacy of the war is the state that it has left the people of Mozambique in. They have been damaged in countless ways and very deeply, as has been catalogued, and are unable in their present state to play a part in the development of their country.

While Renamo fights for power, Frelimo turns to the West for IMF loans, and international aid dumps the consciences of the West onto Mozambique, half abating their misery in an endless cycle of relief, Mozambicans remain helpless. For most, the activities of politics go on dancing around their heads. So many are still unable to produce for themselves and lead settled lives, primarily, for millions, because they are not living in their homes on their own land. The economic recovery promised and begun by the ERP may take place, democracy too, promised by the new constitution passed in November 1990, may take place, but all without Mozambicans, and hence not as well.

Thus far the story of economic success, following the adoption of the ERP in 1987, has been a happy one. The economy has grown considerably, reversing the decline of the early eighties. In 1987 the economy grew at 3.7 per cent, and in 1988 it grew at 5.7 per cent. In 1986, before embarking on the ERP real growth in GDP was measured at 0.9 per cent, and in the years immediately prior growth was negative. Likewise, the story of political reform has been a happy one, with the legalisation of political parties, the constitutional promise of free elections, and the increase in press and personal freedoms, amongst many other things. But until the legacies of the war are overcome, there is a limit to both how much economic growth can take place in Mozambique, how meaningful the economic growth can be to the bulk of Mozambicans, and how deeply democracy can take root.

In terms of economic growth this is quite simply because the success of the agricultural sector is fundamental to Mozambique's economic success, and it cannot develop fully without the participation of Mozambique's biggest economic resource: its people. The ERP recognises the fundamental role of agriculture in Mozambique's future growth and has already focussed on it considerably. The results, reflective not of the return of the mass of Mozambicans to agricultural production, but of foreign investment, the introduction of incentives, and the stress on labour intensive techniques requiring low capital input and informal agriculture, have been significant. The agricultural production growth rate increased from 6.2 per cent in 1987 to 6.6 per cent in 1988.

Further results of the new policies were that cashew nut production reached over 45 000 tonnes in 1988, only a year after the new policy was implemented, and over 50 000 tonnes in 1989, which represented almost a tenfold increase in production since 1984. Maize production at the end of 1989 was heading for its best year since 1983.[7]

However, the normal production of the rural masses is crucial to Mozambican agriculture if it is to return to past levels of performance. The importance of the labour of Mozambique's 12.9 million rural people is very significant to agricultural production levels. During colonial times the official figure reported that peasants accounted for one third of agricultural output, and that the other two thirds of agricultural output was accounted for by workers on company plantations or settler farms. In reality, however, the official figure massively understated the contribution that peasants made to agriculture, because in its accounting it did not include the fact that the family sector fed themselves too. Once this is taken into account it is is revealed that they actually accounted for about three quarters of Mozambique's total agricultural output.

Thus, for the sake of Mozambique's economic growth, the dislocated populations must return to their land and their normal farming lives. Whether the people who have fled their land and others who have been adversely effected by the war are able to return to normal lives, depends of course primarily on the war ending, but also on on their ability to overcome their psychological and physical scars of the war, and, for the external refugees, on the success of the repatriation process too. But the physical and logistical complexities involved with the return of these people to their homes are problematic, as are the challenges of overcoming the deep physical, social and psychological damage done to the human fabric of Mozambique.

Staggered formal repatriation by UNHCR is being organised, but is limited by the amount of funds at the agency's disposal. The tendency for thousands to return at once was demonstrated by the events of 1990/91. Signs of how little it takes to tempt the refugees to undertake the journey back to their homes appeared when large numbers started returning to their homes all over their country as peace talks got underway in early 1990, and as Frelimo opened up zones in Zambezia. The partial ceasefire in late 1990/91 on the Beira and Limpopo corridors, short lived though it was, also lured many back to their homes. If, in the event of a full ceasefire, tens of thousands return at once, as is predicted by aid agencies, the immediate shortages such as food and seed, until the people are able to grow and reap their crops, could be immense. Aid that the refugees were receiving in their countries of refuge will not immediately follow them back into Mozambique, and aid to Mozambique is insufficient to provide for sufficient stockpiling in case of a full scale returnee emergency.

Even if UNHCR had sufficient funds to fully organise such a massive repatriation exercise as may become necessary, it would not be able to organise the tens of thousands of refugees with whom it has never had contact, such as those in South Africa, and the integrated or semi-integrated ones in the other countries. On arrival, practical problems such as the refugees claiming back their old land, will also be faced. The problems of repatriation are great, but at some point they will have to be faced, for one thing is very clear, not least to the refugees themselves, and that is that in order to rebuild their lives and their country they must return to Mozambique. Only once they are home can they begin to tackle the other effects that the war has had on them.

The mental condition of the country is pitiful. Children and adults alike have been disturbed and traumatised; families and communities have been ripped apart. At least a generation of education has been lost. Skills have been forgotten through the lack of an opportunity to use them, and dependency has been learned. Homes, friends and relatives have been lost, and communities have been destroyed. War and banditry, for many, has taken the place of respect for law and order, and for the victims, unpredictability has become the order of the day. All these things serve to limit the likelihood of returned populations contributing much to Mozambique's growth in the foreseeable future.

For the meantime, in spite of improvements in performance, agricultural production is still in a dire position with two thirds of the country unable to feed itself because so many are dislocated, or unable to produce through fear of Renamo reprisals. Mozambique still only produces sixteen per cent of its own food requirements. While reforms go on in the cities, and the face of Maputo changes dramatically, while radios appear in shops and dripping peri peri prawns slip down the throats of foreign investors, the mass of the country lingers in total dependency, perhaps displaced, or in camps; helpless to respond to the latest incentives to produce.

Other legacies of the war which also keep Mozambicans from the developments in their country, pose serious threats to the well-being of Mozambique's fledgling democracy. The most important legacy of the war in this respect is the tribalism that Renamo publicly denies but privately admits that it fosters amongst Mozambicans.[8] With some success, as has been seen, Renamo has manipulated many to support it on the false pretence that its emphasis on the importance of tribal allegiances was linked to a greater political project. Although it is difficult to see the logic, Renamo claims in its public manifestos that democracy is its greater political project. It has been seen all over Africa that if there is one thing that destroys democracy, it is tribalism, because tribalism is usually, as it is with Renamo, linked to a desire to dominate other tribes, not to incorporate them into one democratic nation. The tribally chauvinistic Renamo-affiliated War Lords, Renamo's Mambos, and all those whom Renamo has trained in the ways of traditionalist thinking to believe in the magic of the N'dau tribe, and in the vengeance of neglected tribal ancestors, are those who will not easily fit into a democratic Mozambique. This is particularly true if the war has not been settled before democratic elections take place.

The easy availability of weapons as a consequence of the war is another threat to a stable future, even if the war officially ends. An AK47 sold for a bag of maize meal in 1990, and one wonders if the price has gone down since. Certainly this would not appear to be the case, as pockets of ad hoc banditry, not necessarily part of the Renamo structure, have appeared with great frequency throughout Mozambique. It would be hard to imagine a country of over 15 million people, of whom many have lived lives of war, and survived by looting their enemies and civilians for the last two decades, settling down to peace and democracy with any speed while weapons continue to be readily available.

Not least Renamo leaders themselves in their present form threaten Mozambican democracy. Unless the leaders undergo a dramatic transformation in the near future, it is unlikely that Renamo's goals will change, and their goals, as has been seen, have little do do with democracy. It is the implicit threat that Renamo has made to keep fighting until such a time as its leaders are guaranteed some position in government that is the most worrying. For this would undermine the democratic process right from the beginning. Renamo's apparent lack of concern or understanding of the concept of Mozambique as one nation, and its general lack of any political idea except that of getting and maintaining power, is hardly a recipe for both a settled and democratic Mozambique.

There is yet a more sinister element of Renamo, however, which threatens Mozambique's future development, and it is in this element of Renamo that the problems that it presents for political and economic development coincide dramatically. To understand we must start with South Africa.

Times have not changed in many respects. As always for Mozambique, and indeed for the rest of southern Africa, much depends on developments in South Africa. Depending on the outcome of the current political uncertainty, and the ability of a new government of South Africa to reverse the economic decline of recent years, South Africa could make or break the regional economy. For years South Africa has held the regional economy in a hostile grip, and finally now the time has come for cooperation. 1990 was perhaps the last year when SADCC members would have to be embarrassed at toasting the success of cooperation between the 'frontline states' – which has sought to counter South African dominance of the regional economy – with South African wine.[9]

With a stable South Africa, hopes for the regional economy are high. If the war in Mozambique ends, a massive burden will have been lifted from the shoulders of the region. Not just the South African Homelands, but Malawi, Zimbabwe, Zambia, Swaziland and even Tanzania will be free of the refugees, massive unproductive populations whom they are hosting at great expense. Malawi and Zimbabwe in particular will benefit from the ending of Mozambique's war, because they suffer not only the refugee burden, but other direct and very high economic costs due to Mozambique's war.

How events turn in South Africa has a particular bearing on Mozambique because it is now the recipient of so much new South African investment. In Mozambique today, South Africa is the fifth largest foreign investor. The large part played by South African investors in recent investment in Mozambique is significant, because the nature of their investment is particularly beneficial to the Mozambican work force. Much more than Western investors, South Africans now have a need for a southern African economy that is strong in the long term.

With economic sanctions still imposed by the West, and yet southern African countries beginning to regard the political changes in South Africa as acceptable, South Africa, in early 1990, began to look at the possibilities of investing in the regional economy. Many South African investors are confident that there is great long term potential in the regional economy that they will be in a good position to exploit because of the advantages of proximity. In order to foster a strong regional economy over the long term, it is recognised that local work forces have to be utilised and trained into the requisite technical skills.

Reactions of South African investors to whom I spoke in an investigation into attitudes to Mozambicans as a work force for projects in Mozambique, were, perhaps surprisingly, positive. I asked each interviewee whether or not the low education levels and the skills shortage in Mozambique were a disincentive to invest, and the unanimous reply was that these factors were not major disincentives, as the work force showed many other positive qualities. Amongst these, willingness to work and learn, and a friendliness conducive to good labour relations, were mentioned. Asked about the fifty-three powerless days in Maputo in the first four months of 1990, the investors remained unperturbed.

The potential for extremely beneficial cooperation between Mozambique and South Africa is great, however, there are many difficulties which South Africa must overcome if it is to continue to be economically and politically strong enough to invest so heavily anywhere. There is one particular dark cloud threatening its future which, if it bursts, could have consequences as devastating as those suffered in Mozambique at the hands of Renamo. The danger revolves around the very same South Africans, their colleagues and their successors, who formed and have sustained Renamo in Mozambique for so long, and around their motives for doing so. It is a very real possibility that their activities in Mozambique over the last eleven years have now come home, with disturbingly familiar and characteristic brutality, to roost.

The danger was pointed to by Nelson Mandela in mid-1990 after a particularly gruesome massacre had been carried out by an unknown force on a suburban Johannesburg train. Because the attacks were carried out in a highly professional manner, with the attackers not uttering a word as they shot over thirty civilians, there was speculation that it was the work of an organised force, backed by whites who were paying blacks, probably members of the Zulu Inkatha group, which is the greatest threat to the ANC, to carry out such atrocities. Mandela and President de Klerk agreed that there was what they referred to as a 'hidden hand' behind the violence, and Mandela referred to it as the 'rise of the 'Renamo' movement in South Africa'. A host of other incidents, reports and investigations have all pointed in the same direction.[10]

If bitter whites start in South Africa what was started by the Rhodesians and carried on by themselves in Mozambique, years of destruction and misery may follow, and the whole region will feel the effects. Because southern Africa is so reliant on South Africa economically, the changes in South Africa leading up to multi racial rule of the country represent, in a sense, the beginning of a second independence for the whole region. This is particularly true for Mozambique, the success of whose decision to invite in the capitalists, depends so much on South Africa.

Mozambique's changes towards capitalism, as they were engaged in deliberately and as a consequence of fundamental criticism of the old methods, represent a hope that capitalism can bring to Mozambique an economic growth that Mozambicans can for once participate in. The importance of agriculture to the ERP, and the nature of South African investment indicate that Mozambique's hope could be realised. It is hoped that the strong flavour of recolonisation of following IMF strictures and partially reverting to an export economy can be extinguished by this. However, much relies on South Africa. If Mozambique's history of being ravaged by a military group whose primary purposes are destructive is allowed to repeat itself because of Western and white southern African support, then the telling of history will be will be shown to carry little weight.

If this potential 'legacy' of the war in Mozambique is the most sinister, the most profound must be those which cannot ever be overcome, recovered or compensated for in any way. The most morbid of these is the physical toll that the war has taken on the nation's people in terms of the outright deaths of tens of thousands. There are also some long term effects of the toll of the war on the nation's health, such as the stunted physical and possibly mental growth of an undernourished generation, which simply have to be accepted. Quite apart from the implications of what has happened in Mozambique for its future and the future of the region, a massive human tragedy has occurred, worthy of being catalogued for its own sake.

The war has sucked the lifeblood from Mozambique, and has left a nation whose efforts at development, until the war ends, and its legacies are overcome, resemble the dressing of a skeleton. The skeleton's gowns are expensive, reflecting economic prosperity, and are embroidered with glowing patterns of democracy. But, as so many Mozambicans learned during the days of colonial rule, there is no such thing as the development of a country in which they do not beneficially participate; they know that they are the bones of their country, but, for now, bones bare of muscle.

Mozambique will not come to life until Renamo, and all of its legacies, and all of its ways, have left. This will not be easy to achieve. Worse famines than even those of the mid-eighties threaten the 1990s, and will exacerbate the effects of war and the legacies to be overcome, because their toll will be taken of course on the very people who have been punished for so long. Aid, typically, will fall short just at the wrong time, as it awaits the mournful TV pictures which will arrive, if ever, only when the crisis is in full swing.

Mozambique is in a category of its own as far as suffering goes. The World Bank had to redefine its definition of poverty in order to take Mozambique into account. A survey of the nations of the world conducted for the International Index of Human Suffering, published by the Population Crisis Centre, labelled, not Ethiopia, Somalia, Sudan, Nicaragua or Cambodia, but Mozambique, as the 'Unhappiest Nation on Earth'.[11]

Yet it is a land of such potential. The amount of foreign investment that began to pour in as soon as the economy was liberalised is testament to this. The minerals still lie under the ground, the fish still swim in the sea, the soil still waits to be planted, and the people are waiting to work.

The simple dreams of the boy at the water pump in the Malawian refugee camp who wants only two things, to go to school and to become a driver; the hopes of so many that they can be reunited with their families and villages, and the wishes held so dear by those singing of going home and producing crops for themselves instead of having to rely on aid, might all be realised. For so many years politics of one sort or the other, slavery, colonialism, clumsy government, unconcerned aid, but above all, Renamo's war, have forgotten, ignored or deliberately fought against Mozambique's people. The realisation of their simple hopes depends at its core on the simplest of conditions, that, for once, the people of Mozambique themselves are given a chance to make themselves strong and independent.

Notes

Chapter 1   Background – a Land of War, a Land of Hope

1. *Mozambique File*, no. 169, 1990, reported that there were 16 600 elephants left in Mozambique in 1989, compared to over 54 000 only ten years earlier.
2. In 1965 87.4 per cent were rural farmers, and in 1973 85.8 per cent (World Bank Country Brief).
3. Cashews were not grown in Mozambique prior to the fifteenth century, when they were imported from Brazil by the Portuguese.
4. Knight, 1988.
5. Basil Davidson, 1980.
6. C. F. Spence, 1963.
7. Albeit that Portuguese is spoken in many different dialects.
8. Poor Portuguese often lived in the same areas of town as poor blacks. It is still possible to walk into the slums of Maputo and find shacks as bad as any, in which poor Portuguese live.
9. UN Economic and Social Council, 1976.
10. *Africa Watch*, 11 February 1991, p. 3.
11. Most of Mozambique's military aid still comes from the Soviet Union. The United States is the main food donor.

Chapter 2   Frelimo – Idealism, Discipline, Pragmatism

1. The reshuffle of 3 January 1991 appointed Rafael Maguni to the Ministry of Information. Maguni played a central role in the war, working on the Frelimo radio station broadcasting from Tanzania.
2. Eduardo Mondlane said in 1969 ' . . . what type of social structure, what organisation we would have, no-one knew . . . Now, however, there is a qualitative transformation in thinking which has emerged during the past six years which permits me to conclude that at present Frelimo is much more socialist, revolutionary and progressive than ever and that the line, the tendency, is now more and more in the direction of socialism of the Marxist-Leninist variety. Why? Because the conditions of life in Mozambique, the type of enemy which we have, does not give us any other alternative . . . '. (Bertil Egero, 1987).
3. See Martin and Johnson, 1981, p. 128.
4. Bertil Egero, 1987.
5. Iain Christie, 1989.
6. David Lamb, 1987.
7. The British Ambassador to Mozambique during 1984–86, Eric Vines, refers to the stubborn and impetuous strands in Machel's character,

amongst his better publicised qualities. Machel's biographer, Iain Christie, too alludes to Machel's tendency to demogoguism.

8. Samora Machel May Day Speech, quoted in David Lamb, 1987.

9. These rites often include the crude and unsanitory performance of a clitorectomy on the girl, which prevents her from experiencing any pleasure during sex by severing her clitoris.

10. The payment of bride price by the husband to the father of the bride is taken by many husbands to be their 'claim' on their wife's labour. The wife, because she has been paid for, is expected to do her traditional duties, which, in Africa, usually amount to serving her husband in the way that he sees fit. Disobedience is often punished by beating.

11. For Machel's attitude on race see Iain Christie, 1989, p. 152. Also see Joseph Hanlon, 1984.

12. David Lamb, author of *The Africans*, who visited Codzo, one of Frelimo's re-education camps, described it as follows: 'Codzo was a prison with no walls, no gates, no clanking steel . . . approaching it . . . I saw what looked like a typical African village. There were eight hundred male prisoners . . . some were petty criminals or drug addicts, others were described as enemies of the revolution. No one was ever charged or tried in court, and no one knew how long he would stay. Everyone in Codzo spent ninety minutes a day in sessions devoted to self-criticism and Marxist orientation, and everyone was taught a trade, from carpentry to farming.'

13. The video (made by Prince Johnson, his murderer, and leader of the INPFL rebels) of the murder of Samuel Doe on 10 September, 1990, was shown to Western journalists. It graphically screened the shaving of his head with broken glass and the shattering of both his knees before his death. Doe's own soldiers in 1980, on storming the palace where President Tolbert was President, gouged out the President's right eye, dismembered him, and fired three bullets into his head.

14. *Amnesty Law* (*Law* 14/87) 19 December 1987.

15. See Gervase Clarence-Smith, 'The Roots of the Mozambican Counter-Revolution', *The Southern African Review of Books*, April–May 1989.

16. Middlemas, 1977.

17. As will be seen in the Chapter 3, their discontent was largely material, rather than political or ideological.

18. Geffray, 1990.

19. Geffray, 1990, p. 41.

20. Christie, 1989.

21. Southern Africa Report November, 1989. 'Nampula: What's Left?'.

22. Vail and White, 1980, p. 391.

23. Vail and White, 1980, p. 400 examines this as it relates to the case of the Gurue tea estates, concluding that 'Frelimo was not taking control of the commanding heights of the economy, but rather trying to bail out an endless line of sinking ships'.

24. See Chapter 1, p. 15.
25. See Murray, 1981.
26. Bender, Coleman and Sklar, 1985.
27. There were 317 in 1985.
28. Torp, 1989; *Mozambique* (Marxist Regimes Series).
29. Alex Vines, 1991; 'Renamo in Negotiation and Peace'.
30. Alex Vines, 1991; Confirmed by Fernandes Honwana, Machel's close advisor.
31. 'Building Socialism: The People's Answer', IV Congress, 1983.
32. This lies in sharp contrast to the way Angola, for example, has reformed. In Angola, signs of enthusiasm for the imminent democratisations are considerably less evident. See Herald Tribune, 'Angola, Haunted by Violent Past, Looks Towards Democracy' by David B. Ottaway, *Washington Post Service*, 29 December 1990.
33. Quoted in Bertil Egero, 1987, p. 65.

Chapter 3   The 'Khmer Rouge' of Africa?

1. Ken Flower, 1987.
2. Herman Cohen made this clear in August 1989, as reported by APN, 14 July 1989.
3. UNITA has always refused to have anything to do with Renamo. This was confirmed by an interview with Paul Oliviera taped by Africa Confidential. See Fred Bridgland (1986), *Jonas Savimbi: a Key to Africa* for nature of UNITA.
4. Gordon Winter, 1981.
5. ZANLA is the military wing of the Zimbabwe African National Union (ZANU).
6. See André Thomashausen, *Africa Insight*, vol. 13 (1983).
7. Martin and Johnson, 1981.
8. Martin and Johnson, 1986.
9. Ibid.
10. Winter, 1981.
11. Jaoa Cabrita interviews (1990/91). Cabrita worked with Cristina on the radio station for six years.
12. In interviews with David Martin and Phyllis Johnson in April and June 1984; see *Destructive Engagement*, Chapter 1.
13. Cristina was draughted into the army's military intelligence, reportedly because of his experience in the bush as a big game hunter. There is dispute as to whether or not he was a PIDE agent.
14. He denied that he worked for the PIDE although Frelimo insists that he did. He does, however, admit working for the Portuguese judicial police in Beira.
15. *Magaia* was more or less a monthly publication, and the last edition was printed in 1978. It was not paid for by Jorge Jardim as is commonly believed.

16. Resistência Moçambique.
17. Cristina had told REMO that he was Renamo's leader, so they channelled money raised for the rebels through him. They began to suspect that he was not giving the money to Renamo, but sending it back to his farm in Australia, and threatened verbally to kill him. Cabrita interview.
18. Fernandes has claimed this in interview. However, neither he nor Dhlakama was present at the meeting. Jaoa Cabrita interviews.
19. A senior CIO instructor describes his relationship with Matsangaissa: 'The way I ran them was I always consulted André (Matsangaissa) on everything . . . I didn't always agree with him and if I didn't agree with him I'd say 'No, we don't do that' (*Destructive Engagement*).
20. Colin Legum, 1983.
21. Thomashausen interview, December 1990.
22. Five Reconnaissance.
23. Eschel Rhoodie, 1983.
24. See for example, Knight, 1988, p. 23; Wilson and Shumba, 1990; Geffray, 1990.
25. Wilson and Shumba, 1990; interview in Zambia with refugee from Northern Tete.
26. Saxon Logan's film for *Compass*, screened on ITV London 24 April 1990, 10:35 p.m.
27. Kanji, Richman and Zinkin, 1988.
28. Mozambique Briefing, July 1987, 'Children of the War'.
29. *US News and World Report*, 16 January 1989.
30. A photo in *Die Zeit*, 4 March 1990, reveals that some fighting units are made up solely of children.
31. *The Times*, 22 March 1991.
32. Geffray, 1990.
33. Dhlakama, and José Agosto (Renamo cabinet member), have both admitted in interviews with Alex Vines that support for Renamo in the south is very limited.
34. Geffray, 1990.
35. BBC World Service, *Network Africa*, 25 June 1990, Julian Borgar.
36. Otto Roesch (Trent, Canada) 'Renamo and the Peasantry in Gaza (Southern Mozambique)'. Not yet published.
37. Robert Gersony, 1988. 'Summary of Mozambican Refugees Accounts of Principally Conflict-Related Experience in Mozambique'.
38. K. B. Wilson and F. Shumba, Oxford University Refugee Studies Programme, 'An Account of the Civil War in Northern Tete' (unpublished).
39. Juhba's carried home made guns, and are in charge of collecting maize flour form the villages as 'tributes' to Renamo. Majibha's are 'special groups of volunteers who worked "hand in hand" with Renamo', and despite usually being captives themselves, guard over the other captives for Renamo as their main responsibility.

40. 'Extra' deaths means literally those that would not have died from the drought, because aid was there to help them, but who did die because of the difficulties Renamo created for the efficient operation of aid.
41. 'At Madura they came and demanded money and food. They accused some people of being informers for government forces, and cut off the nose, lips and ear of a number of people. Then they told them to go and report to Frelimo.' (*Argus African News* 1982).
42. Alex Vines, 1991, 'Renamo in Negotiation and Peace.'
43. Alex Vines, 1991, *Renamo – Terrorism in Mozambique*, p. 78.
44. See Sibyl Cline, 1989, 'Renamo: Anti-Communist insurgents in Mozambique: The Fight Goes On'.
45. *Africa Confidential*, 3 February 1989: 'Freedom Inc./Conservative Digest luminaries, while raising money privately for anti-communist struggles . . . also have a tendency to recommend (buying) each other's shares, services and newsletters.'
46. Paul Oliveira Press Conference, 1988. Kaltefleiter was also previously University Professor to André Thomashausen, Renamo policy advisor.
47. *The Weekly Mail*, 30 March–4 April, 1990; Eddie Koch.
48. *The Weekly Mail*, vol. 6, no. 9; Eddie Koch.
49. See *The Weekly Mail* 16 March–22 March, and 30 March–4 April, 1990. Stories by Eddie Koch.
50. *The Weekly Mail*, vol. 6, no. 9; Eddie Koch.
51. Irene Staunton, 1990.
52. 'Constitution for Submission to the Mozambican People' 1991. Document in author's possession.
53. *Daily Mail* (South Africa), 30 July 1990; Karl Maier.
54. Alex Vines, 1991: *Renamo – Terrorism in Mozambique*, p. 130.

Chapter 4 Structure of the War – the Rape of a Country

1. Martin and Johnson, 1981.
2. *Guardian*, London, 23 April 1974.
3. Combined Operations.
4. Martin and Johnson, 1981.
5. *Mozambique Briefing*, February 1987, 'Health Under Attack'.
6. In 1980, 303 village health workers were trained; in 1985 that figure was down to 33 (AIM).
7. Ibid.
8. See UNICEF 1988, 1989.
9. Figures from UNICEF report 1989, and various government sources.
10. André Thomashausen, 1987.
11. *Economist Intelligence Unit*, 1989/90.
12. Ibid.
13. *Mozambique Briefing*, March 1987, 'New Schools for Old'.
14. *The Star*, 22 September 1989. Article by Dawn Barkhuizen of the Star's Africa News Service.

15. UN report for 1990/91.
16. The Gorongosa documents mention that foreigners should be targeted.
17. Alex Vines, 1991, *Renamo – Terrorism in Mozambique*.

Chapter 5   Internal Dislocation – a War against the People

1. Nunes, 1990.
2. United Nations – 'The Emergency Situation in Mozambique 1990/91: Priority requirements for the period 1990–91.'
3. Defined by UNICEF as 'the condition in which it becomes impossible to maintain a minimum nutritionally adequate diet plus essential non-food requirements' (Children on the Frontline, 1989).
4. Nunes, 1990.
5. *The Spectator*, 5 May 1990, 'The Sewer of Africa'.
6. Conversations with residents of Chimoio and Maputo have shown this. MIO reports confirm that there has been an increase in crime. In addition, the strikes of January 1990 were expressions of discontent at the rise in food prices.
7. According to a UNDP report.
8. Nunes, 1990: 'such as business companies, private or public schools, nurseries, training centres, courts of justice . . . '.
9. Nunes, 1990.
10. Richman, Kanji and Zinki, 1988.
11. This was first noted when a temporary drop in armed activity in 1983 was accompanied by a temporary improvement in school performance.
12. Richman, Kanji, Zinkin, 1988. 'Psychological effects of war on children in Mozambique'.
13. Nunes, 1990.
14. See Apendix 1 of the study by McCallin and Fozzard, 1990 which tables childrens' behaviour patterns.
15. *New Internationalist*, February 1989, 'Trauma'.
16. *U.S. News and World Report*, January 1989.
17. *Tempo*. Report on street children, 1990.
18. United Nations, 1990, *The Emergency Situation in Mozambique. Priority requirements for the period 1990–91*.
19. *Noticias* – special end of year supplement, 31 December 1990.

Chapter 6   Refugees in South Africa – a Forgotten People

1. The definition of a refugee adopted by UNHCR is someone who 'owing to well founded fear of being persecuted for reasons of race, religion, nationality, membership of a particular social group or political opinion, is outside the country of his nationality, and owing to that fear is unable to avail himself to the protection of that country'. The more progressive OAU definition extends the UNHCR definition to include 'those compelled to leave their country of origin on account of

external aggression, occupation, foreign domination, or events seriously disturbing public order.'
2. Organisation of African Unity.
3. Zimbabwe Refugee Act (1983).
4. There is a ten kilometer wide band of guarded 'No Man's Land' running along the Zimbabwean border with Mozambique, ostensibly to prevent Renamo incursions.
5. Country Briefing Notes 1990. UNHCR Branch Office, Zimbabwe.
6. Ndumu game reserve, part of KwaZulu, forms part of the border in this area. However, there are no cats in this reserve.
7. In fairness, even if South Africa did want to pull the fence down they would face opposition from Frelimo which sees it as an obstacle to Renamo using South Africa as a rearbase.
8. Operation Hunger.
9. It was verified by an Induna (Headman) in KaNgwane in 1990 that able bodied young men had been put into Renamo training camps as an alternative to imprisonment and deportation, and are taken back as Renamo fighters with promises of good money etc.
10. Phillip Molefe and Eddie Koch from *The Weekly Mail* report 16–22 November, 1990, vol. 6, no. 44.
11. Sometimes the Mozambicans are lured over from Mozambique specifically in order to be sold, and are not refugees to start with. However, because they do not return, and find the condition of slavery preferable to the conditions of war in Mozambique, they can still be considered refugees.
12. Sol Jacobs (SACC) says 1500; Bishop Napier (SACC) says 3500, September 1989; US Committee for Refugees says 2800, November 1989. At the beginning of 1989 there were reports that the South African government wanted to repatriate 40000 of them from the Homelands, but the leaders caused enough uproar to prevent it. Aid agencies working in Chicualacuala, Mozambique, report that in June 1990 1500 Mozambicans had been deported to the town.

Chapter 7   Malawi – the Triangle of Discontent

1. 1988 census. This figure is in theory exclusive of the refugees, although in reality it may include some of the integrated refugees.
2. *Newsweek*, 9 October 1989, 'A World Awash in Refugees'.
3. *Africa Confidential*, 22 March, vol. 32, no. 6.
4. *The Guardian*, 10 January 1991.
5. *AP*, 23 October 1989.
6. Zimbabwe suffers many Renamo attacks on civilians in the Nyanga, Chimanimani and Ghonarezhou areas. Zambia's Lusaka-Chipata road has been the most ferociously attacked by Renamo.
7. Letter from Malawi signed. 'In Jesus, your Missionaries to Mozambique', and dated June 1988 (York Archives). Ellie Hein was present

at a Renamo military base in May 1991.

8. *Washington Post*, 10 August 1988.
9. Figures taken from World Bank Country Report for Malawi 1990, and from *Financial Times*, 30 March 1989, 'Malawi's Economy Needs End to Mozambique War', by Mike Hall.
10. *Financial Times*.
11. It is estimated that 470 000 refugees reliant on aid live in settlements of over 10 000 people of which less than 5 per cent are Malawians. A further 412 000 approximately, also reliant on aid, live in scattered settlements of less than 10 000.
12. UNHCR estimates and figures.
13. MSF coordinator Dr Arnaud Janin.
14. T. O. Bah, a UN deputy in Nsanje province.

Chapter 8   The Limits of Aid

1. Fuel was becoming increasingly expensive at the time of writing, early 1991, both because of the the Gulf war and the consequent fuel price hike, and the expiration of the Soviet agreement with Mozambique in December 1990 whereby Mozambique was provided with the bulk of its fuel requirements cheaply.
2. Iain Christie (Reuters) 01–0947:BC 'Mozambique-Famine', 4 March 1991.
3. CARE/LSU Mozambique Annual Report (1989), p. 3 (2.1).
4. According to the executive Director of UNICEF, James Grant, 18 June 1990.
5. Aid workers from a wide variety of agencies whom I interviewed throughout 1989/90 unanimously held the opinion that funding crises were cyclical.
6. Interview with Care spokesman, Maputo, 27 February 1990.
7. Department of National Calamities.

Chapter 9   Mozambique's Future – the Dressing of a Skeleton?

1. The JVC, made up of countries chosen by both Renamo and Frelimo, accused Renamo of carrying out at least six of the eight ceasefire violations, attacking the Beira and Limpopo corridors, which lead to the breakdown of the Rome agreement.
2. André Thomashausen, December 1990.
3. At Lalaua on 29 June 1991, 49 people were killed by Renamo. One witness said, 'The shelves of the shops were emptied and the severed heads were put there on display' (Reuters, 23 July 1991). Castrations were carried out on 2, 3 and 23 June, 1991. See *MIO*, no. 203 and no. 204.
4. UNAMO (National Union of Mozambique); PALMO (Liberal and Democratic Party of Mozambique). The other parties which emerged

after the law legalising opposition took effect on 6 February 1991, were COINMO (The Mozambique Independence Conference); MONAMO (Mozambique National Movement), the PCM (National Convention Party), MANU (Mozambique African National Union), and the FAP (Frente de Accao Patriotica).

5. Alex Vines, 1991; 'Renamo in Negotiation and Peace'.
6. Renamo communique (Gorongosa) April 1991.
7. World Bank figures 1990.
8. Dhlakama publicly denies that Renamo insists that Shona be spoken, yet a top cabinet member privately admits that it does.
9. This happened at the Tenth Anniversary of SADCC Gala Dinner, 1990.
10. For other evidence of this suggestion see *The Weekly Mail*, December 1990, 'Inkatha's secret training bases' by Eddie Koch; *Cape Times*, 11 December 1989, 'Death Squads: Renamo link?' by Marius Bosch and Barry Streek; *Africa Watch*, 1990, 'The Killings in South Africa'. Mandela's comments came as the result of a conversation with André Thomashausen, policy advisor to Renamo, and one of its main links with South Africa today, the night before.
11. Population Crisis Committee, Washington August 1989.

Bibliography

Africa Confidential (1988–1990): vol. 29, nos 18 and 24; vol. 31, no. 21; vol. 32, nos 33 and 36.

Africa Review (1990, March) 'The Rehabilitation of Beira'.

Africa Watch (1991, 11 February) 'Mozambique'; (1990, 26 October) 'Liberia'; (1990 report) 'The Killings in South Africa – The Role of the Security Forces and the Response of the State'.

Bender, Gerald J., Colman, James S., Sklar, Richard L. (1985, University of California Press) *African Crisis Areas and U. S. Foreign Policy*.

Black, Mabwe, Shumba, Wilson (1990) Ukwimi Refugee Settlement: Livelihood and Settlement Planning. A preliminary report of field research and recommendations (unpublished).

Bray, Ian (1987, Oxfam) *Chicualacuala – Life on the Frontline*.

Bridgland, Fred (1988, Coronet) *Jonas Savimbi – A Key to Africa*.

Cabrita, Jaoa (1983, unpublished) 'A View of the Mozambican Civil War'.

CARE/LSU Mozambique (1989) Annual Report.

Christie, Iain (1989, Panaf) *Samora Machel – A Biography*.

Christian Council of Malawi (1988 reports) 'Church Work with Refugees in Malawi'.

Clarence-Smith, Gervase (1989, April/May) *Southern African Review of Books*, 'The Roots of the Mozambican Counter-Revolution'.

Cline, Sibyl (1989, U. S. Global Strategy Council) 'Renamo – Anti-communist Insurgents in Mozambique'.

Cole, Barbara (1985, Three Knights) *The Elite: The Story of the Rhodesian Special Service*.

Contact USA (1989, vol. 4, no. 6) 'New Opportunities in Mozambique' by Louise dos Santos.

Daly, Ron Reid and Stiff, Peter (1983, Galago) *Selous Scouts – Top Secret War*.

Davidson, Basil (1980, Little, Brown) *The African Slave Trade*.

Economist Intelligence Unit Reports: 1989, no. 4, 1989/90 no. 5.

Egerö, Bertil (1987, Uppsala) *A Dream Undone*.

Financial Times Survey – Mozambique (15 January, 1991).

Finnegan, William (1989, *The New Yorker*, 22 May) 'A Reporter at Large'.

Flower, Ken (1987, John Murry) *Serving Secretly: An Intelligence Chief on Record, Rhodesia into Zimbabwe, 1964–1981*.

Geffray, Christian (1990, Credu-Karthala) *La Cause des Armes au Mozambique*.

Gersony, Robert (1988, U.S. Department of State) 'Summary of Mozambican Refugee Accounts of Principally Conflict-Related Experience in Mozambique'.

Gilbert and Gill (1986) *Refugees and International War.*

Hanlon, Joseph (1984, Zed) *Mozambique: The Revolution Under Fire*; (1986, James Curry) *Beggar Your Neighbours – Apartheid Power in Southern Africa.*

Hermele, Herman (1984) *AKUT 32* 'Migration and Starvation: an essay on southern Mozambique'.

Hoile, David (1988, Claridge) *Mozambique: A Nation in Crisis.*

Kanji, Nazneen (April 1990, *Community Development Journal*, vol. 25, no. 2) 'War and Children in Mozambique: Is International Aid Strengthening or Eroding Community-based Policies'.

Kanji, Naznseen; Richman, Naomi; Zinkin, Pam (1988) 'Psychological effects of war on children in Mozambique'.

Knight, Derrick (1988, Christian Aid) *Mozambique: Caught in the Trap.*

Lamb, David (1987, Vintage) *The Africans.*

Legum, Colin (1983) 'The Counter Revolutionaries in Southern Africa: The challenge of the Mozambican National Resistance', *Third World Reports* (March): 1–22.

Martin, and Johnson (1981, Ravan) *The Struggle for Zimbabwe: The Chimurenga War*; (1986, Zimbabwe Publishing House) *Destructive Engagement – South Africa at War*, chapter 1.

McCallin, Margaret and Fozzard, Shirley (1990, International Catholic Child Bureau) 'The Impact of Traumatic Events on the Psychological Well-Being of Mozambicans Refugee Women and Children'.

Middlemas, Keith (1979, Edinburgh University Press) *Mozambique: Two Years of Independence.*

Minter, W. (1989, *Development Dialogue*, no. 1) 'The Mozambican National Resistance (Renamo) as described by Ex-Participants'.

Morgan, Glenda (1990, *Africa Insight*, vol. 20, no. 2) 'Violence in Mozambique: The case of Renamo'.

Murray, Colin (1981, Cambridge University Press) *Families Divided.*

Nilsson, Anders (1990, ECASAAMA). *Unmasking the Bandits: The True Face of the MNR.*

Nunes, Jovito and Wilson, K. B. (1991) 'Repatriation to Mozambique: current processes and future dilemmas' (unpublished).

Quan, Julian (1987, Oxfam) *Mozambique – A Cry for Peace.*

Rhoodie, Eschel (1983, Orbis SA (pty) Ltd.) *The Real Information Scandal.*

Ruiz, Hiriam (1989, Issue paper U. S. Committee for Refugees) 'Peace or Terror: A Cross-Roads for Southern Africa's Uprooted'.

Spence, C. F. (1963, Cape Town) *Mozambique.*

South African Council of Catholic Churches, Bureau for Refugees (1989, 1990) *Refugees Newsletters.*

Southern Africa Report (various issues).

Staunton, Irene (1990, Baobab Books, Harare) *Mothers of the Revolution.*

Thomashausen, André (1983, *Africa Insight*, vol. 13, no. 2) 'The National Resistance of Mozambique'; (1987, Potchesfstroom University) 'The Mozambique National Resistance'.

Torp, Jens Erik (1989, Marxist Regimes Series, Pinter Publishers, London and New York) *Mozambique: Politics, Economics and Society.*

UNICEF Report (1988, 1989) 'Children on the Front Line: The impact of apartheid, destabilisation and warfare on children in southern and South Africa'.

United Nations (1990, UNHCR Branch Office, Zimbabwe) Country Briefing Notes.

United Nations (1990, New York) 'The Emergency Situation in Mozambique: Priority requirements for the period 1990–91.'

United Nations Development Programme (1988) 'Development Co-operation People's Republic of Mozambique'.

United Nations Development Programme (1989) 'Mozambique: Using Aid to end Emergency' by Prakash Ratilal.

U.S. News and World Report, 16 January 1989.

Vail, Leroy and White, Landeg (1980, Heinimann) *Capitalism and Colonialism in Mozambique.*

Vines, Alex (1991, James Currey) *Renamo: Terrorism in Mozambique*; (1991, not yet published) 'Renamo in Negotiation and Peace'.

Winter, Gordon (1981, Penguin) *Inside Boss: South Africa's Secret Police.*

Wilson, Ken (September 1990) 'An Account of the Civil War in Northern Tete'; (1991, Paper presented to United Nations Research Institute for Social Development; unpublished) 'Social and Economic Aspects of Mass Voluntary Return Movements of Refugees from one African Country to Another' (unpublished)

Other Sources

York University Archives selected documents.

Renamo Statutes; Bulletins 1979–1990; Communiques.

Frelimo Briefings; Congress Reports; *Mozambiquefile* (Mozambique News Agency monthly); Mozambique Information Office News Reviews, *Strategy and Program for Rehabilitation 1989–92.*

Magazines and Newspapers: *Tempo, Soldier of Fortune, The Economist, Newsweek, The Spectator, African Connection, The Weekly Mail, The Daily Mail, The Star, Business Day, The Citizen, The Cape Times, The Guardian, The Times, The Independent, The Washington Post, The Washington Times, The Chicago Tribune, The New York Times, The Christian Science Monitor, Herald Tribune,* and others.

Index